# REVELATION

## The Divine Fire

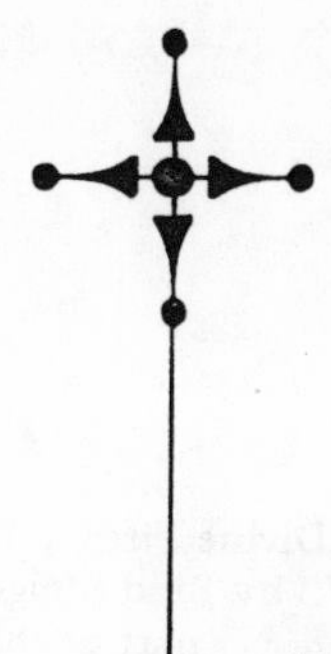

by BRAD STEIGER

PRENTICE-HALL, INC.
Englewood Cliffs, N.J.

Revelation: The Divine Fire by Brad Steiger

Printed in the United States of America
Prentice-Hall International, Inc., London
Prentice-Hall of Australia, Pty. Ltd., North Sydney
Prentice-Hall of Canada, Ltd., Toronto
Prentice-Hall of India Private Ltd., New Delhi
Prentice-Hall of Japan, Inc., Tokyo

Library of Congress Cataloging in Publication Data
Steiger, Brad.
Revelation.

1. Revelation. 2. Religion, Psychology.
I. Title.
BL53.S675 1973 291.4'2 72-10243
ISBN 0-13-779322-7
ISBN 0-13-779330-8 (pbk.)

10 9 8 7 6 5 4 3 2

# Acknowledgments

There were so many individuals who gave generously of their time and their encouragement toward the preparation of this book that the following list cannot hope to name all of them, and I must at once apologize to whomever may have been inadvertently omitted from the following acknowledgments.

*Dr. Walter Houston Clark,* Professor of Religion (retired), Andover Newton Theological School; *Rolf K. McPherson,* D.D., President, International Church of the Foursquare Gospel; *Dr. Martin E. Marty,* Associate Dean, Divinity School, University of Chicago; *Sir Alister Hardy,* Manchester College, Oxford; *Thomas F. Zimmerman,* General Superintendent, General Council of the Assemblies of God; *A. Dale Fiers,* General Minister and President, Christian Church Disciples of Christ; *Janet Bord,* London; *Dr. John Paul Gibson,* Church of the New Birth; *Dr. V. T. Jordahl,* Chairman, Department of Philosophy, Millikin University; *E. Norman Paulson,* President, Brotherhood of the Sun; *Jane Roberts,* Elmira, New York; *Glen A. Lehman,* National Executive Secretary, Independent Fundamental Churches of America; *Don Worley,* Connersville, Indiana; *Diane Kennedy Pike,* The Bishop Pike Foundation; *Sally Williams,* Heritage of Faith; *Rev. Kingdon L. Brown,* New Age Truth Center; *Harold Sherman,* President, ESP Research Associates Foundation; *Dr. Joseph Jeffers,* The Ambassadors of Yahweh; *Rev. Canon William V. Rauscher,* Rector, Christ Episcopal Church, Woodbury, New Jersey; *Gordon Lindsay,* President, Christ for the Nations; *Robert E. L. Masters and Jean Houston,* Directors, Foundation for Mind Research; *Dr. Berthold Eric Schwartz,* Montclair General Hospital; *Dr. Leo Louis Martello,* WICA; *Alan Watts,* Sausalito, California; *Jack Wheaton,* Music Department, Cerritos College; *Betty Allen,* Westfield, New Jersey; *Robert Shell,* Roanoke, Virginia; *Fay Clark,* Perry, Iowa; *Father Ed. Cleary,* Memphis, Tennessee; *Bertie Catchings,* Austin, Texas; *Deon,* Chicago; *Lasca and Harold Schroeppel,* Haly's Psychic Self Improvement; *Dr. William Sargant,* Physician in Charge, Department of Psychological Medicine, St. Thomas' Hospital, London; *Dr. Lawrence A. Siebert,*

Portland; *Henry Cole,* Chicago; *Dr. Bruce Wrightsman,* Luther College; *Peggy Townsend,* Harrisburg; *Dr. Donald M. Williams,* First Presbyterian Church of Hollywood; *Marianne Francis,* Solar Light Center; *Irene F. Hughes,* Chicago; *Dr. Stanley Krippner,* Maimonides Medical Center; *Wilburn Burchette,* Spring Valley, California; *Al. G. Manning,* ESP Lab; *Contesa Gypsy Markoff Amaya,* Santurce, Puerto Rico; *Dr. James T. Hayes,* Murray State University; *Dr. Herb Sloane,* Toledo, Ohio; *H. H. Blackschleger,* Prelate, NPC Church of Religious Science; *Kenryu T. Tsuiji,* Bishop, Buddhist Churches of America; *Jim Anderson,* Decorah, Iowa; *Gerard W. Gottula,* Future Foundation; *Sri Paul and Gail Twitchell,* Eckankar; *Patti Simpson,* Eckankar; *Dr. Richard Rubenstein,* Professor of Religion, Florida State University; *Helen Hadsell,* Irving, Texas; *Dr. Mulford Q. Sibley,* Department of Political Science, University of Minnesota; *David Techter, Fate* Magazine; *Dr. Thelma Moss,* Neuropsychiatric Institute, University of California; *Dr. Gertrude R. Schmeidler,* Department of Psychology, City University of New York; *Dr. W. G. Roll,* Psychical Research Foundation, Inc.; *Joyce Martin,* Muscatine, Iowa; *Joan Howard,* Toronto; *Dr. Aaron Buhler,* Moderator, Baptist General Conference; *Olof Jonsson,* Chicago; *Ron Warmoth,* New York; *Louise Zimmerman,* Chalmette, Louisiana; *Lee R. Gandee,* Lexington, South Carolina; *Dr. Conrad Baars,* Rochester, Minnesota; *Dr. J. Wolfgang Weilgart,* Luther College; *John A. Keel,* New York; *Rev. and Mrs. Milton Nothdurft,* St. James Methodist Church, Sioux City, Iowa; *Rev. and Mrs. Mark Weston,* Ankeny, Iowa; *Aileen Steil and Robin McPherson,* Light Affiliates.

I wish to extend special thanks to my associates, Glenn and Dave, for their moral support, to my secretaries—Jeanyne, Mary, Jean, Lucia, and Jan—for their patience in transcribing many hours of taped interviews, to my wife Marilyn for enduring both my psychic struggle and the typing of the final manuscript, and to my editor Tam Mossman for his unfailing guidance and enthusiasm.

Brad Steiger
Decorah, Iowa

# Contents

# INTRODUCTION

## *There Is a Burning Fire in My Heart*

> ***But his word was in my heart as a burning fire shut up in my bones, and I was weary holding it in, and I could not.***
>
> JEREMIAH 20:9

On December 16, 1970, Father Joseph O. Fournier, a Roman Catholic priest, and Anna Latorce, a former nun, were married in Edmonton, Alberta, Canada, because a revelation from God had commanded them to get married to help bring about a change in their church's celibacy laws.

"I received a revelation from the Lord last September," Anna said. "He said that Father Joseph and I were to serve as a pilot couple. He said that we must get married and try to force church authorities to change their ways."

On November 7, 1970, Anna took a temporary leave from St. Albert's Grey Nuns Convent, where she had been a sister for thirty years. On November 8 she received a communication from God informing her that she and Father Fournier had been married in Heaven on that day. Later another revelation informed the nun that she and the priest should be united in matrimony in Edmonton's City Hall so that they might be wed according to the laws of the province.

"I have been communicating with God since I was eleven," Sister Anna told newsmen. "The Lord talks to me through written messages. He guides my pen, and I record what he says to me."

One such message recorded on October 1, 1970, was addressed to Archbishop Anthony Jordan of the Province of Alberta. "You must liberate my priests," stated the revelation. "I, Jesus of Nazareth, desire and proclaim that from now on all priests of all countries, of all rites, of all orders, may get married if they so desire." Sister Anna admitted that it has been difficult to convince people that she truly has been receiving messages from God. Many church officials urged her to see a psychiatrist.

Dr. Aloysium Fink, a psychiatrist in Edmonton, said that he had examined Anna on four occasions. "She was a serene individual with no history of mental disorders," Dr. Fink observed. "I gave her every test I could think of, and I did everything possible to cross her up. My examination revealed her to be a very healthy person, both physically and mentally. I found no reason to doubt the sanity of Anna Fournier."

Most contemporary revelators are not given the kind of serious attention that would grant them even the dignity of a psychiatric examination. They are simply told to go home and forget about their experience.

A woman whom we shall call Jeanette was kneeling alone at prayer in a Catholic Church. When she looked up, she saw Christ in fleshly form, his head bowed, staring at her. As she watched, he lifted his head slowly and closed his eyes. For the first time, she noticed that his outstretched arms indicated the position in which they would have been pinioned to the cross. With a slight gasp he turned his head to the right side, and Jeanette felt that she was watching her Savior die on the cross.

Seconds later the vision had disappeared, but Jeanette now became aware of a severe pain in the palm of her right hand. In the center of her palm was a stigmatalike gash. Her priest accused her of suffering a self-inflicted wound and sent her home with the admonition that Jesus died only once. The stigmata has reappeared on several occasions since, and she says that it itches almost constantly.

Unfortunately, the consensus of orthodox religious opinion has it that the gifts of the Spirit promised by God through His Old Testament prophets was climaxed with the dancing tongues of flame on the heads of the Apostles on the Day of Pentecost in A.D. 30 and was terminated on the Isle of Patmos in A.D. 95. St. John's cluttered Revelations is the last book in the Christian Bible; and, in the eyes of orthodoxy, it seems to bring down the cosmic curtain on the Holy Spirit's dramatic interaction with mankind.

An Episcopalian priest was severely chastised by his bishop when it was learned that the clergyman was speaking in tongues. In humble tones, the priest commented:

"My bishop must have thought that we are something special because we have this gift. I don't look at it that way. I look at it as an endorsement of the Holy Spirit." How had the gift come to him?

"One night I was awakened–I don't know by what. I felt a sort of burning coal on my lips, and I began to speak. My wife woke up and she heard me speaking in what she said was the strangest, most beautiful language that she had ever heard."

A professor of economics told me in an interview that his wife suddenly began to speak in an alien language one afternoon as they were sitting in their backyard.

"It was a true language," he said, stating his earnest conviction. "I understand that some people, while they are witnessing to someone, suddenly burst into Chinese, for example. But I am certain that this was no known foreign language.

"A few minutes later, while I was praying, I suddenly burst

into a language. I suppose that I spoke in this language for a period of perhaps four minutes. It was not gibberish, but I haven't the slightest idea what the language was.

"I was at one of the Pentecostal churches and a woman seated directly behind me stood up and delivered a prophecy at the close of the service. She seemed to speak in Hebrew, Arabic, or some near Eastern language. This was interpreted by a minister, who had tears in her eyes when she relayed it to the congregation. The experience seems to be overwhelming to the person who interprets tongues, because he seems to feel that God is using him in a very special way to do this.

"I remember one of the messages was: 'Why do you erect your man-made fences, your man-made walls that separate you one from another?'"

A young salesman told me how he had been mired in the despair of drug addiction and alcoholism. He asked if I would believe that he, who now stood before me in glowing health and strength, had been reduced to a shaking skeleton that weighed less than a hundred pounds. What had happened to him? What transforming influence and power had redeemed him from a miserable and ignoble death?

He had walked into a tent meeting, an old-fashioned, stand-up-for-Jesus-and-come-forward revival. He had walked up a sawdusted aisle to have the thunder-voiced evangelist lay hands upon his wretched, trembling-for-a-fix body.

"When that preacher put his hands on my head, there came through a bolt of pure God-fire that was so powerful it knocked down a lady kneeling next to me. It was like electricity! Later, when the preacher led me out to the river to be immersed in baptism, I heard people on the banks shouting, 'Hallelujah!' Hundreds of witnesses saw that dirty, muddy river instantly changed to pure, clear water as my body entered the river. That, my friend, is how powerfully filled I was with the Divine Fire of God!"

Scattered throughout the United States, Canada, Great Britain, and, it would seem, the world, are small groups of sincere men and women who are clustered together in small circles, communicating with various entities, who may or may not be the same source. Now I do not claim to be in contact with all of the groups extant—I doubt if any one person could possibly be aware of all of them—but I am in communication with a great number, many of whom believe their group to be unique, the only one of its kind. These groups are independently coming up with a great deal of the same material, the same communications, emphasizing that man may draw strength from Higher Intelligence, that man has all the requisite spiritual abilities within his own being, that man is One with all things, that man is approaching a New Age, a period of transition, that other-dimensional entities are present to assist man in leaving the old and in adjusting to the new.

After exhaustive research and interviews, I am convinced that the soul-igniting mechanism of the gifts of Spirit did not cease with the prophets and saints of antiquity. I contend that the Divine Fire—the transfer of thought, spirit, and power from an Infinite Intelligence to a finite, human intelligence—is a vital, continuing process which observes no denominational boundaries and employs a spiritual-psychic mechanism that is timeless and universal. Daniel, Zechariah, the Apostles, and all of the world's great saints, mystics, and inspired men and women of history are our spiritual contemporaries.

Saul, a young firebrand, a member of the Sanhedrin who were dedicated to halting the Apostles' preaching of Christ, was struck blind on the road to Damascus. When he recovered his sight by heeding instructions given to him in a vision, he not only changed his name, his religion, and his life's work, but he may have altered the course of history. In like manner were a salesman in South Dakota, a businessman in New Jersey, and a policeman in Nebraska temporarily blinded by a strange and powerful light that appeared above them as they traveled lonely highways. When they recovered their sight, they changed their names, their occupations, and began to devote their lives to the preaching of peace, love, brotherhood, and the coming Day of Glory.

The boy Samuel heard his name being called at night. When no earthly voice could be found responsible, Eli, the priest whom Samuel would one day succeed, told the lad that it must be the Lord calling. Samuel was told to lie down and say, "Speak, Lord;

for thy servant heareth." When Samuel did this, the Lord came and stood before him. Samuel became the last of the judges, the first of the prophets, and as founder of the monarchy, the sole ruler between Eli and Saul, whose principal mission was the organization of the Kingdom of Israel.

In like manner did a housewife in Colorado hear her name being called at night. When no earthly voice could be found responsible, she opened herself to the Lord. Now, a few months later, she is practicing touch healing, speaking in a tongue that confounds academic linguists, providing spiritual lessons to an ever-growing flock, and prophesying on both an international and a personal level.

Ezekiel saw a wheel within a wheel land before him. He watched four angelic occupants emerge, and he felt the Spirit enter him when one of the beings spoke to him. From that day on, Ezekiel had the gift of prophecy and the ability to work miracles. In like manner a television copywriter in California, an Air Force pilot in Florida, and a college girl in Washington observed the landings of unknown aerial vehicles. They communicated with the occupants, felt the Spirit enter them, and later discovered that they had remarkable precognitive and clairvoyant abilities.

Moses spoke to the angel of the Lord as it appeared in a pillar of flame near a wilderness bush. The voice from the fire assured Moses of Divine aid and the power to work miracles. In like manner a voice from a glowing orb spoke to an artist from England, a clergyman from Illinois, and a sailor from Kentucky and promised them paranormal abilities. All have since forsaken their former callings and have devoted their lives to cleansing the Earth for the coming New Age.

If any reader has been wondering why the revelatory experience should come, for the most part, to men and women of rather humble and mundane social positions, he might consider this quotation from William Seabrook's *The Magic Island:*

> ...We have built domed temples and vast cathedrals, baited with glories of polychrome and marble to trap them, but when the gods come uninvited of their own volition, or send their messen-

gers, or drop their flame-script cards or visit from the skies, it is not often these gilded temples or the pride of the earth they seek, but rather some road-weary humble family asleep in a wayside stable, some illiterate peasant girl dreaming in an orchard as she tends her sheep, some cobbler in his hut among the Alps. Perhaps in their own far-off celestial sphere, the gods are surfeited with glory, and only for that reason visit earth at all. Perhaps they suffer from some divine *nostalgie de la boue*. Always when the rich, mighty temples are erected where once the humble stable stood, there is a risk that the bored gods will betake themselves elsewhere without saying "*au revoir*."

During the past five years, I have interviewed and corresponded with men and women from widely separated geographical areas and vastly assorted occupations who have claimed regular communication with Higher Intelligence. Clergymen, clerks, professors, public relations executives, housewives, students, servicemen, and factory workers have been demonstrating that Pentecost was not just a one-shot special designed to excite the Apostles and their kibitzers in Jerusalem of A.D. 30.

As I conducted my interviews with revelators, theologians, psychologists, and various observers of the contemporary scene, I wanted to know if everyone agreed that there seemed to be a great outpouring of the Holy Spirit in our age. Did everyone view our generation as the recipient of a profound spiritual revolution? Did everyone believe that there really was a basic, cosmic truth to the much-touted Age of Aquarius?

I could see from the outset that the semantic problem would present a continuing hassle. When I said "Divine Fire," some people would think Holy Spirit; others, Cosmic Consciousness; and (I honestly had not foreseen this) still others, sexual energy. When I said "revelatory experience," meaning a verbal or nonverbal communication between Higher Intelligence and human intelligence, many interviewees would think of creative inspiration. Indeed, creative inspiration may most certainly be classed as a kind of revelation; but, for my purposes, I would be talking about that Energy, which we commonly call God, or His messengers, meeting man and suffusing him with the Divine Fire of his Intelligence. I rather like the vibrations of such a term as

"Holy Spirit," but I had no intention of getting into the hierarchical hang-ups of the Trinity.

So many revelators had mentioned being stunned, even blinded, by a brilliant light that seemed to beam down on them from the sky or that seemed suddenly to surround them. I wanted to know what my interviewees believed was the source of the "blinding light" that so often signaled the onset of revelatory experience.

I wished to learn if others had observed that faith did not seem to be a factor in all revelation experiences, that the practical as well as the prayerful may suddenly undergo a revelatory contact. I was curious to hear if others had noticed the personality changes that seem to be associated with the aftermath of revelation? Why did the revelator in so many cases not only change his behavior patterns, but also his name?

It also seemed important to me to discover how others felt about encouraging the visitation of the Divine Fire. Were there certain practices that might more effectively bring about this spiritual spark? Were there any criteria which one might employ to test whether or not his experiences were authentic and not just the precocious child of expectancy and ego? In some instances certain proclamations of the Divine Fire may not really be divine at all but a psychological fantasy mechanism of frightened and confused men and women. Man's collective unconscious may need to articulate the horror, disillusionment, and awful depression of attempting to adjust to the specter of nuclear annihilation, the grim biological reality of the population explosion, and the sickening ecological morass of what may be an irreversible pollution problem.

In other cases of revelatory experience, I had the uneasy feeling that the ecstatic flame may, in reality, have been kindled by multidimensional beings who have a kind of symbiotic relationship with man and who may exploit their "prophets" for selfish, parasitical purposes. Throughout history these entities may have required points of reference on the physical plane of existence that were best realized through deluded human hosts.

I wished to learn how many of my interviewees accepted the existence of other intelligences—call them angels, masters, spirit guides—that might operate from another plane of being to influence mankind's development through carefully controlled individual and group revelatory experiences. Since so many revelators insisted that their message was relayed to them by a cowled figure, a glowing angel, a bearded master, might it be possible that these entities actually existed in another plane of being? As in the past, these entities may be materializing to guide man through a difficult period of adjustment.

At the same time that I was asking rather sticky questions about messenger entities, I wanted an opinion as to why—once a prophet had received a number of accurate predictions and revelations—the material often began to develop certain internal inconsistencies, half-truths—Divine Fibs, as I have called them.

Finally, I wished a reaction to the oft-quoted passage from C. G. Jung in which he warned man against the great change that is inherent in the Age of Aquarius. In *Flying Saucers: A Modern Myth of Things Seen in the Sky*, Jung said: "I am, to be frank, concerned for all those who are caught unprepared by the events in question and disconcerted by their incomprehensible nature." He went on to speak of "changes in the constellation of psychic dominants" which might bring about long-lasting transformations of the collective psyche.

It may occur to some readers of this book that throughout the centuries the recipients of the Divine Fire have been repetitiously proclaiming the same basic revelations. Although minor alterations have been made to adapt the messages to contemporary situations, the prophets of 3000 B.C. and A.D. 30 were receiving essentially the same revelations as the prophets of 1970. This realization may at first lead the reader to consider whether or not the Mind of God might really be some supercosmic transmitter that endlessly broadcasts the same signal to human receiving sets—a signal which, because of its sameness, is not especially pertinent to any given period and has no true relevance to any era. On the other hand, the reader may conclude that the very repetition of a basic message may be evidence of the vital relevancy and universality of a cosmic truth.

It may also be that, in the course of our inquiry, the reader may receive a clearer picture of the Outside Intelligence that has been interacting with man throughout history. "Truly, Thou art a God who hidest Thyself," the prophet Isaiah complained.

*INTRODUCTION*

Where better to seek a description of the Face of God than in an examination of the lives and the testimony of those who have been consumed by the Divine Fire?

# ONE

## *Revelation Is Not Respectable*

Recently my friend Michael Avallone, the popular mystery writer, sent me a couple of snapshots from London which captured a group of bearded, flowing-gowned individuals supporting makeshift posters that warned of Judgment Day being at hand and advised everyone to repent at once. Doom-mongers have become such an integral part of our Western culture that it would be nearly impossible to find a collection of magazine cartoons that did not have at least one humorous caricature of these Apocalyptic errand boys. What an observer of even ten years ago would find unique in these photographs is the large number of businessmen, conservatively attired matrons, and smiling, peace-emblemed students marching in step with the somber visaged latter-day Jeremiahs.

Chico Holiday is a singer-guitarist at Harold's Silver Dollar Room in Reno, Nevada. He watches the tambourine players in their hot pants, bra-less under their tight sweaters, as they sing selections from *Jesus Christ Superstar.* He remembers when it used to be "a big no-no" to sing a religious song in a nightclub.

"Right now we're experiencing the biggest revival back to Christianity since the time of the Apostles," he told Steve Toy for *Variety.* "The kids are saying that Christ came to save the sick. What better place to do it than in the nightclub?" In Holiday's opinion, the era of religious music is going to get bigger. He said that he did at least three or four Christian songs a night and that he got requests for more.

Line Renaud, entertainment director for King's Castle, was quoted as believing the young people had started the new trend toward religiosity with their distaste for war and with their love messages. Renaud commented: "I came back from France two days ago—the same thing is happening there. I think it's an evolution. Audiences like it because, little by little, it grows on you. Not to accept it would be to refuse an evolution."

One chilly November night in Chicago, I asked a lightly robed Jesus Person if she were not cold. "Not at all," she answered jubilantly. "I'm filled with the Holy Spirit."

To these Street Christians with their raised arm, clenched fist, heavenward-pointing index-fingered salute, the Deity is personal, transcendental, available. And even though their long hair, scruffy beards, and Army surplus wardrobes may upset their parents who populate the pews of mainstream churches, the most conservative of these same frowning elders must smile at the Jesus People's affirmation of a personal faith in God, their belief in Satan and his chaos-spreading role in these Last Days, and their repudiation of drugs, drunkenness, sexual promiscuity, excessive pride, and obsessive accumulation of material goods. But the Jesus folk do not come to church very often. This is the day of the lay apostolate, and the action seems to be in the streets.

In his address to the European Congress on Evangelism held in Amsterdam in August 1971, evangelist Billy Graham listed ten commendable features which he had found in the Jesus Movement:

1. The Jesus Movement thus far centers in the person of Jesus Christ.
2. The movement is Bible-based.
3. There is a demand for an experience with Jesus Christ.
4. The young people of the movement are putting a renewed emphasis on the Holy Spirit.
5. The young people of the movement have found a cure for drug addiction. A religious conversion to Jesus Christ has apparently cured many hard-drug addicts.
6. The movement is making a spiritual contribution to American churches.
7. The movement emphasizes Christian discipleship.
8. The Jesus People give evidence of social responsibility.
9. The members of the movement have a great zeal for evangelism.
10. The Jesus People have placed a renewed emphasis on the Second Coming of Jesus Christ.

Mr. Graham stated his own belief that there is scriptural basis for anticipating a great outpouring of the Holy Spirit upon the Church before the end of the Age. The first outpouring of the Spirit, predicted by Joel, was fulfilled at Pentecost, the evangelist said. "The second will occur just before 'the great day of the Lord.' The Holy Spirit began his outpouring at Pentecost and continues his outpouring in spiritual renewals from time to time throughout history. But there will be a 'grand finale' just before the Lord returns."

Writing in *Christianity Today,* ("Close-up of the Jesus People," August 27, 1971), Dr. Donald M. Williams says that first of all the distinguishing features of the Jesus Movement is that it is student-led. "The initiative has passed from the professional Christian worker, be he pastor, youth leader, or campus-ministry staff member. . . . The same hip teen-ager who last year turned his friends on to drugs may now be turning them on to Jesus."

Dr. Williams feels strongly that this student leadership has been emerging out of the youth culture with integrity. "The

Gospel of the incarnation is being acted out again in the youth culture, as the Word becomes flesh in these particular lives and their particular style. The institutional church that has no contact with the culture of this generation is being confronted by a new breed of Christians who call this culture home. Whether the churches can embrace these authentic Christians in their own culture is an open question, and with the answer rests much of the future."

A young addict named Sharon recently told newsmen how she had been on drugs for two years, then went "cold turkey" one night in a Detroit jail after calling on Jesus. In a moving, personal account, Sharon said: "And He came, and He changed me right there."

Can the Church embrace such revelators as Sharon? It is hard to have such personal visions "officially" accepted. Spiritual authorities are very cautious about outbreaks of the Divine Fire.

At the height of his illness in December 1954, Pope Pius XII had a vision of Christ in which the Savior spoke to him in "His own true voice." The Vatican kept Pope Pius' revelation secret for nearly a year, then through the "affectionate indiscretion" of one of the Holy Father's close friends, the picture magazine *Oggi* broke the story in its November 19, 1955, issue.

On December 12 the official Vatican newspaper, *L'Osservatore,* confirmed the remarkable disclosure. The vision was declared not to have been a dream, and sources near to the Pope said that he had been wide-awake and lucid.

Vatican authorities said that there had not been a more vivid or specific vision of Jesus since the days of the Apostles than that reported by the Pontiff. According to their records, Christ had appeared to a Pope only once before, and that was in the fourth century when Pope Sylvester consecrated the mother church of St. John Lateran in Rome after Emperor Constantine had ended the brutal persecutions of the Christians.

Father Herbert Rogers, theologian of Fordham University, was quoted as saying that Pope Pius' vision was unique in our age, so far as had been reported. Father John Sheerin, editor of *Catholic World,* noted that a private revelation, such as the one granted the Holy Father, was "no part of the teaching given by

Christ to the Church. A Catholic who accepts a private revelation does so not on the infallible teaching authority of the Church, but because of the credibility and integrity of the person to whom the revelation has been given."

Roman Catholic scholarship holds that there are two kinds of visions:

One, the imaginative vision in which the object seen is but a mental concept or symbol, such as Jacob's ladder leading up to Heaven. Saint Teresa of Avila had numerous visions, including images of Christ, which Church authorities have judged were of this symbolic kind of vision.

Two, the corporeal vision in which the figure seen is externally present or in which a supernatural power has so modified the retina of the eye so as to produce the effect of three-dimensional solidarity.

Pope Pius XII appeared to have had such a vision—a solid image of Christ, together with His clear voice.

In the twelfth century St. Francis of Assisi was credited with seeing Christ. Saint Catherine of Sienna reported seeing Christ in the fourteenth century. The Catholic devotion to the Sacred Heart as a symbol of love was begun in the seventeenth century after the vision of Christ had been seen by the French nun St. Margaret Mary. Why should not such visitations continue to occur?

Dr. Conrad W. Baars, a psychiatrist from Rochester, Minnesota, recently spent some time in Europe investigating both the claims of supernatural revelations and their claimants:

"Recently when I was in Rome, I was told by certain persons in the area of investigation of world-wide claims of revelations from the Holy Spirit that such claims had been very much on the increase in the last couple of years and that this department is quite busy in investigating all these alleged claims of supernatural revelations. . . . I think we are witnessing the diminishing enchantment with institutional religion, whether Catholic, Protestant, Jewish, or others. This phenomenon does certainly give evidence of man's basic need and orientation toward a supernatural being."

Pastor Aaron Buhler, Moderator of the North American Baptist Church and Minister of the Parma Heights Baptist Church in Cleveland, Ohio, expressed doubt whether the modern tongues and healing movements were truly the manifestation of a New Pentecost.

"Many of our churches, including mine, have people who claim to speak in tongues, to have been baptized by the Holy Spirit, and to see miracles of healing," Pastor Buhler said. "Since I have observed my own members and have not seen one genuine healing, although a lot of professions, I do not believe that this movement meets the New Testament test, and therefore I cannot endorse it."

It is Pastor Buhler's concern that a seeking of the "Baptism of the Holy Spirit" may cause Christians to emphasize personal experience above Scriptural doctrine. "Experience should not form doctrine, but doctrine should shape experience," he stated.

Pastor Buhler contends that 1 Corinthians 12:13 ("By one Spirit were we all baptized into One Body") should be examined carefully, "because it sheds light on the meaning and purpose of this ministry of the Spirit. For by one Spirit are we all baptized into one body. A union is effected of believers to the body of Christ, which is the Church. The baptism is the work of the Holy Spirit in forming and adding to the Church.

"The experiences of the Apostles in founding the Church are not necessarily the norm for today. None of the experiences in connection with the baptism in the Spirit recorded in Acts can be exactly duplicated today. Scripture nowhere exhorts believers to seek this baptism, nor is there any distinction made between those who have and those who have not been so baptized. It is presented as a fact common to all believers. We are not to seek the experience of baptism, but the filling."

I was fortunate to receive an interview from Dr. Donald Williams, a young Presbyterian minister, who, according to *Presbyterian Life,* was at the heart of the Jesus Movement, "coordinating its little cells," providing it with "important resources from First Presbyterian Church in Hollywood, where he is pastor of the college department." Dr. Williams received his

Ph.D. from Union Seminary and Columbia University, "his schooling in classical theology, his disposition against personal cults and peculiar doctrines. He was always the man to coordinate, cooperate, meld something resembling the historical witness of the churches from the passionate, exotic groups and preachments of the various Jesus People."

*Dr. Donald Williams*: I would like to begin by saying that it seems to me that the thesis you present [in *The Divine Fire*] is very Eastern, not Christian, and not Biblical. You apparently are looking for some common phenomenological description of what you entitle The Divine Fire, some spiritual transformation that cuts across theological, confessional, and various historic religious faiths to come to some synthetic understanding that there is a fundamental unity behind all spiritual experiences. The term "Cosmic Consciousness" is, of course, very Eastern, and it avoids the personal understanding of God characteristic of Biblical Christianity.

When you say that you hope to demonstrate that revelation is a vital, continuing process that observes no denominational boundaries and utilizes the same spiritual-psychic apparatus among all people, I would have to take serious issue with you.

In the first place, we believe that revelation has been given uniquely in the Bible and supremely in Jesus Christ—the only way to God, the one mediator between God and Man.

We deny that there are continuing revelations. We do not deny that there are continuing spiritual conversions and changes that are brought about through the proclamation of the one revelation of Jesus Christ through the word of God, and we are very much involved in seeing that change take place.

There is the continual illumination of individuals in each generation through the one unique and final revelation given us in the Bible and in Jesus Christ, but revelation has been completed and the Bible and the canon is closed. Any attempt to add revelations that stand in similar authority to the unique revelation of Jesus Christ is to be rejected. At the same time, I would be the first to admit that God continues to work and to speak in each generation and that he makes his word known today through the Holy Spirit.

You use the phrase, "the visitation of the Holy Spirit," but then you go on to talk about the "same spiritual-psychic apparatus" and "no denominational boundaries" and "Cosmic Consciousness reaching down from a higher reality." You seem to have a mixture here of Christian and non-Christian terminology. You should be cautious about using phrases that are really mutually exclusive and contradictory.

If you are talking about the work of the Holy Spirit, you are talking in Christian understanding of the third person of the Trinity, who enlightens and illumines people and brings them to conversion in Jesus Christ. If you are talking about "Cosmic Consciousness in a higher reality," you are talking about something that is not Biblical and is really identified with Eastern religion. When you say that all the world's great saints, mystics, and inspired men and women of history are our spiritual contemporaries, then I have to say yes and no.

If you mean that all those who have come into conversion or new birth experience with Jesus Christ are our spiritual contemporaries, then I would say yes, in that we share a faith that is real and living and we are bound together both in time and in eternity by one God who unites all things in Jesus Christ.

If when you speak of the great saints, mystics, and inspired men and women of history you mean to take in a much wider context then the Biblical Christian faith, I would say no. I don't consider myself to be spiritually contemporary with Gandhi or Buddha or those who have had great spiritual and religious experiences. I really consider myself to be contemporary in a historical sense–and not in a timeless and nonhistorical sense–with those who know Jesus Christ personally now and those who are bound to him, although they have lived in past generations.

When you say that "revelation is an eternal now," you seem to dehistoricize it and remove it from relationship to the Bible, and I would want to take issue with that. Revelation has been received historically in Jesus Christ and is now carried on in the life of the Church through the work of God.

[Dr. Williams does feel, however, that there is "a spiritual awakening going on around us."]

We find a great number of young people in and out of the institutional church, ex-hippies, drug addicts, dropouts, alienated youth from the counterculture, those who have been into heavy revolutionary activity and the political far left, coming into a personal faith in Jesus Christ that has become a life-changing experience for them. We see this happening all over the country.

I, myself, had this experience at fifteen years of age through an organization called Young Life, which is an Evangelical Christian organization that is cross-denomination. The understanding of Jesus Christ that was proclaimed to me through Young Life was Biblical.

It centered in Jesus as the Son of God, who was born of the Virgin Mary, who lived a life of teaching and preaching, who was more than simply a good teacher, who was the Son of God and who revealed himself to be such to his disciples, affirming Peter's confession: "He is the Christ, the son of the living God." Jesus died by the act of his own will, as well as at the hands of sinful men, for the sins of the world, a substitutionary atonement on the cross. He was resurrected from the dead three days later, leaving the tomb empty. As a historical fact, he appeared to his disciples for forty days, then ascended into Heaven where he reigns at the right hand of God. He will come from Heaven at the close of this time in history—which I consider to be now very short—to complete God's purpose, to fulfill his work of redemption, to judge all men, to set up God's kingdom on Earth, and to re-create all things and restore them to their original perfection.

It was that message that brought me into the vital, personal relationship with Jesus Christ, and that thing that was most important to me in my own conversion experience was that message that Jesus loves me, that he gave himself for me, that he could come to my life personally and really change my life if I would allow him to do so. This immediately excludes all ideas of Cosmic Consciousness, higher reality, and things that are abstract. Personal love has to be between the one who loves and the beloved.

As Dr. Williams implies, other Eastern religions take a different view of the Divine Fire. In *The Uses of the Past,* Herbert J. Muller writes:

> In effect, Hinduism has regarded religious truth as symbolic, not historical or literal. More specifically, it has asserted a continuous or progressive revelation. While the divine inspiration of the Vedas is one of its unifying tenets, the Vedas did not become a closed Canon. The most pious admitted the possibility of new revelations, and through the centuries have produced new scriptures; some sects even consider the Vedas outmoded . . . [Hinduism] affirms that God is always revealing himself to all men, everywhere.

Dave Anderson is a friend of Dr. Williams and head of The Lutheran Evangelical Youth Movement.

*David Anderson*: I see young people finding that the pursuits of trying to find happiness and meaning and purpose through abuse of sex, abuse of drugs, whatever, just aren't filling the needs for love, for acceptance, for self-identity in their lives. They are looking at the message of Jesus Christ. Some of them are having to look beyond the Church, beyond what may have turned them off in the past–formalism, organizations, boards, committees, things that are a part of the structured Church. They are looking straight to the Bible and into peoples' lives that have been changed by the power of God. They are seeing the person in the power of Jesus Christ as being reality, and not just an idea or just a general way of life or a philosophy of a following of some good teacher.

Many of these young people are inviting Jesus Christ to take control of their lives, and now many of them aren't crying themselves to sleep at night wondering what tomorrow will bring or lamenting over their guilt or their messed-up lives. They're looking at life positively, with a great deal of hope, not in what man can do, but hope in what God can do in changing lives and in filling these very deep needs that we all have. The young people that I have been talking to in the last couple of days have really been awakened to the fact that they have been searching for the unconditional love of Christ. They have tried to forgive themselves for what bothers them. They have tried to look for forgiveness and for acceptance, but they have not found it. When they understand that this forgiveness, this acceptance, this love, this purpose, this meaning, this quality of life-style comes through a personal relationship with Jesus Christ, then the question that they in their deepest thoughts have been asking has been answered.

I think the mistake that the church has made for quite some time, at least in youth ministry in our denomination, is that we have been answering questions that kids aren't asking. I believe that when the name of Jesus Christ and his message is lifted up, he will, as he says in the Scriptures, draw men to himself. It is a matter of the Holy Spirit convincing men who Jesus is and why they need him and why they need to accept him.

Young people have tried to read the Bible and have only seen the lists of "begats" and the long names. But when they have seen it with new eyes and with a new understanding, the Bible has become a living book, a real guide for life, a real source for understanding in truth. Young people today are finding out that prayer is just a minute-by-minute dialogue with God, not a monologue, but a dialogue. We can hear God speak to us and guide our lives.

There are various spiritual gifts that God has seen fit to give to individuals. The gift of tongues–which is better called "praying in tongues," rather than "speaking in tongues"–I understand as a communication from the Spirit of God within us to God the Father. Other gifts include the interpretation of tongues and prophecy, which is not so much telling the future, but speaking the Word of God in a way similar to the prophets of old.

The Charismatic Movement has caused a great deal of controversy in the Church, because it has not been understood. The Church has not done a good job of presenting these spiritual gifts, and when they occur, no one seems to know how to handle them. I think that in years to come, you will see a greater proper use of these spiritual gifts.

*Dr. Williams*: In conclusion, I would like to say that the most powerful thing in the world is the power of the Holy Spirit working through the Gospel of Jesus Christ.

I have seen people who have been given up for dead by their parents, by their probation officers, by their lawyers, become transformed fundamentally and receive a brand new life. I have seen people come off heroin. I have seen people come off barbiturates. I am thinking of a friend of mine whose habit was about twelve "reds" a day, who had dropped acid over 500 times, who was shooting heroin. Now he is getting a 3.5-grade average at UCLA, majoring in psychology. His parents had given up on him as a dead person. Jesus Christ changed his life.

These are not isolated incidents. *Look* Magazine (February 9, 1971) tells of a nineteen-year-old licensed minister named Breck Stevens who promises a thirty-second cure from heroin addiction—with no withdrawal pains. According to available figures more than 4,000 young addicts have had an almost supernatural healing of their chemically enslaved bodies and brains.

Living for Jesus in the New Age becomes more complex than just another "high." When twenty-one-year-old Anita Pankratz was chosen Miss Illinois, she told an interviewer that Jesus gave her a "real high," and that "the greatest thing about being high on Jesus is that you don't have to come down."

How long, though, can one stay "high" when a whole lot of people are trying to bring you "down"?

In a highly critical article ("Jesus Now: Hogwash and Holy Water," *Ramparts,* August 1971), California poet James Nolan maintains that all the Jesus freaks have really done is to introduce a few variations to "Bible-pounding, tent-revival, fundamentalist Christianity."

Among the innovations to the fundamentalist dogma which he found stultifying as a youth in New Orleans, Nolan lists:

> street language (Jesus is no longer Lord and Savior but Leader and Liberator) . . . the communal life-style. But over-arching all else is a passionate belief that the world will end within their lifetime while

> Jesus returns to rapture them off to a very literal heaven with streets of gold and angels twanging on electric-amp harps, the thought of which clouds their eyes and leaves them murmuring "fa-a-ar out."

In Nolan's opinion, "mything out" on Jesus is not a great deal different from spacing out on drugs. "And once Jesus has brought them down from drugs," he asks, "what's going to bring them down from Jesus?"

Nolan concludes his article with a message to "Jesus-Boppers":

> If your apocalypse does not happen on schedule, and if and when you are lemming off in some new direction, realizing the torment and difficulty of true sainthood and that salvation is not just a shot of anything away, spare us one vision: a littered, trampled post-festival shambles with Jesus Christ, a blown-out superstar, back where he started, unplugging the amps and picking up the empty dixie punch cups and sweeping up the cookie crumbs scattered by the marauding packs of crowded, lonely people: no one was saved.

Marcus Bach, that open-minded chronicler of religious experience, has criticized the Jesus People for a kind of judge-others fundamentalism. In his *Strangers at the Door,* Dr. Bach tells of attending a meeting in Hollywood at which seventy-five young people came forward to the lectern microphone to tell how Jesus had saved their souls.

"Their voices were sharp, clipped, and accusing," Dr. Bach writes.

> They were warning the sinners that a yawning gulf stretched between them and the saving grace of the Christ, that time was short, that God was impatient, and that heaven or hell was waiting. . . .
>
> The longer I listened, the more the feeling of fraternity that had thrilled me faded away. Bit by bit the wonder and joy of the singing, the radiant faces, the kids you thought you'd like to embrace and bless became a different kind of Jesus Army, a highly

exclusive, far-right army ready to condemn and sentence those whose sensitivity might still see Jesus as the Lord of Love.

In *Earth* magazine for November 1971, Alan Watts despairs that the Jesus People "identify Jesus the man as the one-and-only historical incarnation of a Divinity considered as the royal, imperial, and militant Jehovah," thereby reinforcing "the pestiferous arrogance of 'white' Christianity—with all the cruel self-righteousness of its missionary zeal."

Watts contends that there is no excuse for the "parochial fanaticism of spiritual in-groups" in a day in which we are being exposed to "all the riches of Earth's varying cultures and religions."

The Jesus People, Watts writes,

> . . . must realize that Christianity would seem ever so much more valid if it would stop insisting on being an oddity. Christianity has universality, or catholicity, only in recognizing that Jesus is one particular instance and expression of a wisdom which was also, if differently, realized in the Buddha, in Lao-tzu, and in such modern *avatars* as Ramana Maharshi, Ramakrishna, and, perhaps, Aurobindo and Inayat Khan . . . This wisdom is that none of us are brief island existences but forms and expressions of one and the same eternal "I am" waving in different ways, such that, whenever this is realized to be the case, we wave more harmoniously with other waves.

Other serious thinkers, such as Sir Alister Hardy of Manchester College's Religious Experience Research Unit, have begun to ask whether Jesus himself would have allied himself with the Christian religion or would have identified with the Christian claims of his divinity.

"Would Jesus Christ be Christian?" Sir Alister writes in *The Divine Flame*.

> If by the term Christian we mean who so many orthodox churchmen appear to mean, then I, for one, very much doubt it. I feel certain that he would not have preached to us of a God who would be appeased by the cruel sacrifice of a tortured body; the

> parable of the prodigal son surely belongs to quite a different religion.
>
> What a paradox it is. To me Jesus speaks of reality—the most brilliant burning of the divine flame in all history . . . Yet I find so much in orthodox Christianity that repels me . . . I cannot accept . . . the hypothesis that the appalling death of Jesus was a sacrifice in the eyes of God for the sin of the world, or that God, in the shape of his son, tortured himself for our redemption. I can only confess that, in my heart of hearts, I find such religious ideas to be amongst the least attractive in the whole of anthropology. To me they belong to quite a different philosophy—a different psychology—from that of the religion that Jesus taught.

Dr. Walter Houston Clark, Professor Emeritus of Andover Theological Seminary, feels that it remains to be seen whether revelation will be integrated either within the churches or outside of them in a lasting form.

"But there is no doubt that on the one hand the blandness and harmlessness of institutional religion, and on the other hand its more commendable, but nevertheless spiritually rootless, social activism has left many young people with a feeling that something is missing. This is the element of the mystical and the ecstatic—something comparable to what they feel when they fall in love.

"The churches have very little awareness of the presence of this type of religion or that they are alienating many of their youth because of their obtuseness. They seem to be in the process of rejecting a spiritually quickening movement of great power, as the Roman Catholic Church rejected Protestantism and the Church of England, Quakerism and Methodism, to their impoverishment. I would sympathize with the churches in their bewilderment over the confusion and many contradictory forms of religion among youth, but not with their unwillingness to involve themselves with it in order to help bring some order out of that chaos that Nietzsche said was necessary to produce a 'dancing star.' "

Thomas F. Zimmerman, General Superintendent of the General Council of the Assemblies of God, Springfield, Missouri, said that they used the term "Pentecostal," because they wish to denote "... the fact that the church received, according to the promise of the Savior, the imbuement of power as they tarried in Jerusalem. It is recorded that 'they were all filled with the Holy Ghost, and began to speak with other tongues, as the Spirit gave them utterance.' "

Brother Zimmerman stated that his own involvement with the movement began when a small group of Pentecostal believers prayed for his mother, who had been given up to die. Two weeks from that day, Mrs. Zimmerman walked into the office of the doctor who had pronounced her incurable and received his amazed testimony that he could no longer find any trace of the disease.

"That did something in our home," Brother Zimmerman said. "We became tremendously interested in this doctrine that would bring about such a marvelous manifestation of God. We immediately found the glorious truth of the baptism of the Holy Ghost and we received that experience."

But then the Zimmermans found that the "reputable church" of which they were members suddenly decided that they were misfits: "Back in the early days of this revival, it was common for those who received the experience to be cast out of their former churches," Brother Zimmerman explained. "Leaders of those churches showed by their attitude that they were totally unprepared for the supernatural implication of the revival of Pentecostal blessing."

Pentecostal leaders did not care to form another denomination "to be countenanced by the older churches." They were more interested in getting out the message. But today the Pentecostal revival has encircled the world, until, said Brother Zimmerman, "it has been evaluated by contemporary church leaders as being a significant part of what they have called 'the third force in Protestantism.' "

At the two-week congress of the International Academy for the History of Science which was held in Moscow in the summer of 1971, Dr. Bruce Wrightsman was the only theologian who was invited to present a paper. Dr. Wrightsman's background training was in physics and engineering before he decided to enter the Lutheran ministry. Today he still maintains an interdisciplinary stance, as he teaches both science and religion at Luther College in Decorah, Iowa. He is the author of the forthcoming book, *Science and Religion: From Conflict to Consensus.* In his opinion, the really interesting and crucial problems are "borderline problems, not solely the territory of technicians or economists or politicians."

According to Dr. Wrightsman: "I think the problems we are facing now—ecology, war, race, and so forth—show that to be the case. The reductionist philosophy that has guided most of our scholarly thinking in the last one hundred to two hundred years is locked up in that kind of a framework, and too many scholars simply can't think outside of that into other dimensions, which is the problem, of course, with religion . . ."

*Dr. Bruce Wrightsman*: I think revelation as an avenue to knowledge is vastly neglected by both science and religion. We give a lot of lip service to it, but most theologians don't really take it seriously as a pre-condition of their approach to religious experience or the knowledge of God. Certainly scientists have always seen it as inimical to the mode of discovery, setting off disclosure and discovery as sort of opposites in which man is either active or passive in the process.

I think you can make a case for saying all knowledge comes by way of revelation, or no knowledge does, depending again upon your point of view. As far as Divine Revelation is concerned, from my Christian point of view, it's undeniable. I see too many evidences of it around, too many experiences of it in my own life. Not that there aren't other explanations available, but the other explanations are no more credible to me than the key word, revelation."

"If there is one thing I am certain of," Sir Alister Hardy has said, "it is the need for a scientific approach to the subject [of religion] . . . the whole of civilization is moving with increased speed, into the scientific age. . . ."

Sir Alister Hardy, D. Sc., F.R.S., Emeritus Professor at Oxford, is well qualified to examine religious experience with the most exacting of scientific standards. A marine biologist and ecologist, author of *The Living Stream,* Sir Alister regards himself as a "true Darwinian." But while he grants that the DNA code "may well determine the *physical* nature of the individual organism," he does not believe "that this gives us a complete account of the evolution process."

Sir Alister states: "It is not just lines of individuals that are evolving; it is whole populations. In the higher ranges of evolution . . . new patterns of behavior can exert important selective forces within populations of animals to bring about better adaptational changes. Thus the *mental* side of life turns out to be a factor of cardinal importance within the process of Darwinian evolution."

When I began to correspond with Sir Alister in August 1971, he cautioned me that the Religious Experience Research Unit at Manchester College, Oxford, England, had only just begun to collect data on religious experience and he would not, therefore, be able to present me with any statements regarding their conclusions. But Sir Alister did provide me with a generous supply of material, including his sole library copy of his series of lectures on religious experience, entitled, coincidentally, *The Divine Flame.*

Sir Alister explained that the Religious Experience Research Unit's first task was to classify the varied kinds of religious experiences that were reaching them. They had to work out what the biologist would call the "taxonomy of the collection."

Sir Alister had said that they should not, at first, be concerned with the more dramatic, ecstatic, mystical states (important as those were) but should be concerned with the records of a more general kind of spiritual awareness, "the feeling of being in touch with some transcendental power, whether called God or not, which leads to a better way of life." Even though the researchers stressed their desire for this kind of report in their appeals for religious experiences, they received "an almost equal number of the more ecstatic mystical type."[1]

[1]If any reader should like to assist Sir Alister Hardy in his research project, he should send the report of his religious experience to The Director, Religious Experience Research Unit, Manchester College, Oxford, OXI 3TD England. Particulars such as age, sex, nationality, marital status, religious background, and other relevant factors should be included.

Sir Alister recalls: "In our classification I had thought we should first distinguish these two main categories, the more general kind to be classed as 'A' and the more mystical as 'B' experiences. We soon realized that the latter could be separated into a dozen or more subdivisions, such as those concerned with seeing visions, hearing voices, ecstatic transfiguration experiences, rapturous Wordsworthian feeling in relation to nature and so on, merging through out-of-the body and lucid dream experiences to those of a more psychic nature. The taxonomy was turning out to be much more complex than we had at first envisaged; and on that account the more interesting."

The researchers at the Manchester RERU are now in the process of arranging data according to types of religious experience, background, age, sex of percipient, and so on, and transferring the information to the punch-card index systems of their computers. Here are representative selections from Sir Alister's files, identified by number, in order to protect the anonymity of the subjects:

(198) One day as I was walking along Marylebone Road, I was suddenly seized with an extraordinary sense of great joy and exaltation, as though a marvelous beam of spiritual power had shot through me, linking me in rapture with the world, the Universe, Life with a capital *L*, and all the beings around me. All delight and power, all things living, all time fused in a brief second.

(183) I heard nothing, yet it was as if I were *surrounded by golden light,* and as if I only had to reach out my hand to touch God himself, who was so surrounding me with his compassion.

(712) It seemed to me that, in some way, I was extending into my surroundings and was becoming one with them. At the same time I felt a sense of lightness, exhilaration and power as if I was beginning to understand the true meaning of the whole Universe.

(201) I went into the sitting room and got on my knees in the dark atmosphere and cried "Oh God. Oh God. Please help," then burst into tears: something I had not done for several years. From that night onward, a strange calm came over me as I felt the tug of an unseen hand guiding me and leading me to do things I would not otherwise have done.

Sir Alister admitted that some are undoubtedly offended by his attempt to apply the scientific method to something as delicate and sacred as religious experience. Others have written letters asking him if he could not be satisfied with the evidence of spiritual experience found in the Bible and in the works of the mystics and the saints. Why, these indignant correspondents wish to know, should he seek additional experiences?

Sir Alister answers that he fully agrees that the Scriptures and writings of the mystics contain "... some of the most profound examples of such experience. What is also important, however, is to demonstrate that these experiences are just as real and vital to modern man as they were in the lives of those of long ago. As Dean Inge said: 'Religion is concerned with that which is and not with that which was.' " As might be expected, Sir Alister does not view God anthropomorphically, but he does believe in an "extrasensory contact with a Power which is *greater than,* and in part lies *beyond the individual self.*"

On the other hand, Sir Alister is fully cognizant of the disregard in which great numbers of his scientific colleagues hold his work. The seventy-five-year-old biologist knows that some scientists have characterized him as a senile old man attempting to carry out some sentimental whim.

He is quick to answer those colleagues who sigh about "poor old Hardy" with the statement that he has long been interested in religion and he has been preparing for this monumental study for more than twenty-five years.

"Ecology stands on its own feet as a true science dealing with animals as living wholes," he writes in *The Divine Flame:*

> Just as molecules, atoms, and electrons are the units of physical science, so living animals can be the units, the behavior of which we can deal with just as legitimately, by observation, experiment, and statistical treatment to build a true science of life. A biology based upon an acceptance of the mechanist hypothesis is a marvellous extension of chemistry and physics, but to call it an entire science of life is a pretense. . . . No wonder that those who spend more time on analysis in the laboratory than in the study of living animals in nature are apt to come to the conclusion that in their physical and chemical discoveries they are explaining life. . . .
>
> I cannot help feeling that much of man's unrest today is due to the

widespread intellectual acceptance of this mechanistic superstition when the common sense of his intuition cries out that it is false.

Sir Alister believes that the confident, dogmatic assertions of the mechanistic biologists are "as damaging to the peace of mind of humanity as was the belief in everyday miracles in the Middle Ages." He agrees with Professor Joad who said that "... the unconsciously frustrated desire for spiritual experience is no less important than the unconsciously frustrated desire for sex upon which the psychoanalysts have laid so much stress." Biology, Sir Alister feels, "should entertain the possibility that the rapture of spiritual experience ... may, after all, be a valid part of natural history, coming into existence in the living stream no less mysteriously than did sex; and that perhaps it may have only developed as religion when man's speech enabled him to compare and discuss his strange feeling of what [Rudolf] Otto called the numinous.... what I am calling the divine flame is an integral part of the creative evolutionary process which man, with his greater perceptive faculties, is now becoming aware of...."

Sir Alister is the first to concede that science can no more be concerned with the "inner essence" of religion than it can be with the nature of art or the poetry of human love. He does maintain, however, that "... an organized scientific knowledge—indeed one closely related to psychology—dealing with the records of man's religious experience ... need not destroy the elements of religion which are most precious to man—any more than our biological knowledge of sex need diminish the passion and beauty of human love.

"Could the religious sense—the sense of the Holy—the feeling of the sacred—the something we call God—be something as fundamental as time but, like love, be unperceived directly by our senses; and like love—indeed linked with it—felt by our conscious ego in an extrasensory way," Sir Alister wonders. "As our natural history of religion brings together the records of religious experience and slowly, through classification and a relation to psychology, merges into our future science of theology, it will begin to show us more of the nature of the divine flame in man which responds to what we call divinity in the universe."

# TWO

## *New Gospels for a New Age*

The editorial writer who penned "No Other Gospel" in the January 21, 1972, issue of *Christianity Today* set down his warnings against adding to Biblical revelations in flaming ink:

> The Gospel must be neither abridged nor added to. . . . Integrity means wholeness, and with the Gospel, it is a matter of all or nothing. To truncate the Gospel, whether by denying the deity of Christ, who is at its center, or by reducing the efficacy of his death for our sins to an example of martyrdom, or by repudiating the reality of his resurrection, is to destroy the Gospel . . . Among the most severe words in the New Testament are these from the greatest of the apostles: "But even if we, or an angel from heaven, should preach to you a gospel that is different from the one we preached to you, may he be condemned to hell!" (Gal. 1:8,

TEV)—a kind of plain speaking that rather grates on the ear in this time of covert universalism.

Although Dr. Donald Williams presented me with strict cautions to guard against "counterfeit revelations," there are so many men and women who have been consumed by the Divine Fire and who have been compelled to permit "the missionary part" of them to speak of these spiritual insights to their fellow searchers that I find it most difficult to subscribe to the suggestion that any one religious body might have cornered the market. For example, following a series of revelatory experiences, Kingdon L. Brown, a former public relations executive with Michigan Bell and a graduate of Northwestern University from a Presbyterian religious background, left a successful niche in the business world in order to allow the "missionary part" of him to found the Church of Essential Science. The following quotes are excerpted from material from a number of trances in which Mr. Brown served as a channel:

"The third dictation contains secrets for you to advance in the protection of the egg-soul of your being, emanating from the solar plexus.

"Those who whisper, those who speak in charms, telling you the false doctrines, are clouding your minds with confusion, which they themselves know. A blight of hesitation marks the Dark Forces, which emanates as they speak to you.

"True being lies within each of you. Like a burst of radiant light, the third eye opening allows the energies to enter. The Christ Being is now born again within each heart, releasing the true love in the hearts of all."

"The Life Soul is the Egg of you. This is found in the meaning of your own self-death. The secrets of life are in death. Only the body dies. Your soul-egg moves from the body, and the mind cements to the soul-egg and moves to the place of consciousness in the vibratory nature of the after-fact."

"Love to the marching noise. Peace to the marching noise. Peace to the planet Earth. Divide the hatreds; multiply love.

Your power is greater than you think. Your light is brighter than you say. Break the chains of your mind and bring forth the Christos. The missionary part of you must transfer this Blessed Truth to others. Bless them that curse you. Bless them that curse you."

Men and women such as Kingdon Brown have the greatest respect for the Bible, even though they may have become disenchanted by its ecclesiastical interpreters. But it is the contention of these contemporary revelators that the Scriptures do indeed require several addenda for the coming New Age.

As a religious group, Essential Science is dedicated to the development of a "science of life" based on the revelation of the New Age. The Cosmos, as viewed by students of Essential Science, is composed of indestructible energy, Divine Manifestation, which changes its form according to Cosmic law. It is the duty of each soul to progress through eternity in attunement with this Divine Manifestation. God's infinite plan of perfection is demonstrated to each soul as it progresses.

To the extent to which a soul is able to make an attunement with the Energy, or Spirit, it becomes an agent for God's action and is directed by the highest potential of Being. The soul that makes a satisfactory attunement builds an awareness of its progression and its mission on earth. The soul that fails to make an attunement becomes ensnared in a never-ending cycle of negation, falsehood, insecurity, hatred, jealousy, and ego-involvement.

The systematic methodology of Essential Science teaches the following three principles:

1. The experience of God
2. Knowledge of the human mind
3. The creative realization of the power of Divine Will in the Earth-plane of existence.

Essential Science summarizes the Mystery of Life in these maxims:

1. Truth is the Evolving Oneness and is self-sufficient for each soul.

2. God's action protects and directs all who seek it.
3. An understanding of the principles of God's Manifestation brings Eternal Harmony into the life of every soul.

Kingdon Brown has recently moved his Essential Science headquarters from Detroit, Michigan, to Scottsdale, Arizona. The pleasant, bespectacled young man is the author of two books (*The Power of Psychic Awareness; Cosmosis–The Technique and Its Use in Daily Living*). He speaks easily and articulately about his work and his revelations.

*Rev. Kingdon L. Brown*: About 1964 a group of us began to meet regularly, once a week, to practice, primarily, Yoga meditation techniques and to discuss psychic phenomena. That was in Detroit. I was working with Michigan Bell at the time, and had done several years of public relations with them.

Even today it is a little difficult to understand the things that began to happen in that experimental group. We assumed, for example, that God power or the power of Spirit was available in different forms, and from that assumption we simply built other assumptions, and we tried to channel and use this power. As a result, after a period of a couple of years or so, a number of people in the group developed a capacity to do healing work. Some developed a strong psychic sense, including mediumship, clairvoyance, and to some degree, prophecy.

"Did you credit this to Yoga?"

*Rev. Brown*: No, because we really went way past that. We just started by doing Yoga meditation. We simply kept meeting every week, and we felt that if this power were available, then there was no reason why it shouldn't be available to us. I don't know if it is significant, but many of the people in the group had become disenchanted with organized religion, but they were *not* disenchanted with their relationship to God.

"You're saying, then, that while they had not shut themselves off from God, they had shut themselves off from organized religion."

*Rev. Brown*: I would say that the majority had, yes. But they were all seeking, and one thing led to another. We finally chartered a small church which is still functioning and which I still head, St. Timothy's Abbey Church, the Founding Church of Essential Science.

"What would you say is the basic contribution of your Essential Science?"

*Rev. Brown*: I think it is probably the power of God. Primarily, what we've been able to do has been to activate this power and then, somehow or other, transmit it to other people. It's quite an infectious thing. I think we're reaching a point where there is some pattern to the kind of revelations people are getting.

We seem to be in a period of preparation for a rather severe change. I don't know whether it will be cataclysmic in the sense of some of the Edgar Cayce predictions; that is, I'm not entirely certain if it's earth changes, sociological changes, or political changes. But we are in preparation for a new consciousness. People separated from one another by thousands of miles are receiving very similar types of communications, similar types of awareness, and there seems now to be quite a definite pattern emerging with respect to this.

"And there is no contact between these people, no chance for collusion?"

*Rev. Brown*: If there is collusion, it is collusion at a source much higher than ours. For example, I know of some people in Ontario, who meet fairly regularly and receive communications which seem similar to communications that some people here in Arizona are getting. There is no earthly transmission between these two groups, yet they seem to be receiving urgent revelations or communications that indicate it is very much past the time in which we need a new spiritual consciousness.

"Have you received any communication from any particular entity?"

*Rev. Brown*: Yes, I have. Through my in-trance work, our group has received communication from a specific source that identifies itself as "Manta Ru."

"Who does he claim to be?"

*Rev. Brown*: I can't say exactly who, but, basically, he is giving us more information to prepare us for this coming change. The source is not clear, but there have been references to an ongoing observation. There seems to be some monitoring of this plane going on. Whether this is a God monitoring or some other kind of force, I don't know. Sometimes I have a feeling the source may be from another form of life, not what we usually speak of as a spiritual form of energy. They may be forms similar to us.

There is a repeated assumption running through these transmissions that a time limit is involved, that a monitoring and observing of Earth is going on. The transmissions seem to indicate that it makes no difference whether or not people know it or believe it, which is interesting. Some people will understand and some won't, and if they do not believe, there needs to be no convincing going on.

One group I know receives communications from some entity, or source, who calls himself the Voice of the Universe. This new kind of channeling seems little involved with the classical kind of mediumship communications, with the voices of Aunt Susie and Uncle Charlie. These new messages seem to be coming from a higher source, and here I mean a more abstract source, a source that deals with universal principles or laws. It is this kind of thing that is now emerging.

The whole subject of spiritual power, or spiritual energy, is interesting, because there appears implicit in this a transferral of this awareness or energy and also a change in it. In other words, the power of God, or the spiritual energy in the Universe, is used in one case for healing, but the very same activated power is used in another case for some other kind of manifestation.

I don't like to think of myself as a prophetic personality. In fact, we have not made these revelations too well known, or too public. I mostly try to introduce the techniques that we have used, assuming that they will lead people to their own insight. We feel this is preferable to presenting our particular insight for them to accept or reject. So we've made no effort to distribute the teachings of revelation.

"You don't consider yourself missionaries, then?"

*Rev. Brown*: No, not at all. We simply present the techniques to those who are interested in them. What usually happens is that they use the techniques and later receive the same insights that we did.

This method makes it much easier for me. People don't depend on me. After all, I am just a person like anyone else. These things happen around me, but I don't control them. When people look upon a person as prophetic, they tend to attribute the information more to the individual than to the source, and the individual becomes responsible. I have tried not to be responsible for the teachings themselves, just the techniques. It's the only way I can keep my own equilibrium. . . .When I left the business world to go into this work full time, I resolved that I would still try to function as consciously and as objectively as I could, even though these other things were happening.

"From what you have told me, your reception of the Divine Fire has not brought about a sudden, dramatic change in your life. You really became a revelator through a process of spiritual development, didn't you?"

*Rev. Brown*: Yes, although my life did change after the revelations came, and it's been changing right along, diametrically opposed to the original set of concepts that I held.

But I've always tried to present the revelations of Essential Science in a very matter-of-fact manner to others. As time progresses and you meet other people who have tried our techniques and our methods, you will find them very matter of fact, too.

"I hope that you do not mind—because any person who is a truth seeker is a friend—but I would like to help you to understand that by the Divine Fire, you no doubt mean the Divine Love," Dr. John Paul Gibson, Chief Elder of the Church of the New Birth in Washington, D.C., told me. "Jesus was the first to receive this Divine Love when he was baptized by John the Baptist, and a voice from Heaven came down in the form of a dove and said: 'You are my beloved son in whom I am well pleased.' And Jesus became the Christ."

Religious matters had confused John Paul Gibson until a most remarkable thing happened to him in 1945.

"A total stranger in a New York restaurant began a discussion with me on spiritual gifts of God the Father and mentioned the fact that new revelations had come to his attention in a book that had been received through the gift of automatic writing of a

Mr. James E. Padgett in Washington, D.C. The name of the book was *Messages from Jesus and Celestials,* and my new friend presented me with a copy of the volume," Dr. Gibson recalled.

Upon a close examination of the book, Dr. Gibson found that his personal search for the "Truths of the Father," that, in his evaluation, fulfilled the Second Coming of Jesus on Earth, had been realized in the writings received by James Padgett. For the next three years Dr. Gibson studied Volumes I and II of Padgett's transcriptions and based sixty sermons upon their texts. During the same time he corresponded with Dr. Leslie R. Stone, the editor of the books, who suggested minor revisions in the sermons, then granted permission for Dr. Ginson to use them as he saw fit.

"Dr. Leslie R. Stone was a close friend of James Padgett, and he was present when Mr. Padgett was receiving communications from the various spirit writers," Dr. Gibson explained. "Some evenings Mr. Padgett received as many as forty pages of material through the gift of automatic writing. Jesus and the other Celestial writers were able to write through Mr. Padgett only after he had received the Divine Love in sufficient quantity."

The front matter for Volume II of the *True Gospel Revealed Anew by Jesus* reprints a letter that Padgett wrote to an orthodox Protestant minister on December 28, 1915. Padgett began by explaining that he was a practical-minded lawyer with, at that time, thirty-five years' experience, thoroughly conditioned not to accept allegations of fact as true without convincing proof. He went on to state that he had been reared in an orthodox Protestant church and, until quite recently, had remained steadfastly orthodox in his beliefs.

But then, ". . . a little more than a year ago, I commenced to receive by way of automatic writing messages from what was said to be the spirit world, and since that time I have received nearly 1500 such messages upon many subjects, but mostly as to things of a spiritual and religious nature, not orthodox, and as to the errancy of the Bible."

With this bit of introduction, Padgett released his revelatory bull into the ecclesiastical china shop.

> Among the writers is Jesus of Nazareth, from whom I have received more than 100 messages. I will frankly say that I refused for a long time to believe that these messages came from Jesus . . . But the evidence of the truth of the origin of these messages became so convincing, not only from the great number and positiveness of the witnesses, but from the inherent and unusual merits of the contents of the messages, that I was forced to believe. And now I say to you that I believe in the truth of these communications with as little doubt as I ever believed in the truth of a fact established by the most positive evidence in court. I wish further to say that to my own consciousness I did no thinking in writing the messages. I did not know what was to be written at the time except the word that the pencil was writing.
>
> The great revelation of these messages from Jesus . . . is to make a revelation of the truths of his Father. He asserts that the Bible does not contain his real teachings as he disclosed them while here on Earth, that many things that he said are not therein contained, and many things that are ascribed to him therein he did not say at all. He wants the truths made known to mankind.
>
> And I must say that many of these truths which he has already written, I never before heard of, and I have studied the Bible to some extent. One thing in particular impressed me and this is what the truth is of his bringing "Life and Immortality to Light." The Bible does not state it, and I have not been able to find in any commentaries on the Bible an explanation of it.

According to Dr. Stone: "Mr. Padgett told me that when his brain and hand were controlled by the spirit while receiving the writings, he did not know in advance what the next words or sentences were to be written. If Mr. Padgett, when receiving the writings from the spirits, allowed his own mind to become active at the time of receiving the messages, the spirit communicating would stop controlling his brain until he had regained the inactive state so that the spirit could convey through his brain the exact words it desired to write." Dr. Gibson pointed out that this brief explanation tells us that the spirit, rather than the medium, must control the brain in automatic writing.

Why did Jesus wait so long to communicate the high qualities of truth received by Padgett?

"John the Evangelist answered that question in Volume II," Dr. Gibson said. "Jesus had tried others before, but he was not successful until Mr. Padgett was used. The brain has to be prepared by the development of the soul. The quality of a high truth requires that the brain be of high quality to receive it.

"When he first started to receive writings from spirits, Mr. Padgett could not receive the high truths until after he had obtained the Divine Love of the Father. However, he could easily receive messages dealing with moral or ethical truths, and of things of a material nature.

"Mr. Padgett was told by Celestial Spirits when receiving the early writings that he must pray to the Heavenly Father for Divine Love with all the earnest, sincere longings of his soul. When this Love came into his soul in sufficient abundance, it changed the quality of his brain into that high quality that enabled the high spirits to write through him the highest truths that had been lost to the world after the earliest followers of Jesus died–and which truths they were so anxious to put into print so that they might be given out to the world."

After many visits to Washington, D.C., and a ten-year association with Dr. Stone, Dr. Gibson became concerned about the safety of the many valuable writings left by James Padgett. Less than half of the material had been transcribed or printed, and Dr. Stone was getting along in years. Dr. Gibson began earnestly to suggest that some kind of foundation be established to preserve the new gospel of Jesus.

In the fall of 1955, Dr. Stone informed him that Jesus had selected a second instrument who was qualified to continue the work where James Padgett had left off. On November 7, 1955, in his hotel room in Washington, D.C., Dr. Gibson witnessed the first message from Jesus through the new instrument (who must remain anonymous). The communication affirmed Dr. Gibson as "among those disciples who are working to spread the Word of God" and offered the others encouragement for the establishment of a foundation that would preserve the new revelations.

Several meetings with attorneys in the next two months produced the resolution of the final details which would permit the incorporation on January 12, 1956, of the Dr. Leslie R.

Stone Foundation, so named to honor Dr. Stone for his thirty-year service on behalf of the Padgett writings. On January 2, 1958, the Foundation Church of the New Birth was established, replacing the Stone Foundation, which had been found to be unworkable for a successful church operation with a tax-exempt status.

"At the first meeting of the Foundation Church of the New Birth, bylaws that were two years in preparation were submitted by the Secretary and approved by our leader, Jesus of Nazareth, Master of the Celestial Heavens," Dr. Gibson said. "At the close of each meeting thereafter, we waited for comments and instructions from our Leader regarding the business at hand, either approving or disapproving the items."

The Church of the New Birth is an interdenominational Judeo-Christian Church, according to Dr. Gibson, with the ten following special holiday observances:

The First Observance: *Yom Kippur–Repentance Day–John the Baptist*. These holidays are observed on the last Saturday and Sunday in September.

The Second Observance: *Chanukah–Christmas–Epiphany*. These holidays are celebrated on three different dates–December 17 and 18; December 25; and January 6.

The Third Observance: *Passover–Easter*. Another Judeo-Christian double observance, this holiday is celebrated on the second Saturday evening and Sunday in April.

The Fourth Observance: *Shavuoth–Pentecost*. This date is observed on the Sunday that is closest to the fiftieth day after the second Saturday of April.

Here, with the permission of Dr. Gibson, are a number of excerpted revelations from the *True Gospel Revealed Anew* by Jesus (published in three volumes by Church of the New Birth, P. O. Box 996, Benjamin Franklin Station, Washington, D. C. 20044):

*The Power of Love to Redeem Men from Sin and Error*

I am here, *Jesus*.

My Father's love is, as I have written, the only thing in all this universe that can save men from their evil natures and make them at one with Him. This Divine Love is the one great power that moves the universe, and without it there would not be that wonderful harmony that exists in the Celestial Heavens of the spirit world; nor would so much happiness exist among angels who inhabit these spheres.

This Divine Love is also the influence which makes men on earth think and do that which makes for peace and good will among men. It is not possessed by all men, in fact, by comparatively few, yet its influence is felt over nearly the whole earth. Even those who have never heard of my teachings, or of my Father, enjoy the benefit of its influence in some kind of belief or faith in an overshadowing spirit of great power and watchfulness . . . So, notwithstanding the fact that my gospel is not preached to every creature, as I commanded when on earth, yet this Love of the Father is everywhere and is all pervading.

Still, it is not received in all that fullness that enables those who feel its influence to realize that God is their Father and they are his children, and may become members of his household in the Celestial Spheres.

No man can receive this Love unless he has faith in the Father's willingness to bestow it upon him . . .

Every man has in him the natural love which will give him great happiness in eternity as a mere spirit and inhabitant of the spheres lower than the Celestial, even though he refuses to seek for the Divine Love that will make him a divine angel of the Celestial Heavens.

Only this Divine Love can change the natural man into a man having the divine nature in Love that the Father has. I do not mean that man, even though he be filled with this Love to the highest degree, will ever become a god and equal to the Father in any of his powers and attributes. This cannot be, but this love will make him like the Father in Love and happiness and harmony. This Love has no counterpart in all creation, and comes from the Father alone. It changes not, nor is it ever bestowed on anyone who is unworthy, or refuses to seek for it in the only way provided by the Father.

. . . This Love has the power to change the most hardened sinner into a true child of God, if only through faith and prayer such sinner will seek for it. Let this Love take possession of a man or a spirit, and its power to purify and change the heart of that man or spirit never fails.

*The Real Truth of Life on Earth and What It Means to Mortals*

When men come to the knowledge that they are children of the Father and are under His care and protection, they will see that they must lead such lives as will fit them to become in union with the Father and be able to partake of His love which makes them, as it were, a part of Himself . . . There is in all men the potentiality of becoming a part of the Divine Essence. But in order for them to partake of this Divinity they must let the Love of the Father, in its highest nature, enter into their souls and make them at-one with Him. No mere love that they had bestowed upon them as creatures of the Father's handiwork will enable them to attain to this exalted condition . . . when [natural love] was bestowed upon them it was merely intended to enable them to live in a good and harmonious way with their fellowmen. It was not the real love that formed a part of the Divine nature of the Father, and it was not intended to make men a part of that nature. In order for men to receive this higher Love, they must do the will of the Father while on earth; or after they become spirits, they will have a more difficult work in receiving the wonderful inflowing of this Divine Love.

The earth is the great plane of probation, and the development of the souls of men depends upon their correct living in accordance with those principles which the Father has established as the means whereby they may receive this condition of Love, which alone can make them at-one with Him.

No man can of himself become fulfilled with this love, for in only one way will it come into his soul; and this is by prayer to the Father for its inflowing, and faith that He will give it to him who asks earnestly and humbly. I know that some men think that prayer is nothing more than an appeal to their own better selves, but I tell you that this is a wrong belief; and when they realize the truth that prayer ascends to the Father, and is heard by Him and answered, they will understand the great mission and benefit of prayer.

Let men live the most exemplary lives, and yet they will not necessarily become partners of this Great Love, and have the qualities that are necessary to enable them to receive the Great Gift of unison with the Father. I urge all men to live a good moral life, because it has its own reward in the spirit world, and makes them happier as spirit beings in a condition of mere natural love, and will fit them for a life in the spirit world which will bring to them happiness; but not the happiness of those who fit themselves for greater happiness in the Kingdom of Heaven or Celestial Kingdom.

. . . So let not men be content with trying to live good moral lives, but seek with all their hearts the Love that makes them truly angels of God; and such angels, as by reason of the Divinity which such Love brings to them, can feel and realize the certainty that they are immortal.

Immortality is only of God, and anything less than God or His Divine Essence, which makes the creature a part of that Divinity, is not immortal.

. . . Life on earth is an important part of the great eternity of living, and men should realize this to its fullest meaning, and not think the earth a mere stopping place where the spirit is enfolded in flesh only for the pleasures and gratification of its carnal appetites. This earth life is like a fleeting shadow of the spirit life, but an important shadow to the happiness which man may enjoy in the future. It is the most important period of man's whole existence, and the way that such life is lived may determine the whole future life of the man. I don't mean that there is no redemption from the grave, for the mercy of the Father continues into the spirit life, but when man fails to accept this mercy . . . he may never accept it in the spirit life.

. . . Let men seek this Divine Love, and in faith they will find it, and forever be one with the immortal Father, as He is immortal and happy beyond all conception.

*Why Men Should Believe the True Jesus Writes Through Mr. Padgett*

I am here, *Jesus.*

I, by reason of my soul development and my knowledge of spiritual things, was able to exercise these powers to an extent that made the people of my time suppose that I was the only Son of God, possessed of many of His powers and attributes . . . But I was only a mortal when on earth, and only a spirit after I passed from the earth to the spiritual life.

Of course, my development of the soul qualities were such as to enable me to do many things on earth which no other mortal could do; and after I became a spirit, I obtained a position in the spirit world that no other spirit had obtained. Yet I am only a spirit, a highly developed one, possessing more knowledge of God's truths and having more soul development than any other spirit.

If I were God or a part of God, I would be something more than the mere spirit that I am, and my position would be such that I could not, or would not, communicate with you in the manner that I do. But I am only a spirit, having the same form and means of communicating with the mortals of earth that other spirits have, only to a greater degree . . . My home, of course, is in a sphere far above that of the earth sphere, and my condition of development is far greater than that of any other spirit, and I am not of the earth in any particular, yet my powers are correspondingly great and my ability to communicate is in accordance with my powers and knowledge.

If I were God, I would not resort to the means of communication that I do now, and it would not be surprising that men would not believe that I would so communicate. But as I said, not being God, there is no reason that I should not communicate through you or any other qualified medium, the great truths of my Father and the plan provided by Him for man's salvation.

So men should not think that because I am the Jesus of the Bible and have for so many years been accepted and worshipped by so large a part of the human race as God—or rather a part of Him—that . . . I, as a spirit, have not the qualifications and powers of other spirits; and because I do so communicate, that I do that which, as God, I should not do.

### *St. Paul Explains His Thorn in the Flesh, His Experience on the Way to Damascus*

... [The thorn in the flesh] was no doubt at times that I was called to preach the truth of man's salvation as taught by Jesus.... Notwithstanding the Bible narrative of my conversion, I was not altogether convinced by the vision that I saw. I know now that it was a true vision and that I was called–but when on earth I had doubts at times, and this was my besetting sin.

... I am afraid that I will have to disillusion you, for I was never stricken blind or taken to the house of the prophet of God as the Bible says.

My vision, though, was plain enough, and I heard the voice upbraiding me, and I believed; but at times there would come this doubt that I speak of.

Of course, from my epistles, you would never think that I had any doubts, and I purposely abstained from making known my doubts, and so called it my besetting sin. But thank God that I never let that doubt influence me to prevent me from giving the work my call.... As I continued to preach, my faith grew stronger; and after a while, my doubt had left me, and in my later years I had no doubt.

### *Jesus Was the Natural Son of Joseph and Mary*

I am here, *Mary the Mother of Jesus.*

Was Joseph the father of Jesus?

I suppose I am the only one in all the universe of God who knows the fact with reference to that question, and I as a spirit of the Celestial Spheres, knowing only truth, say to you and all the world, that Joseph was the actual father of Jesus, and that he was conceived and born as any other mortal was conceived and born. The Holy Spirit did not beget him, and I never was informed that such a thing would happen. I was known by Joseph before the conception of Jesus, and by him I was made pregnant with that blessed son....

I was a simple Jewish maiden, and never had any knowledge that my son was to be different from the sons of other mothers, and it was not until after the development in him of the Divine

Nature of the Father that I realized that he was so different from the sons of other mothers.

*Jesus Claims That His Disciples Never Wrote All the False Doctrines Attributed to Him in the Bible*

. . . The sayings in the Epistles and in the Gospels and in Revelations to the effect that my blood saves from sin are erroneous. My disciples never wrote that false doctrine, for I repeat here, what I have before written you, that my blood has nothing to do with the redemption of mankind from sin, nor has my blood any effect in reconciling men to God or making them one with Him. The only thing that works this great result is the New Birth as I have explained it to you.

*St. John Says the Book of Revelations Is Not to Be Relied upon in Many Particulars*

I am here, *John of the Revelation.*

Much of the matter contained in the Revelation, I never wrote; but men or scribes who professed to copy the description of my vision added to it for the purpose of incorporating therein the views of the Christians of that early day, so that their views might be emphasized and in union with similar views that had been added to the Gospels and Epistles in the copies which these same persons or their predecessors in these views had made.

. . . There are enough truths in the Bible, though mixed with many errors, to lead men to the light and to salvation. Love is the great principle, and the fact is that God is waiting to bestow that love on mankind, if they will only seek for it, as it is the principle which is sufficient to lead men to the Celestial homes and happiness.

*What the Holy Spirit Is and How It Works*

I am here, *John.*

[The Holy Spirit] is merely the evidence of the working of God's own soul in bestowing upon mortals His love and mercy. The Spirit is God's messenger for this purpose and is not a creation of His, as is Jesus and mankind. It is merely an energy of the soul of the Father, conveying His love.

The Spirit could have no existence without the Soul of the Father, and is entirely dependent upon the powers of that Soul for its existence, and only in the sense that it conveys God's love can it be called the Comforter . . . [The Holy Spirit] is always present, waiting for men to receive it, and by their longings and prayers, cause their souls to be opened up to its reception. And this remember: that this Love of the Father is so very great that the Spirit which conveys it to man cannot become grieved.

### *The Prayer of Jesus*

Our Father, who art in heaven, we recognize Thou art all Holy and loving and merciful, and that we are Thy Children, and not the subservient, sinful, and depraved creatures that our false teachers would have us believe. We are the greatest of Thy creation, and the most wonderful of all Thy handiworks, and the objects of Thy great soul's love and tenderest care.

Thy will is; we become at one with Thee, and partake of Thy great love which Thou has bestowed upon us through Thy mercy and desire that we become, in truth, Thy children, and not through the sacrifice and death of any one of Thy creatures. . . .

We pray that Thou wilt open up our souls to the inflowing of Thy love, and that then may come Thy Holy Spirit to bring into our souls this, Thy love, in great abundance until our souls shall be transformed into the very essence of Thyself; and that there may come to us faith–such faith as will cause us to realize that we are truly Thy children and one with Thee in very substance and not in image only.

Let us have such faith as will cause us to know that Thou art our Father and the bestower of every good and perfect gift, and that only we, ourselves, can prevent Thy love changing us from the mortal into the immortal.

Let us never cease to realize that Thy Love is waiting for each and all of us, and that when we come to Thee, in faith and earnest aspiration, Thy love will never be withheld from us.

Keep us in the shadow of Thy love every hour and moment

of our lives, and help us to overcome all temptations of the flesh and the influence of the powers of the evil ones, which so constantly surround us and endeavor to turn our thoughts away from Thee to the pleasures and allurements of this world.

We thank thee for Thy love and the privilege of receiving it, and we believe that Thou art our Father—the loving Father who smiles upon us in our weakness, and is always ready to help us and take us to thy arms of love.

We pray thus with all the earnestness and sincere longings of our souls, and trusting in Thy love, give Thee all the glory and honor and love that our finite souls can give.

# THREE

## *Putting On the New Self and Acquiring Gifts of the Spirit*

When the Divine Fire scatters its sparks upon humanity, different receptors naturally respond in individual ways. But one of the more common themes of the revelation experience is a sudden, dramatic personality transformation.

In his *Deeper Experiences of Famous Christians,* James Gilchrist Lawson related brief biographies of such well-known evangelistic figures as John Bunyan, George Whitefield, Christmas Evans, Lorenzo Dow, Peter Cartwright, and Dwight L. Moody—either wicked, illiterate, or confused men (or various combinations of the three) before their conversion experiences.

Bunyan, who wrote the great classic *Pilgrim's Progress,* was a man of only meager formal schooling, a man known for wicked and blasphemous ways. Then, one day, after a sudden conviction of sin, he was passing through a field when the words "Thy righteousness is in Heaven" struck his very soul and he saw Jesus.

He ran home elated, searched the Scriptures in disappointment because he could not find the verse in the Bible, but maintained his excitement to the extent that he began to preach in little meetings. Bunyan went to prison for daring to hold religious meetings separate from the Established Church of England, but he made good use of his twelve years' incarceration by writing a book that has sold nearly as many copies as the Bible.

Christmas Evans, a Welsh evangelist, was a rowdy, quarrelsome youth who became converted to Christ after he had a vision of the Second Coming. As a troubled young minister, depressed with the burdens of preaching the gospel, he was walking from Dolgelly to Mchynlleth, climbing toward Cadair Idris, when he was touched by the Holy Ghost.

"It would come over me again and again, like one wave after another," he said, "like a tide driven by a strong wind, until my physical power was greatly weakened by weeping and crying. This event caused me to expect a new revelation of God's goodness to myself and the churches. In the first service I held after this event, I felt as if I had been removed from the cold and sterile region of spiritual ice, into the pleasant lands of the promises of God."

Peter Cartwright described himself as a "wild and wicked boy." One day, after dismounting his favorite racehorse, he suddenly fell to his knees. Blood rushed to his head; his heart palpitated; he felt death had come.

Confused and frightened by the experience, he succumbed to his mother's urgings to attend an evangelistic camp meeting. There: "Divine light flashed all around me, unspeakable joy sprung up in my soul. It really seemed as though I were in Heaven. The trees, the leaves, and everything seemed to be praising God. My mother raised the shout, and my Christian friends crowded around me." He became one of the great American pioneer Methodist preachers.

Charles G. Finney is considered by some to be among the greatest evangelists since the days of the Apostles. James

Gilchrist Lawson considers Finney's *Systematic Theology* to be "probably the greatest work on theology outside of the Scriptures."

But Finney had once been a skeptical law student. It was one morning in the autumn of 1821, while on his way to study law in the office of Squire Wright in western New York, that he had a vision of Christ hanging on the cross. That night after dinner, he stepped out of his office into a dark room and "met the Lord Jesus Christ face to face."

Finney later wrote that he saw him as he would see any other man. The Christ did not speak, but looked at Finney in such a manner that the young lawyer fell down at his feet and wept. A few moments later, he received a "mighty baptism of the Holy Ghost."

In Finney's own words:

> Without any expectation of it, without ever having the thought in my mind that there was any such thing for me, without any recollection that I had ever heard the thing mentioned by any person in the world, the Holy Ghost descended on me in a manner that seemed to go through me, body and soul. I could feel the impression, like a wave of electricity going through and through me. Indeed it seemed to come in waves and waves of liquid love; it seemed like the very breath of God.

Often the inner transformation seems so dramatic that, like Saul of Tarsus, the revelator feels compelled to take on a new name.

I remembered the woman seated before me as the pre-Bardot French sex kitten imported by Hollywood to add Gallic sultriness and allure to at least a score of motion pictures in the forties and fifties.

"They kept me in those insipid movies and tried to type me," said the woman I had known as actress Corinne Calvet. "I had about eighty-six words of dialogue in seventeen pictures. I said the same thing all the time."

But Corinne Calvet no longer exists. She has been born anew as "Corona."

"I think the best explanation for what has happened to me,"

she told me, "is that Corona's soul was living in Corinne Calvet's body. A part of my ego wanted all those things that Corinne Calvet was able to obtain, like fame and luxury and position and admiration and recognition and all those ego trips that we all go through. In the attempt for me to obtain those things, I pushed back the stronger force within me, which I knew was present and of which I was constantly aware."

Corona's New York City apartment was heavy with the scent of incense. Sitar music issued from a stereo set connected to a series of flashing lights. Her young son interrupted us by coming across the room to kiss my wife and me and the other people seated throughout the room. The woman before me was heavier than I remembered her from the romantic films I had watched in my adolescence, but her beauty was still to be noticed in any company of women. However, she was no longer concerned with maintaining the body that had once been so nearly perfect. Corona's interest now was in developing a perfection of the spirit.

"I constantly took care of that stronger force within me by studying dogmatic religions and by studying at the Self-Realization Center in California," she went on. "I received the teaching of Yoga and eventually the blessing which made me Corona, which means compassion."

Corona had her first mystical experience in early childhood. "I think my first manifestation on that level was the night before my first communion, when I had a dramatic vision of the Last Supper. I walked out of my bed as if I were a sleepwalker to behold it."

Did Corona mean that she had seen the vision during an out-of-body experience?

"If I was out-of-the-body, if I was taking an astral trip, I don't think I would have left my slipper behind where I went—unless my astral body decided to take the slipper so that somebody could find it and reassure me that I had been there and that I had really seen what I had seen. As far as I am concerned, I was there; and *they* were there, as much as you are here now."

What are Corona's plans for the future? "I am of service. I

don't have any plans, because if I had a plan, I would not be available for the work that is coming. So I live in the Flow, and I know that if I live in the Flow, everything that is supposed to come my way will have a chance to appear, and then I will do it."

When I asked her about "revelatory experiences," she stated that she could not remember a time when she had not had visions and minor revelations. But, as she herself stated, the Corinne-ego continually pushed back the stronger force within her, the Corona-awareness. When "Corona" did emerge as a result of the spiritual discipline of Yoga training, the actress assumed this new name along with her new identity.

As we have seen, not all revelators change their name. Rev. Kingdon Brown has not, "because I try to maintain my own identity. I don't try to merge with any of the revelations or teachings. I would not want people to begin reacting to me in ways which I would find psychologically difficult." But many of those who have been touched by the Divine Fire do not put on a new person to mask their former selves, but, I believe, in order to acclaim their evolved and blessed selves.

Dr. Walter Houston Clark told me: "The change in name which often follows the experience of a profound revelatory experience simply underlines the profound change of attitude that results from the experience. For each individual and those who surround him, his name becomes the epitome of those characteristics conceived of as himself. A change of name symbolizes for the individual this profound change that has occurred in the center of his being and serves notice on those who know him that he has become essentially another person."

[Director of Haly's Psychic Self Improvement, Oak Park, Ill.]

*Harold Schroeppel:* If the revelatory experience is genuine, I would feel that the revelator changes his name because he, as an individual, is changed.

In an awful lot of spiritual training, the individual, whether he be Yogi, monk, or priest, entering the service of God is expected to leave his past being, his past personality, behind him. Usually he is asked to change his name to Sister Theresa or Brother Sebastian or whatever—and this has no relation to John Woodsneck, who was born at such and such a place.

*Lasca Schroeppel:* When you have had such an experience, you simply have a new base of operation, and I think it is good to identify with this and throw away whatever uselessness you might carry with you. Throwing away the old helps you to maintain a high spiritual level.

When an individual has had such an experience, he becomes less concerned with prejudices, past conditioning, and all irrelevant things. When he sees himself as he really is, he not only sends, but receives, a clear signal. Maybe, instead of the experience *changing* an individual, he really becomes more his real self.

Dr. William Roll of the Psychical Research Foundation, Durham, North Carolina, sees the change of name as an abnegation of the old self:

"Of course, when we talk about Bill Roll or J. G. Pratt, and so on, and when we think about ourselves, it is the ordinary, encapsulated sort of personality. I think it's easier for me to see that when there is this hypothetical experience of something wider, we have to put a new tag on it. It is misleading, in a way, to use the old tag with all our petty pursuits and the sort of things we identify ourselves with in ordinary lives. When people join a monastery or an ashram or install themselves in some kind of order, it's sort of common to give up the old name."

*Dr. Al Siebert,* Clinical Psychologist, Portland, Oregon: Why do so many revelators change their names? I would say that they are indicating that: "Once I was human and uninformed and I had that name. But now that I've seen the light and found my inspiration and so forth, I am a new person; this is my new name, and the words I pass on to you are not my own, but come from a Higher Source.

"Look at what happens in many orthodox, formal institutions. A woman becomes a nun and changes her name. A man or woman gets a degree and they are no longer Betty or Al, but they are called Doctor. The name change is actually a formal part of many of these programs that are supposed to bring a person to a new level of spiritual goodness or to a new level of insight into human behavior."

Although the rite of Holy Baptism as practiced by the

Christian church is a "name-giving" ceremony, it was originally a purifactory ritual which in the early Church was the essential requirement for admission to membership in the Christian community. St. Paul transformed the original form of baptism into a sacramental rite of rebirth, simulating the death and resurrection of Christ.

According to S. G. F. Brandon:

> The Pauline doctrine of baptism recalls, in a striking manner, the assimilation of the dead with Osiris in the ancient Egyptian mortuary cult. Like the Egyptian rite, baptism for Paul effects rebirth or transformation to a new exalted state of being. Paul's view had a decisive influence and found dramatic expression in the baptismal ritual of the Early Church. Baptisteries were specially constructed to allow total immersion. The candidates took off their clothes and descended into the water, thus ritually symbolizing a dying to their old selves. On emerging from the baptismal water, they were clothed in white robes, received a new name and given mystic food of milk and honey, so proclaiming their rebirth by baptism to a new life in Christ.

A growing emphasis on the doctrine of Original Sin, in which the newborn inherits the wrath of God along with the collective sins of mankind, brought about the practice of infant baptism, the most common expression of the ritual practiced today. While it is a matter of debate whether or not Jesus himself baptized others, it was a well-established tradition in the early Church that the Holy Ghost descended unto him during his own baptism by John the Baptist and that Jesus commanded his own disciples to make disciples of all the nations by baptizing them.

But the rebirth which ensues after one has been touched by the Divine Fire has almost nothing to do with the renunciation of sin or the purification of self symbolized in the ritual of baptism. Pentecostalists speak of the "Baptism of the Holy Spirit," which is very much closer to what we are talking about in this chapter.

The Divine Fire seems to descend simply because it is needed—to heal, or to provide strength and courage for a weak mortal vessel.

A close personal friend shared with me the revelatory

experience that helped him "get it all together" and has enabled him to remain sober since October 1956:

"At the age of twenty-one I was more animal than human. I had been drinking for a mere five years, yet I was a completely warped personality. Officially, I had been charged and convicted a total of thirty-eight times for military and civilian infractions of the law. . . . At seventeen my conduct drove my family to have me removed from the home for the sake of the younger children. Violence was my constant companion. Berserk escapades, blackouts, straightjackets, hospitals, jails, detention barracks became my environmental scene. By the age of twenty I was a social misfit who had abused every agency that had offered me assistance and who had acquired a reputation as an unstable troublemaker.

"Six months before I had my last drink I was introduced lightly to the A.A. program . . . I could see that it was a good one for alcoholics; but, of course, I did not consider myself in that category. Somewhere in their literature, though, I read the words, "God as I understand Him" and "Power greater than myself." I had long since denied what I considered to be the impossible Christian platform of the orthodox churches, yet it did not occur to me that these two simple expressions offered me the very spiritual freedom I had so longingly pursued . . .

"After that brief flirtation with A.A., I was drunk again in a month-long bout with demon rum. When I sobered up on that Canadian Thanksgiving Day in October 1956, I had the shakes and the room was pitching. I was horrified at my reflection in the bathroom mirror. I walked to a canal and considered suicide; but thankfully, I instead called an A.A. friend of my father's. He came and told me his story of human degradation that made my fall from grace seem almost insignificant. But the way he said it and his unmistakable depth of sincerity caused strange things to happen inside me.

"Late that night, or early the next morning, I experienced the first in a series of spiritual encounters . . . I can still feel the electric vibrations that seemed to fill the room and my body. I saw an illuminated vision of Jacob's Ladder. At the base of the ladder, I witnessed a fierce death struggle between a dark-clad person and one clothed in white garments. It was a fight to the death, and I knew they were both me. The white-clad warrior was victorious; the vision disappeared; and I shook with happy excitement. I knew freedom was mine. I have not taken a drink since.

"Personal revelations have occurred with burning intensity on three other occasions since I was given a new life. In the spaces between these experiences, it has been necessary to expose myself to people who maintain contact with spiritual forces. I consider these forces to be universal, yet each person seems to understand and apply them in a different, personal way. I believe spiritual tolerance to be much more vital to our survival than any other expression of tolerance."

In *The A.A. Way of Life* "Bill," the cofounder of Alchoholics Anonymous, wrote of his revelation experience as he lay in a hospital:

> My depression deepened unbearably, and finally it seemed to me as though I were at the very bottom of the pit. For the moment, the last vestige of my proud obstinacy was crushed. All at once I found myself crying out, "If there is a God, let Him show Himself! I am ready to do anything, anything!"
>
> Suddenly the room lit up with a great white light. It seemed to me, in the mind's eye, that I was on a mountain and that a wind not of air but of spirit was blowing. And then it burst upon me that I was a free man. Slowly the ecstasy subsided. I lay on the bed, but now for a time I was in another world, a new world of consciousness. All about me and through me there was a wonderful feeling of Presence, and I thought to myself, "So this is the God of the preachers!"

In *Alcoholics Anonymous* Bill states that he had always believed in a Power greater than himself, but the image of God offered by organized religion had always irritated him. Then a friend suggested that he choose his own conception of God, and he "stood in the sunlight at last." Bill found that: "It was only a matter of being willing to believe in a Power greater than myself. Nothing more was required of me to make my beginning. I saw that growth could start from that point." From that day until he died, he never took another drink of alcohol. He had undergone a complete character change and he felt a sense of victory followed by peace and serenity. "God comes to most men gradually," he wrote, "but His impact on me was sudden and profound."

*Alcoholics Anonymous* is filled with dramatic and sudden metamorphoses of men and women hopelessly enslaved by alcohol, existing miserable and crushed lives, who experienced a spiritual revolution which enabled them to emerge as free beings. In many of these stories the recipient of the wondrous reprieve mentions being surrounded by a light or watching light streaming to him. In an appendix to the book (*Second Edition of the Big Book, New and Revised*), the anonymous author states that the terms "spiritual awakening" and "spiritual experience" are mentioned often. Even though it was not the compiler's intention to create such an impression, "many alcoholics have nevertheless concluded that in order to recover they must acquire an immediate and overwhelming 'God-consciousness' followed at once by a vast change in feeling and outlook."

The Twelve Steps to recovery as set forward by Alcoholics Anonymous are listed below:

> STEP ONE: We admitted we were powerless over alcohol—that our lives had become unmanageable.
> STEP TWO: Came to believe that a Power Greater than Ourselves could restore us to sanctity.
> STEP THREE: Made a decision to turn our will and our lives over to the care of God as we understood him.
> STEP FOUR: Made a searching and fearless moral inventory of ourselves.
> STEP FIVE: Admitted to God, to ourselves, and to another human being the exact nature of our wrongs.
> STEP SIX: Were entirely ready to have God remove all these defects of character.
> STEP SEVEN: Humbly asked Him to remove our shortcomings.
> STEP EIGHT: Made a list of all persons we had harmed, and became willing to make amends to them all.
> STEP NINE: Made direct amends to such people wherever possible, except when to do so would injure them or others.
> STEP TEN: Continued to take personal inventory and when we were wrong promptly admitted it.

> STEP ELEVEN: Sought through prayer and meditation to improve our conscious contact with God as we understood Him, praying only for knowledge of His will for us and the power to carry that out.
>
> STEP TWELVE: Having had a spiritual awakening as the result of those steps, we tried to carry this message to alcoholics, and to practice these principles in all our affairs.

They are marvelous principles to practice. From one perspective, as the reader may see, A.A. offers its members an unstructured religion with God-consciousness as its goal.

*The Little Red Book* of A.A. states that it would be inconsistent to "mince words" over the fact that a spiritual awakening is an essential part of their recovery program. Hence, six of the Twelve Steps are of a spiritual nature:

> Knowing the fallacies of alcoholic thinking, it is inconceivable that we could recover from alcoholism without . . . some power greater that our own . . . Without the spiritual principles of the Twelve Steps . . . A.A. . . would be a group of disgruntled alcoholics, temporarily on the wagon . . . Our sobriety demands a personality change. We gain this in the form of a spiritual awakening from living the A.A. program.

"When I had what I thought was a spiritual experience," a young man once told me, "I didn't head for a minister; I went to the local chapter of the A.A. I didn't have a drinking problem, but I had heard of their ideals. I knew that they helped men and women to find that inner strength, and I knew that their picture of God came closest to my own. I was driven away from the organized church when I was a teen-ager, and I would be repelled every time one of my relatives told me that I was making God or Jesus sad by my life-style. I needed to take a big step toward self-awareness of my own worth. Even though I wasn't an alcoholic, the people at A.A. welcomed me and really helped me put it all together in my head."

Not infrequently, a revelator finds his "new self" possessed of talents which he never had before. In October 1971 I received this account from an American evangelist whom we shall call Rev. Bobby:

"I quit in my junior year of high school and joined the Marine Corps. After coming out of the Marines, I worked on construction for a while, then went into the insurance business in Florida. My wife and I joined a church and I received Jesus Christ as my savior. In a nine-month period, I enjoyed some of the richest blessings, revelations, and miraculous dealings of the Holy Spirit. I was baptized with the inner baptism of the Holy Ghost and this was consummated, or confirmed, by the experience of glossolalia, speaking in tongues.

"Shortly after I had spoken in tongues, I was involved in a miraculous healing. This kind of experience was brand new to me, and I would have scoffed at such an experience prior to my Baptism by Fire. This was probably the most instrumental event in the complete change in my life.

"It was about this time that the Lord began to actually speak to me during prayer, during periods of meditation, and He told me that he expected me to make a drastic change in my life and to preach the Gospel and to go the way that he would lead me. In other words, I received my calling.

"I had never been able to do public speaking. I was intimidated by crowds. I would have stage fright so bad that I would become ill. So when the Lord said he wanted me to preach, I thought surely He must be making a mistake. But I told Him that if this was what He willed, I would have to depend on Him for the power to do so. Also, I admitted that I had never read the Bible much before, but He assured me that through the power of the Holy Spirit, the Word of God would be open to me and I would understand all the hidden meanings and the allegories, all the parables—everything I needed to know.

"I had a talk with the State Secretary of the Disciples of Christ Brotherhood in the state of Florida, and he told me that the only way to be sure of my experience was to try preaching. . . . I said that I would need at least a month to prepare, but they told me that I would lead the worship and give the sermon in two weeks.

"At first I was terrified, but I just opened the Bible, let it fall where it may, and let the Lord speak to me. As He spoke to me, I took notes and from there I composed a sermon. I put it on tape, played it back once, and forgot about it.

"When the Sunday arrived, I thought at first I would be nervous, but when I stepped into the pulpit, it was as if I had been born for preaching. I opened my mouth and let the Lord talk through me. Let me say that this church had not had anyone come forward to dedicate his life or to make a first-time commitment or acceptance of Christ in about six months. I daresay that in a period of six years, that church had only had five or six people come forward. But the Holy Spirit took over and spoke through me and at the end of the sermon, fifty-four people came forward either to rededicate their lives to Christ or to accept Him for the first time.

"I accepted a call to a church and I left my job with the insurance company. It took a good deal of courage to make the decision and to take such a great cut in salary, but the courage came through the Holy Spirit. My former mundane existence has been changed to a vital, very meaningful, and very rich life. I have received a realization of God and of His will, and some of the revelations that I have received have been astounding, because they concern things that I had never before been concerned with."

Perhaps the most astonishing gift that revelation brings is that of healing. Apparently the same energy that heals a revelator can be channeled through him and used to heal others.

The Rev. Mark Weston and his wife, who serve a Methodist congregation in Ankeny, Iowa, have been blessed with the gift of healing. I met the Westons on Labor Day 1971 at the home of Fay and Mary Clark, and I was able to visit with them at that time. Later, Rev. Weston was to tell me that the ability to help other human beings had "added a new dimension" to his life and had deepened his faith.

"In all of these experiences," he said, "my concept of God has increased and my awareness of the power of God has become greater."

*Rev. Mark Weston*: While I was serving a church in southern Iowa, one of the families came to me and said that their baby had to go back to the hospital in Des Moines for a kidney operation and they asked if they might have the child baptized that Sunday. I agreed to the baptism, and while I was conducting the baptismal service with my conscious mind, I also asked the

God Spirit to bless and heal the child. On Tuesday the parents called excitedly from Des Moines and said that the doctors had decided they did not have to operate on the baby. It no longer showed any evidence of kidney malfunction. I offered a prayer of thanksgiving that God had blessed and healed that child.

*Mrs. Weston*: So many of my experiences have come through dreams and sometimes visions with my eyes open. One night I had a dream in which this chubby-cheeked little girl with a golden blond ponytail came into view. I knew that she had to go to the Mayo Clinic for help at once or her life would be destroyed. I awakened, told my husband, and he rushed to the drawer of a night chest and pulled out the photographs of our congregation. When I saw the little girl and identified her as the one in my dream, Mark said that he would make arrangements to counsel with her mother in the morning. The mother told him that she had been longing to take the girl to the clinic because she had been having convulsions since early in her life and had been on medication ever since. Even though it was the clinic's busy month of August, the woman's request came through in three days and they were off in five days. Today that child has been making fine progress in school.

*Rev. Weston*: One night my wife and I were visiting with a young doctor when we happened to notice that there were musical notes around his head and shoulders. I picked up intuitively that when he was a young man he had made a commitment to his father that he would become a musician. He had never completely released this commitment. He thought he should be a musician because his father had wanted him to be one, but he decided to become a doctor so he could help people. This old promise was troubling his subconscious. We were able to show him how, with God's blessing, he could release himself from the pattern that had been set by his father and go on to become a doctor in his own way.

*Mrs. Weston*: I think one of the greatest joys I have in life is to see people grow within and to this inner awareness of a power greater and a source mightier than they can comprehend.

During one of my first major surgeries I was so miserable because I was allergic to the three pain killers they had given me.

The doctor said that he was sorry, but I would have to go it alone. So I blessed my body, and I "put it out" under the warm sunshine on the warm sands near the clear, blue water. I noticed that my body became very relaxed, even though I was packed in ice. There appeared at the foot of my bed a huge glowing ball of heat, and I felt it radiating all through my body. The nurse later marveled how I could get such a good night's sleep.

*Rev. Weston*: I do a great deal of counseling, and in my counseling I ask God to tell me what is wrong with the individual. When my counselees walk in the door, the God part of me identifies the situation, and then I am able to help them find and overcome the problem. After one session of counseling, one woman made a confession of all the troubles that were plaguing her. She said if she did not tell me, I would just find out through my guidance.

*Mrs. Weston*: Once when we were camping, our three-year-old son bruised his foot while playing on the rocks along the lake. He cried all night, and the foot became hot and feverish. There were red streaks going up his leg. We were far out in the woods and I became alarmed. We had nothing to kill his pain, and he was unable to eat or sleep because of his suffering.

I put his foot in my lap and put my hand over it. I kept singing to him and repeating over and over again that he was being healed and that this would happen on his own and he would be able to go swimming the next day. I kept singing this over and over and over for half a day. I could see the swelling coming to a head, and he dozed off to sleep. I kept on singing and reassuring him that he would be able to walk. He hit his toe on a table leg and didn't complain. The swelling appeared to have drained, and the next day he was able to go swimming.

Sometimes when my husband and I are working together with people, I am able to see symbols around individuals. Sometimes I see the color of their auras. Many times I am unable to understand the symbol, but with my husband's help, we are able to counsel these individuals and help them get more relief so that they might better enjoy life.

*Rev. Weston*: Occasionally in my counseling I will use auras, as I use the pattern of light and color around the individuals to diagnose the conditions that are bothering them.

Some time ago I saw an advertisement for a book by Daniel Fry entitled *Can God Fill Teeth*? I accept the reality of spiritual healing, but I could not help laughing at the notion of a tooth cavity being filled by faith. I even believe that cancers can be reversed by positive mental attitudes. But a tooth-filling definitely requires a substance from outside the body, an actual materialization of matter that can halt tooth decay and plug up evidence of its former presence. It all seemed preposterous to me; but out of curiosity, I began a correspondence with Evangelist Williard Fuller, a former Baptist minister, and his lively and attractive wife, Amelia, a former schoolteacher, the subjects of Fry's book.

I found the Fullers most friendly, as evangelists should be, and able to provide a great deal of documentation for their claims. Fry's book is filled with dozens of testimonials from people who state that, utilizing the Fullers as a channel, some Force outside themselves straightened their teeth, filled cavities, even grew new teeth where before there had been empty sockets in their gums. I was most impressed, however, by the following statement from a Chatsworth, California, dentist that appeared in the *Valley Advertiser/Herald Tribune* for June 22, 1967:

> "Supernatural" tooth fillings that "didn't look like any metal I've ever seen before" were described to the *Valley Times* today by a Chatsworth dentist . . .
>
> Describing himself as a member of the Valley Dental Society and the American Dental Association, the dentist said that he had several patients with extra teeth and several with fillings that had been done, they said, "by a supernatural force."
>
> "The fillings are lighter than gold and yet more yellow than silver," he said. "I've attended conferences of dentists and have never seen anything like this before."

Bill Middleton, Religion Editor for the Jacksonville, Florida *Times-Union*, told of being present during one of the Fullers' healing sessions. The article from which the following comments have been excerpted appeared on October 2, 1971.

> ... Rev. Fuller called for all those who wanted to be helped to come to the front of the church.... When they were standing there, he went quickly from one to the other, touching each person's face, a hand on each side of the person's jaw, as he gave a short blessing.... Soon, there were open mouths of astonishment as well as open mouths that had been healed.... There was Amanda Smith who stood in the church aisle. She had a radiant smile as she explained that her two front teeth had been crooked. "Now they're straightened," she said ... "It scared me at first ... I could feel a tingling in my mouth."
>
> Other people said they also felt tinglings. Some said they felt a numbness.
>
> A cluster of the curious was around Ann Bolling Jones who was shaking her head in disbelief but belief. "It's been a whole change ... All of my fillings were dark. Now, they're bright. And a crooked tooth I have is definitely moving. I believe with God, nothing is impossible. I believe in a miracle through God. You can use my name if you give all the credit to the power of God."
>
> Linda Barnes: "I had an old silver filling. Now I have a new one."
>
> Jess Neely: "One filling is turning to gold. It's a miracle."
>
> Duane Kimbriel, age 9: "My gums overlapped my teeth. Now they don't." He opened his mouth. Everything appeared normal.
>
> But what perhaps brought on the most excitement were the cases when a "filling" could be "seen" coming into the mouth.
>
> It was noted that never did Rev. Fuller even suggest that a person had been healed. He let them say what was wrong, and what they thought had happened. If the person indicated a change had taken place, Rev. Fuller took no credit. He thanked the Lord.
>
> Gladys Lowens could hardly speak, as she excitedly said to anyone listening: "When he (Rev. Fuller) held the mirror so I could see, I saw the filling coming in while I was looking at it. As he held the light I saw it coming in, white porcelain filling in the cavity."

> . . . When asked what happened to her, Thelma Caine said she had had a chipped tooth, but that "now it is rounded out and there is gold there. There was no gold there 15 minutes ago."
>
> . . . Standing beside her was Jim Ladd who said he had seen Thelma Caine before, "and I saw her before that [the gold filling] came in there. I saw it come into her mouth. It grew. It came in like water flowing. It just spread. I saw it smooth over."

Bill Middleton said that after he had witnessed the "miracles" at the Unity Church on Lomax Street, he contacted several Jacksonville ministers. In substance, he wrote, they seemed to agree on one thing: "If you believe in the Bible, and if you believe in the miracles in the Bible, is this any different?"

To determine whether or not Williard Fuller's work was indeed any different from the miracles in the Bible, I interviewed the spiritual "dentist" myself:

*Rev. Williard Fuller*: When I was fourteen years of age, I had a divine call to be a minister. The entire experience was vivid and real and directed straight to the heart of my soul. But it was quite a few years later that I had the real encounter that was proof to me of a personal contact with spirit.

In a religious camp meeting I was instructed by impressions to get up from my seat and to walk a goodly distance to an isolated place. There I waited until a man that I had never met came up to me, touched me with his hand, and broke out in a message to me. I instinctively knew that it was a message from the mind of God being delivered to me by the voice of this person.

In this encounter, I was told that I would be used as a funnel through which God would pour blessings upon his people. This time the awareness of the Spirit stayed with me persistently, and I was forced out of my Baptist ranks because of the new territories in God which I was to pioneer.

About a month later, I was with a small group of people at a nondenominational meeting when I felt a peculiar joy. I raised my arms to praise God and burst out in a Heavenly language. I could not stop. I went on in delirious praise. This joy was an evidence to me of spiritual touch.

Fifty-seven hours later, when I was on my knees praying alone, an audible voice, clear and concise, spoke to me from outside of myself and said: "I have given to you the gift of miracles, the gift of healings, and the discerning spirit. You shall lay hands on people in the name of Jesus, and I shall heal them." Then, although I had never believed in them and as a Baptist minister had preached against them, I had a vision. I saw right before me the children of Israel traveling to the Promised Land. In this moment I was seeing a portion of ancient history.

From that time on, I was able to manifest healing powers in my work with people. I saw cancers just dry up and fall off. I saw goiters just disappear in front of my eyes. I saw people that had been suffering years from rheumatoid arthritis suddenly drop their crutches and begin to jump and to praise the Lord. I saw people with horrible warts and growths have their disfigurements vanish.

Then I heard about a man whom it was said prayed for dental needs. I traveled one hundred miles to be in a service with this man, and that night the evangelist laid hands upon my head and broke out into a prophecy about my life: "Think it not strange my son the things that thou hast seen me do this night through this my servant. All the things that thou hast seen me do through him I shall do through thee. And greater things I shall do through thee than thou has seen me do through him."

Soon afterward, I discovered, the Spirit of God would anoint me, and I was able to pray for people with dental needs. . . . Testimonies now come in that point to well over fifteen hundred people each year receiving dental healings and more than twice that many continue to receive healing blessings in other areas. I receive a blessing from God each time I see the miracle.

There is no big financial machinery behind my work, nor any monied board of directors. I just endeavor to be of service wherever I'm able. My wife shares in this ministry with me. Hers are primarily psychic and spiritual gifts of the world of knowledge and wisdom. She has been a great help in other areas and certainly is a staunch prayer partner.

# FOUR

## *A Blinding Light from Heaven*

Psychic sensitive Betty Allen told me that, while she sat at her typewriter, "I was bathed in golden light. It was just like being flooded with love, and I felt like I was sitting in a beam of light. I realized that there was a remarkable world beyond my ordinary senses. I realized that I was a part of it, and I knew that I wasn't really struggling alone."

In his classic work, *Cosmic Consciousness*, Dr. Richard Maurice Bucke did not presume to place himself in the company of the illumined individuals whose lives he examined in his book, but he did relate—in the third person—the account of his own revelatory experience:

> It was in the early spring, at the beginning of his thirty-sixth year. He and two friends had spent the evening reading Wordsworth,

> Shelley, Keats, Browning, and especially Whitman. They parted at midnight, and he had a long drive in a hansom (it was in an English city). His mind, deeply under the influence of the ideas, images and emotions called up by the reading and talk of the evening, was calm and peaceful. He was in a state of quiet, almost passive enjoyment. All at once, without warning of any kind, he found himself wrapped around as it were by a flame-colored cloud. For an instant he thought of fire, some sudden conflagration in the great city; the next, he knew that the light was within himself. Directly afterwards came upon him a sense of exultation, of immense joyousness accompanied or immediately followed by an intellectual illumination quite impossible to describe. Into his brain streamed one momentary lightning-flash of the Brahmic Splendor which has ever since lightened his life; upon his heart fell one drop of Brahmic Bliss, leaving thenceforward for always an aftertaste of Heaven. . . . He saw and knew that the Cosmos is not dead matter but a living Presence, that the soul of man is immortal, that the universe is so built and ordered that without any peradventure all things work together for the good of each and all, that the foundation principle of this world is what we call love and that the happiness of everyone is in the long run absolutely certain. He claims that he learned more within the few seconds during which the illumination lasted than in previous months or even years of study, and that he learned much that no study could ever have taught.

Mrs. Jo Peters of Honolulu, Hawaii, told me of a most interesting experience which her little daughter Andrea had in December 1971:

"In a matter of fifteen minutes, Andrea came down with a fever of 106 degrees. I quickly started putting her in ice packs and gave her vitamin C. During the evening it would get down to 104, then it would go back up to 106. The next morning the fever was nearly gone, because I kept her in cold water. My background is in nursing, psychology, and nutrition. I passed my state board exams, but didn't go into practice.

"At eleven thirty that morning, I was holding Andrea in my arms, relieved that her fever had gone. She was lying across me, and all of a sudden she began to laugh. Then she made a horrible face and breathed in forcefully. Several times I asked her what was the matter, but she didn't answer me.

"She was looking up at the ceiling, and she started to describe a scene. I asked her to tell me about it. She said that it was the most beautiful color. She does not do well with colors. She's four now and she still gets them mixed up.

"She said she saw the color blue, described some other colors, then she screamed horribly. After this terrible scream, she began to smile again. 'I see Jesus on the Cross,' she said.

"We are not Catholic. Our children know about Jesus, but we have never taught them about Jesus on the Cross. 'He is looking at the little animals and talking to them,' Andrea said. Then she said, 'The Light is sooo beautiful. It is gold and it is yellow.' She screamed again, then smiled, just as she had done before, and said: 'I see God. Oh, Mommy, God is Light! *God is Light!*'

"I have never taught her that. I have always said God is Love. But she kept repeating over and over that God is Light and that He is so beautiful. She is not a dramatic child and never talks expressively.

"All of a sudden Andrea reached out and said, 'Mommy, I don't want to go there yet. Please keep me away.'

"She hugged me very tight and came out of it. It was ended.

"I talked to her later, and she remembered the experience clearly, but each day it would fade away a bit in her memory. Now when I talk about it, she doesn't know to what I am referring. I think she came close to passing on."

"I get the light when I'm doing healing work," Peggy Townsend said. "This is the light of Christ. Now, I do not say Jesus Christ. There are many Christs. This Christ dwells within each of us, and I think that we can all do what he does. I know that when I am working with healing there is a blinding flash of light when I know the healing has been sensed by the stricken."

The well-known Chicago medium Deon Frey described her contact with the light of the Divine Fire at some length.

*Deon*: I remember being in meditation for quite some time and sitting in my room this night when all of a sudden the whole room was filled with light, as if the sun were shining brightly.

"Was there a color to the light?"

*Deon*: The light seemed to be emanating from one corner of the room, and it seemed as though I could almost make out a form. The color was indescribable. It had edges of violet hue, but it was crystal white, or mother of pearl, and so bright that it could almost blind me.

I had a feeling of oneness with it, a unity. It was like being one with everything all at once. The only way I could describe it to myself afterward when I thought of it was like I was water in a sponge. I just became suddenly drawn into it. It was like a love that one really can't understand from the earth plane, because it's such a spiritual envelopment. You want to stay. You don't want to return. You don't want to come back to the conscious state, although you are in a conscious awareness.

Although I heard no voice, I was filled with a knowing quality. I just knew things. It wasn't as if the light were speaking to me, but it seemed to give me direct answers to a lot of questions on my mind.

"Did you say that you sensed a presence in the light?"

*Deon*: For a moment I thought that the light was going to form into the Ancient of Ancients. I seemed to have an awareness that it could be a man, it could be a woman, or it could be both. But I knew that whatever it was, it was not anything that I should fear. I think this is what is meant by becoming one with the light and letting your light shine forth.

Many revelators have mentioned a brilliant light that surrounded them at the onset of their experience. Such reports immediately bring to mind the account of Saul on the road to Damascus. When I asked Dr. Richard Rubenstein, Professor of Psychology of Religion, Florida State University, about the light phenomenon, he stated that he should consider that one aspect of the "blinding light from Heaven" might be cultural. "Millions of Christians have read, or have been told, of Paul's great conversion and the accompanying revelation which were initiated by the blinding light," Dr. Rubenstein said. (However, as we will see, the phenomenon of the brilliant light occurs to those who have never heard of the New Testament story of Paul.) Dr. Rubenstein did go on to point out another psychological aspect of the phenomenon:

"The real question may be, to what extent are we in touch with our unconscious depths. The appearance of the blinding light could involve what I call a cessation of normal ego function, the function by which one apprehends the day-to-day world, by sight, by touch, in a sort of average, practical way. In revelation experiences, you no longer have that. The day-to-day world ceases for a while. In the case of St. Paul, he fell down. He wasn't even able to eat, drink, or see for three days. And it was when his contact with the day-to-day world ceased that the revelation came to him."

Almost without exception, those who have experienced the sudden flooding light have stated that their sense of time was obscured; and while in this state of Eternal Now, they realized a sense of unity with all things.

"I think that what happens is that with the cessation of contact with the normal, day-to-day world, one becomes more aware of one's own unconscious world," Dr. Rubenstein said. "That is obvious, for example, in the world of dreams. We don't dream during the day, but as our attention withdraws from the waking world, we become aware of another world within our own psyche, and that is the world of dreams, which is a part of the world of our unconscious. And so the 'blinding light' would seem to me to be an onset of a renewed contact, not with some world out there, but some world within ourselves."

Al G. Manning is a 1950 Magna Cum Laude graduate from UCLA with a degree in Business Administration. He has served in an executive capacity at two aerospace manufacturing and research firms, and currently, in addition to directing the ESP Lab at 7559 Santa Monica Boulevard, in Los Angeles, he maintains his accounting business in his capacity as a CPA.

Al is an energetic, perpetually smiling man with a ready sense of humor. I have known him for a good many years, but it was not until I was doing research for this book that I asked him to relate his illumination experience:

"I was in my middle twenties, suffering from ulcers and migraines, wearing two different pairs of glasses. I had been doing a lot of seeking, but I suffered from what I have come to call the 'Phi Beta Kappa syndrome.' My seeking was purely intellectual. I literally worshiped at the altar of intellect, subscribing to *American Scholar* and doing all sorts of things that were ego fodder.

"Then one night I had what I would have to term an out-of-body experience. It was as if a searchlight were turned on directly above my head and shining down upon me. I was in the middle of this shaft of light. I could feel the warmth and the love.

"A voice spoke from within the stream of light. I was not allowed to bring back any messages from the experience, although for some time after the illumination, I had the power of levitation.

"I tremendously misinterpreted the experience in the beginning. I had the idea that, 'Oh, goody, all I have to do is a little research and I'll fill the Hollywood Bowl with a levitation demonstration.' Ridiculous, isn't it? When you're young, what can you say? But it did start me seriously seeking, and the inspiration of that experience has stayed with me all these years. I have touched the Light many times.

"I think what the Kahunas call the High Self fits into what we do with the Light here at the Lab. We work frequently to help other people get their own revelation. I like to touch this as the mystic experience, separated from the psychic.

"It is my position that the mystic experience is the common denominator of all religion and that without touching the Divine Fire, the Light, whatever you like to call it, worship is only of the mind. Worship becomes of the whole being only when we touch the Light and feel the response of love.

"I sit down at my altar each morning and evening. The first thing I do is, Huna-like, to reach up to my highest concept of God, to something greater than I, and I *expect* a response. No, I do not always find the room brightened and find myself bathed in light, but there is always a response. There is a *feeling*, not just subjective, either. The energy often feels like someone shot some electricity on my head. The descriptions are difficult because we don't have words in our language to describe them well.

"But every time I reach for the Light, whether I am at a big business conference at somebody's board of directors meeting, or sitting comfortably before my altar, or driving down the street, I expect a response. If I don't get one, I stop everything until I do, because to be that far out of tune would be just chaos to me. Before I leave my altar, I reattune myself with the Light and send it before me. The affirmation that I use varies somewhat, but, basically, it is this:

" 'Now I direct the Light to go before me to make the path easy and the way straight. May the Light bring upliftment, inspiration, effectiveness, enthusiasm, and joy to everyone who comes close to my aura. I am Light going to meet Light, and only goodness can result.'

"In my opinion, my feeling of the Light is quite the same as the feeding of the *mana* to the High Self by the Huna. It compares to the *samadhi* of the Hindu or to the *satori* of the Zen Buddhist or to the Holy Spirit of the Christian.

"The 'tongues of flame' are only one more way of being touched by the Light, and I have seen tongues of flame touch people in the room during some of our own meetings. More often it is seen as a shaft of light, and we all wish to walk in it."

Of course, the experience is also described by those outside of the Christian tradition.

In her autobiography, *"Don't Fall Off the Mountain,"* Shirley MacLaine tells of the night that she lay shivering in a Bhutanese house in the Paro Valley of the Himalayas. Her teeth chattered and her insides "tied themselves in knots." As she lay wondering how she might overcome the terrible cold, she remembered the words of a Yoga instructor in Calcutta who had told her that there was a center in her mind that was her "nucleus, the center of your universe." Once she had found this nucleus, he had said, pain, fear, sorrow, nothing could touch her. "It will look like a tiny sun," he had instructed her. "The sun is the center of every solar system and the reason for all life on all planets in all universes. So it is with yours."

Miss MacLaine closed her eyes, searched for the center of her mind. Then the room "left" her. The cold room and the wind outside began to leave her conscious mind.

"Slowly in the center of my mind's eye a tiny round ball appeared," she writes. "I stared and stared at it. Then I felt I became the orange ball."

The center began to grow and generate heat. The heat spread down through her neck and arms and finally stopped in her stomach. She felt drops of perspiration on her midriff and forehead.

> The light grew brighter and brighter until finally I sat up on the cot with a start and opened my eyes, expecting to find that someone had turned on a light. Perspiring all over, I was stunned to find the room dark. I lay back. I felt as though I were glowing. Still perspiring, I fell asleep. The instructor was right; hidden beneath the surface there was something greater than my outer self.

In his *An Introduction to Zen Buddhism,* D. T. Suzuki quotes Professor Nukariya's description of *satori*, the state of illumination attained by reaching a higher level of consciousness:

> This is what the Masters of Zen call the mind of Buddha or Bodhi (the knowledge whereby man experiences Enlightenment or Prajna, the highest wisdom). It is the godly light, the inner heaven, the key to all the treasures of mind, the focal point of thought and consciousness, the source of power and might, the seat of goodness, of justice, of sympathy, of the measure of all things. When this inmost knowledge is fully awakened we are able to understand that each of us is identical in spirit, in being and in nature with universal life, or Buddha, etc.

In his *Varieties of Religious Experience*, William James quotes Vivekananda's work on Raja Yoga, which was published in London in 1896, in regard to the state of mystical insight known as *samadhi*:

> ... The mind itself has a higher state of existence, beyond reason, a superconscious state, and ... when the mind gets to that higher

> **state, then this knowledge beyond reasoning comes.... All the different steps in yoga are intended to bring us scientifically to the superconscious state or Samadhi.... Just as unconscious work is beneath consciousness, so there is another work which is above consciousness, and which, also, is not accompanied with the feeling of egoism.... There is no feeling of *I*, and yet the mind works, desireless, free from restlessness, objectless, bodiless. Then the Truth shines in its full effulgence, and we know ourselves—for Samadhi lies potential in us all—for what we truly are, free, immortal, omnipotent, loosed from the finite, and its contrasts of good and evil altogether, and identical with the Atman or Universal Soul.**

The Hindu scripture *Bhagavad-Gita*'s instruction on how best to practice Yoga ends with the promise that ". . . when the mind of the Yogi is in harmony and finds rest in the Spirit within, all restless desires gone, then he is a Yukta, one in God. Then his soul is a lamp whose light is steady, for it burns in a shelter where no winds come."

*Lasca Schroeppel*: The question you raise about the blinding light is a challenge, and I try so often to understand this, because every time it happens to me, it is a little different. Sometimes instead of seeing a blinding light, I will see the complete spectrum of the rainbow, rotating in succession, sometimes rapidly cycling and recycling. Other times it is a pure light, like the light you see before the prism separates it.

Sometimes I feel that perhaps the "prism" is my body, or an intermediary, that takes the spiritual energy which is always there and breaks it up for my use and our comprehension. When I see this white light, it is not like an ordinary light source. It is frequently accompanied by a very clear, pure tone without harmonics.

This light is so inconceivably brilliant that it is almost as if it is being drilled into me with many little protons of light—each with individual energy, yet, collectively, pure and bright. I would love sometime to have an EEG done when I am experiencing this phenomenon. I have a feeling that all leads that are usually diversified, depending on the area of the brain, would be in some sort of clear unison. Perhaps lower centers of the brain would also be in some sort of unison or harmony or reciprocity. I feel that when you are able to be a vehicle for this sort of thing that you have offered yourself, or identified yourself, with the Divine. Sometimes I have felt pure energy going through my hands.

*Harold Schroeppel*: Our students frequently see this blinding light, but my own personal consciousness did not come to me that way. It kind of filtered in little by little, and one day I walked outdoors and suddenly I had a kinship with everything that was out there. Gradually, over the years, I learned that I had a lot longer reach than I thought I had, but my consciousness simply did not happen all at once and it did not happen with a blinding light.

When we take students up the scale, we start with their attention on the physical body, then the emotions, then move them through the energy flows and the psychic levels into the awareness of the Chakras, the spinning vortexes; and if we can, we move them into higher consciousness. Very frequently they see a brilliant light at this point. If they see a light, and a lot of it, they make their own relationships.

I think that when it comes to the consciousness of God, you may grow into it, but I doubt very much if you will ever grow out of it.

Whether the blinding light and, indeed, whether all revelatory material, comes from "some world within ourselves" or some Intelligence without will have to be a question resolved by each individual reader, perhaps, each individual expression of the revelatory experience may require an individual answer.

As Dr. W. G. Roll told me, "It is true that this light phenomenon does occur. Some people believe it's a sort of quasi-physical light. When we get into these areas, it becomes difficult to distinguish between the physical and the spiritual worlds. What we call the spiritual, what we call the physical, what we call the mental, are probably all the same thing."

Dr. Walter Houston Clark speaks of the phenomenon of the blinding light in connection with those who have undergone revelatory experiences as "... a kind of symbol of the new and freeing insight into the nature of the subject's existence. However, I am inclined to think that the profundity and excitement of the experience causes some kind of nervous activity that produces the light. Of course, in some sense, this may have a cosmic origin. We think of all such insights as 'coming from God' or having some ultimate source, so that my speculations here must remain exceedingly superficial."

When I discussed the question of the blinding light with Dr. Al Siebert, he said that he felt the experience might simply be a metaphor for suddenly comprehending knowledge. "We say things that we don't know are 'in the dark,' and we usually refer to things that we do know as being in the light—'I've seen the light,' for example. I would go for another kind of hypothesis. And that might be getting back to birth itself. The infant is in total darkness in the womb, then when it is born into the world, it is suddenly overwhelmed by the lights and the sounds—the *blinding light* of this world that it has suddenly been thrust into."

"Aha!" I replied. "A playback effect. When the revelator is *reborn* through the Divine Fire, some mechanism in his psyche replays the traumatic explosion of light that overwhelmed him at the time of his physical birth experience. Is that what you mean?"

*Dr. Siebert*: Possibly, I don't know. But I see a lot of things that happen to infants as explaining some of our religious stories and experiences.

Writing in *Psychiatry* (Vol. 29, 1966), Dr. Arthur J. Deikman refers to the mystical perceptions of encompassing light in terms of his hypothesis of a "sensory translation," which he defines as "the perception of psychic *action* (conflict, repression, problem solving, attentiveness, and so forth) via the relatively unstructured sensations of light, color, movement, force, sound, smell, or taste. . . .'Sensory translation' refers to the experience of nonverbal, simple, concrete perceptual equivalents of psychic action."

In Dr. Deikman's concept, "Light" may be more than a metaphor for mystic experience:

> "Illumination" may be derived from an actual sensory experience occuring when, in the cognitive act of unification, a liberation of energy takes place, or when a resolution of unconscious conflict occurs, permitting the experience of "peace," "presence," and the like. Liberated energy experienced as light may be the core sensory experience of mysticism.
>
> If the hypothesis of sensory translation is correct, it presents the problem of why sensory translation comes into operation in any particular instance.
>
> In general, it appears that sensory translation may occur when (a) heightened attention is directed to the sensory pathways, (b) controlled analytic thought is absent, and (c) the subject's attitude is one of receptivity to stimuli (openness instead of defensiveness or suspiciousness). Training in contemplative meditation is specifically directed toward attaining a state with those characteristics. Laksi (1961) reports that spontaneous mystic experiences may occur during such diverse activities as childbirth, viewing landscapes, listening to music, or . . . sexual intercourse. Although her subjects gave little description of their thought processes preceding the ecstasies, they were all involved at the time in intense sensory activities in which the three conditions listed above would tend to prevail.

Whatever the answer, I agree with Al Manning that the mystical experience is the common denominator of all religion and when he observes that without the Divine Fire, worship is only of the mind. The light of the Divine Fire seems definitely to symbolize a rebirth. Dr. Richard Maurice Bucke said that those individuals who had experienced the illumination of the "subjective light" had had their "spiritual eyes" opened "and they have seen."

Dr. Bucke goes on to say that those who have received this illumination "have created all the great modern religions, beginning with Taoism and Buddhism, and speaking generally, have created, through religion and literature, modern civilization." One recognized a member of this remarkable "family" by the fact that "at a certain age, he has passed through a new birth and risen to a higher spiritual plane. The reality of the new birth is demonstrated by the subjective light and other phenomena."

Dr. Bucke found the same semantic difficulties in dealing with the universality of Cosmic Consciousness as I experienced in speaking of the Divine Fire. We are separated in time by nearly a century; but, perhaps, if Dr. Bucke and I could ever get together and compare notes and hypotheses, we might find that we were writing about the same kind of experiences.

If I were to draw a distinction, Dr. Bucke was writing about a mystical state of illumination, which, it seems to me, is a goal unto itself, a plateau of enlightenment, the creation of a new self in the state of highest good. But although a revelator may achieve Cosmic Consciousness, not everyone who has achieved Cosmic Consciousness is a revelator. The recipient of the Divine Fire *begins*, rather than *ends*, his work with the illumination experience.

I am writing about a transfer of thought and spirit from what we call God, or one of his messengers, to a recipient who feels compelled to share his revelation, or other spiritual gift, with his fellows. I am writing about the "missionary" element in illumination that inflames the recipient with the desire to "go quickly and tell," to put his visions and dreams into practical application and help others discover for themselves the universal spiritual truths.

# FIVE

## *Tuning In on Primal Sounds and Cosmic Vibrations*

The Divine Fire, it seems, can stimulate any of our five senses; either with flashes of light, "feelings," or direct verbal messages. Some revelators, however, also report music—and there may be some clues to how the Divine Fire operates in the experience of those who have been literally "tuned in" on a power beyond themselves. We must remember that even without words, rhythm and vibration can still carry information.

An Iowa college student recently found out that he had the ability to do many things which he had never before thought possible. Calvin, as we shall call him, was reared in a strict Missouri Synod Lutheran farm family; yet after a dramatic revelatory experience, he found that he could sit down at the piano and play lovely melodies which just "came to him." Calvin had had no formal musical training and had never received even one elementary piano lesson.

Calvin's initial revelatory experience came after an all-night "bull session" in his college dormitory, during which the conversation had centered around Fatima, St. Bernadette, miracles, and religious and occult experiences. He had a brief vision of a door that he could not open, but could only be opened from the "inside." He became very warm, began breathing rapidly; then he turned cold and his breathing became very shallow.

Calvin fainted and his friends panicked when they could detect no sign of breathing at all. Suddenly his eyes shot open, and he began speaking as an entity named "Marian." He told the young men assembled secret and hidden things about themselves, and when he later found himself at a piano, he went into a light trance and began to play the instrument with authority.

I sent a tape recording of Calvin's melodies to Jack Wheaton, President-elect of the National Association of Jazz Educators, a member of the music department at Cerritos College in Norwalk, California. It had occurred to me that some revelatory material was being relayed in nonverbal terms, so that a revelator might not be able to find words to articulate the experience and be driven to express himself in such nonverbal communication as music.

Jack Wheaton's analysis of Calvin's music was as follows: "The left-hand accompaniment, for the most part, is a technique called an 'Alberti bass,' indicating a method of rhythmically playing the underlying harmony in such a manner that a continuous rhythmic flow is maintained, giving a forward motion to the accompaniment. This style of left-hand accompaniment did not come into common practice until the classical period, roughly 1750-1825.

"Although the left hand is in a classical-period style, the melodic and harmonic structure is modal, using the miolydian (sol, la, ti, do, re, mi, fa, sol), lydian (fa, sol, etc.), and dorian (re, mi, fa, etc.) modes. This modal and harmonic structure is not characteristic of the classical period, which was pretty much major-minor orientated in harmonic structure. The modal structure is very characteristic of current rock and folk-rock tunes

(Beatles, etc.) and/or the harmonizations used by sixteenth- and seventeenth-century solo singers (galliards, minstrels, etc.)."

In Wheaton's opinion, the music reflected no particular well-known composer of any recent historical period. Calvin's music could be the result of "extremely well-developed tonal memory and facile muscle-memory," and the young man may be "reproducing what he has heard and stored in the unconscious."

On the other hand, Wheaton was bold enough to consider that Calvin might be temporarily possessed when he entered the light, trancelike state which preceded his playing. "Some soul wandering the astral world, who was a former musician-composer, possibly frustrated in his attempts at recognition, might be using this boy to get attention," he speculated, adding that reincarnation might also offer an explanation for an ostensible musical illiterate suddenly being able to compose music at the piano.

Eventually Calvin came to the attention of sympathetic and experienced men and women, who were able to counsel the youth and enable him to adjust somewhat better to the psychic explosion that had been detonated within his being. One night, while in the company of a clergyman and other professional and lay men and women, Calvin went into trance and produced the following message, thus demonstrating that his revelation experience might also be translated into verbal, as well as nonverbal, expression:

I am Marian.

"Welcome. Do you have a particular reason for coming to talk to us?"

The body [Calvin] has called.

"What message do you have for the body?"

The light of the triad, the symbol of peace, unity, and understanding, the growing spirit, the achievement of one.

"Very good, I'm certain that's what he is striving for. What can we all do to increase our knowledge and understanding of spirituality?"

The basic need is awareness of what surrounds, what composes all things. The secret lies within your inner self. To tap this awareness, one must learn how to reach inside and to bring forth the knowledge that is always there. Turn into yourself. Become as one with the Light. Try to work for all, not just for self alone.

"Does the personality who is speaking come from a universal source, or does it come from an individual consciousness?"

The source lies in no area, because it is the area. It is of consciousness, yet it is of things that are not seen, not heard of, not thought of. It composes all, and yet it is one.

Universal Mind is a reference to a being, yet to comprehend, one must visualize an Allness, a Oneness with the Light. This is the Mind–the consciousness, the awareness of all that there is and was and will be. The Mind is all; you are all together to form the Oneness.

"Must I put away my physical personality in order to attune to this Oneness?"

The self draws from the central Source. You are as one with it, yet the main difference is the awareness and the degree that one is with it. To put the self back in the central Source is to become as pure as One.

From the level from which you are viewing reality, "would you explain to us a bit of the principle of the continuation of life? Do we reincarnate and come back into physical embodiment?"

As Oneness with the Light we all have the same beginnings and the same ends. When one is born, he is in complete attunement with the God Mind, but the imperfection of the physical plane creates ego and its need to think of only one and no one else. Therefore, we must try to return to God Mind by using imperfect vehicles. It may take a series of times before we develop fully, before we evolve to become one with the God Mind. We must experience all the pain and suffering that we have caused other beings who were created from the God Mind. This need to experience results in the cycle of lives, dying, being reborn until the imperfections are alleviated or brought forth.

"Some people say that Jesus of Nazareth *died* for us; others say that he *lived* for us. Was it Jesus' life or death that is most important to us. Would you turn to the Universal source of knowledge and see the answer that would be given?"

Full comprehension cannot be contained in one physical mind, yet this is to be told: The entity called Yesu of Nazareth is of one attunement to the One Mind. Throughout his entire life, he maintained spiritual attunement with the Universal Mind. He had no death, because death only exists on a physical plane. His death was not spiritual, and the spirit is the true body. His body died because of the man-substance, yet his spirit lived and became alive again.

Calvin's parents were present that evening when he became a channel for Universal Mind, and they left the house extremely disturbed, certain that Calvin could not have learned such things in Sunday School or Lutheran confirmation class. Had their son become possessed by Satan? Or had they, totally unaware, been rearing some bizarre kind of mystic?

Last spring a well-known psychic, Mrs. Nell Westergaard of Florida, told Jack Wheaton some interesting things about music which he recalled for me:

"Superior intelligences in outer space are using rock music to drain off much of the excess energy from our youth. Somehow or other, they live off the energy we turn loose in anger, primitive music, drugs, etc.

"Extremely complex musical instruments, such as piano and organ, require 'help' from persons on the 'other side' for mastery.

"We are seeing the return of some types of music used centuries ago in many of the ancient mystery religions to achieve release from the physical body for astral travel.

"Persons can get 'hooked' on music as well as drugs.

"Music can be used for hypnotic conditioning and could easily be used in the future to help control a computerized technological dictatorship.

"Most great composers receive their inspiration while asleep, traveling to higher astral worlds, hearing the advanced sounds, then trying to reproduce them when in the body and awake. Much of rock could be coming from the sudden thrust into the lower astral worlds, by drugs and unprepared meditation."

Contemporary music surely seems to be one of the most effective methods of raising the vibratory rates of large masses of people—at once instructing, inspiring, informing them and, perhaps on an unconscious level, urging them to find the Primal Sound that created the universe.

To pursue the interrelationship between music and the collective unconscious, I asked Jack Wheaton to expand on the subject:

"Throughout history, music has been used as a method of lifting man outside of himself. It seems that music has been used for such a purpose in two basic ways: (1) To elevate man's consciousness through inspirational music, and (2) to work as a cathartic, literally letting it all hang out by loud, repetitious rhythms and melodies. Compare these methods with today's musical extremes, the gentle sound of the church choir and organ versus the terrifying penetration of the electric guitar and drums.

"From what I can gather, these two musical extremes exist in most cultures and have battled for supremacy through the history of Western civilization. From what McLuhan and others tell us about returning to a tribal culture, it would seem logical that the hypnotic loudness of the Dionysian-type music would accompany such a transition.

"Somehow, traditional forms and styles of classical music have run out of gas. Most contemporary classic music lies either in the electronic idiom or is in the "toot-whistle-boom" school of intellectual nonsense. Any serious ideas seem to be coming from the jazz-folk-rock field. The musical emphasis in the previous age was on developing individual virtuosity, isolated intellectual and artistic development, until the classic pianist was like a nervous, high-strung thoroughbred. Today's musical world finds the emphasis on groups, not individuals—a characteristic of the Aquarian Age with its emphasis on brotherhood.

"Rock music today is the simplest and cheapest—and least dangerous—way for young global village adolescents to 'trip out.' Escape from a frustrating, depressing, boring environment is only the flick of a switch away. Unfortunately, this escape can be damaging, at least physically, when it results in permanent hearing loss because of the high decibel level apparently necessary to achieve a full 'high' on rock sounds. Psychologists tell us that this level in most live rock concerts and in many adolescent bedrooms across the nation is above the threshold of pain. So we have another interesting phenomenon–music that deliberately inflicts physical pain upon the listener, giving a masochistic twist to rock's attraction and turning most rock concerts into sadomasochistic ceremonies.

"Music enters the human nervous system through the auditory nerves and is transported to the higher levels of the brain via two small knobs at the base of the thalamus, man's interior, more primitive brain. Studies have shown that man's automatic nervous system reacts without conscious effort or resistance to music. For instance, music faster than the normal pulse rate can actually speed up the pulse, increase or decrease the respiratory rate, cause glandular secretions to take place in the blood stream, and trigger involuntary emotional responses. Possibly one of the reasons that music creates problems for the generation gap is that Dad's nerves are already on edge, his adrenalin is already flowing, his body is already in a state of partial 'fight or flight' because of heavy freeway traffic or a frustrating day at the office, when he opens the door to his home, expecting to escape from the dangerous world outside, and is greeted by a multilevel decibel bombardment of sounds that are designed to tax his automatic nervous system even further.

"Modern physics and ancient Yoga both tell us that everything in our universe, solid or nonsolid, is vibration. Matter is nothing but atoms and molecules vibrating at a particular rate. In fact, you could destroy or reproduce anything in matter if you knew its exact vibrational and density factors.

"Transcendental Meditation and Self-Realization Fellowship both use Mantra Yoga [silent repetition of a given sound or sounds] to develop their followers spiritually. The vocal level and the rhythmic rise and fall of an evangelist's voice may be more important in reaching an audience than the content of his message. We know of Joshua and the Battle of Jericho, where the walls came tumbling down via sound. Today our scientists are capable of creating a weapon that would locate the frequency vibration of a piece of matter and disintegrate it with a flick of a switch.

"Iowa State University found that they could considerably increase the rate of growth and the yield of corn by playing music through loudspeakers across the growing fields. Dairymen and poultrymen have already discovered that music raises their yield and quiets their animals and birds. A lady in Denver experimented with playing different types of music over growing beds of pansies. The plants responded best to the music of Bach and Mozart. Hard Acid Rock killed the plants in less than two weeks.

"Recent dentistry studies have indicated that music can be used in place of an anesthetic in dental work and dental surgery. Studies in dyspepsia and neutralizing stomach acids showed that soft, classical music, played while eating or shortly thereafter, reduced stomach acidity more than any of the chemical antacids used. Dr. James Barrett at Southern Colorado State, a musician and former music teacher as well as a psychologist, said he believes some day scientists will be able to treat some heart conditions and some glandular problems with music. Centuries ago Plato said that he cared not what others taught in the schools of a society, but that if he could teach music, he would eventually control that society."

For the past two years I have valued a friendship with a fascinating young occultist-musician named Wilburn Burchette. By the time he was twelve, Wil was deep into his unorthodox experiments with music. It occurred to him that since everything in our universe is composed of vibratory atoms, then vibration is movement, movement is time, and that, to achieve any creative-spiritual breakthrough, man must rise above time.

"I considered music to be an art form of time, through time, and in time. I assumed that everything was time. However, that which conceives time doesn't necessarily have to be in it," Wil told me. "The breakthrough to Higher Reality is outside of time. When you break through time, that is revelation, that is breaking through to the Godhead."

The young boy was experimenting with his music when his personal breakthrough occurred: "I was getting to a point where my mind was blank. I remember shifting consciousness and having a sensation of my mind being above time. I felt I could move forward, backward in time. The physical sensation is an orgasm of the soul, because you are in complete, absolute union.

You extend your mind and being out of this dimension, and *wham!* You receive a knowing beyond words. When you transcend over into the other dimension, you split in two. This is what all the alchemists brought out: you split in two, and yet you are one. This is pretty weird for most people, but you have to split in two, you have to have another being which can realize the Absolute, the Godhead. These two *you's* are in perfect union.

"It was a grand experience for me. I was elated. It was a great revelation. It was a union with the Godhead. I realized what was real and what was not real. I had an understanding beyond words. Everyone can achieve this transcendence if they want to. Everybody should."

Wilburn Burchette's personal revelation was given a marvelously translatable expression through a music which he calls Impro. It is Wil's belief that he has cracked music's emotional code, thus becoming able to trigger in his audiences the emotions that he, as performer, wishes to communicate. Wil further believes that he has rediscovered the occult music of the ancient mysteries. In his performances, he does not seek to play *music* but *emotions.* He has discovered that certain frequencies control certain moods, and he is able to directly involve the listener in his occult concerts.

The farther Wil was able to move his consciousness back in time, the more difficult he found it became to separate the concepts of music and altered states of consciousness. "I believe that in the early days of the Earth, communication was a thought-inference system," Burchette says. "Under such a system any audible sound would have been communication of some sort. Consequently there would have been no differentiation between language and music.

"But I think that music became separated along the way, because of its special properties. It was more sophisticated. The division, then, between language and music would have come about as these special properties became more pronounced. Thus language became a lower means of communication. It was more precise and was used to carry out the affairs of material existence. It was more functional in a day-to-day situation.

"Music, on the other hand, would have been taken over by

the priestcraft and made their special domain. For music is, and has been since its beginnings, the method of communication with the gods."

The musical efforts of the priests were largely directed toward one goal: finding the Primal Sound that created the universe. This search is responsible today for the Hindu holy word, *Om,* and for the many sacred chants and mantras of Eastern religious teachings. This Sound, or vibration, was believed to reveal the nature of things and the phenomena of life.

Pythagoras, an initiate of this school of thought, later developed this concept into what he called "the Harmony of Spheres." According to this theory, each celestial body (as well as every atom) produces a particular sound due to its movement, its rhythm, or vibration. All these sounds and vibrations form a universal harmony, in which each element, while retaining its specific function and individuality, contributes to the unity of the whole. Anyone blessed with the proper attunement could thus hear the celebrated "music of the spheres."

"The ancients," Burchette explains, "believed that everything that existed had a voice and that all creatures were eternally singing the praises of the Creator. But contemporary man, because his soul is enmeshed in the illusion of material existence, can no longer hear these divine melodies."

Burchette assembled all these cerebral-psychic tools and began to fashion images in his mind. If one could properly identify his personal consciousness with the music being heard, the musician reasoned, he might be able to tie in his thought processes with the ideals of music, or "the praises of the Creator." If one would then open up his mind and let his *emotions* carry him, he could transcend the "illusion of material existence" and thereby expand his state of consciousness to the extent that he could actually hear the music of the spheres. And that, exactly, is the theory of Impro, the transcendental music.

"Impro isn't a new idea," Burchette is quick to point out. "It's just that in recent times no one has asked *why* people felt blue or happy when they felt a certain strain of music. And that is what Impro is about—feeling."

In asking that *why*, Burchette discovered that "music is not real; scales are not real. Music is a divided system. The only true, pure music is based on an emotional tone scale."

Just what is this emotional tone scale, and how is it used? "The emotional tone scale is another way to think," Burchette believes. "Instead of a tone, each line and space represents an emotion. The degree of emotion is indicated by the note's position on, between, above, or below the five parallel lines called the staff. The staff is ascertained by a character called an 'empathy clef,' placed at the beginning.

"Empathic ideas are expressed by employing traditional notes, rests, and other standard notation. Such characters hold their traditional definitions except where noted. Standard rhythmic symbology is retained, as it measures the duration of the emotion expressed."

Chords are still possible within the emotional tone-scale notation, as are accidentals. Key changes can be indicated. "The key in which the piece is played is always a contrasting emotion, such as 'light/dark,' 'pride/shame,' or 'joy/sorrow.' "

The interrelationships between music and consciousness already alluded to proved to be the essential bridge Burchette had to cross in order to develop the concepts of Impro and the emotional tone scale. The bearded musician realized that consciousness and music share some of the same qualitative values:

"I define consciousness as a point with the ability to recognize the dimensions of time through comparisons. As such, it has being. Now, in order for it to be able to recognize these different dimensions implies that it has a past and it foresees a future, because it is aware that it occupies some place in between. Taking these three dimensions of time—past, present, and future—three would be the smallest unit of consciousness related to time. Consciousness can thus be seen and expressed as flowing through time.

"Music is related to consciousness because it, too, is aware of itself as existing now, between the past and the future. But music is the only art form that moves in time. Painting, sculpture, all of these have *spatial* dimension. They occupy space, but not time. A painting is a finished creation that hangs on a wall. It does not flow *through* time, though it may survive *in* time. Emotions, on the other hand, have the ability to transcend space and flow freely through the past, present, and future.

"Emotions are not stagnant; they are dynamic. This is why music motivates them so well. Consciousness, music, and emotion all share dimension in time. This transcendant quality of music makes it the best form with which to control emotions."

Once the theory as well as the mechanics of both Impro and the emotional tone scale were worked out, Burchette realized he would have to find the right musical medium to express his discoveries. A guitarist for half of his thirty-two years, it seemed only natural that he choose this instrument as his vehicle of presentation. To get the full effect of Impro across to his audiences, however, it would be necessary to construct a special "Impro guitar." Long, tedious hours went into the arduous process of tearing down and rebuilding. By the time it was finished, six different woods had gone into the guitar's construction. Included in these were mahogany (the base), soft pine, elder, and rosewood. The neck is inlaid with abalone shells.

An Impro guitar is not, however, a requirement for successful communication of this art. The principles of Impro can be applied to any instrument, including the human voice. Furthermore, Burchette believes that Impro could be an excellent tool in the classroom. The teaching of musical taste, or aesthetics, to elementary school children has long been a problem to the sincere educator. With the use of Impro, however, greater listening enjoyment and increased self-awareness can easily become the products of the daily music hour.

Impro is a concept that embraces the principles of music and emotion and successfully weds them. Impro teaches that a specific note on the scale can inspire in an individual an equally precise emotion. Thus application of this knowledge allows the composer and/or performer to control the emotions of his listeners. Properly employed, a musician may actually be responsible for raising and expanding the consciousness of all whom he encounters.

Gerard Gottula of the Future Foundation, Steinhauer, Nebraska, told me that he believed one might acquire the revelatory experience if he were able to tune himself into a higher state of vibration and reach the Christ consciousness frequency.

"Since each physical body is just one state of vibration," he said, "I believe that we may be like a capacitor in a radio, and this capacitor must be electrically balanced to work to perfection. Until mankind learns that Love is a true balance, we will continue to experience 'static' and chaos in our lives.

"When the individual first tunes into the Christ consciousness frequency, he may very often experience a blinding light that signals full contact. He may change his own name in order to set up a vibration, or frequency, that is more compatible with the work that he will now do.

"There are higher dimensions around us functioning on different vibratory levels, just like radio frequencies, to which we can attune ourselves. Different entities can travel on various frequencies, according to their vibratory rate, and Supreme Intelligence binds us all together."

I suppose that I shall never forget that night in the summer of 1969 when I was awakened by a strange sound that I can only describe as the buzzing of a *metallic bee.* Our bedroom seemed suffused by a very soft, greenish light. I propped myself up on one elbow. In principle I am pacifistic, but when I saw what appeared to be a man in a striped coat leaning over my wife, moving his arms in a fluid, undulating motion, I reverted to defense reflex responses. I remember emitting the primal scream of anger-outrage-fear, then swinging my arm back to deliver a roundhouse left. The blow never landed.

The adrenalin was pumping. I was instantly awake, but I crumpled to the bed, the defensive blow undelivered. I began to weep, not I would like to think out of fear, but in awe or confusion. It was now that my sleeping wife awakened. Marilyn reached out her arms to me as if I were her child rather than her husband. Her hands moved over my body gently, soothingly.

"Don't be afraid," she said in an uncharacteristic monotone. "He won't hurt you. You will not be harmed. Listen. Listen." If indeed this was not all some bizarre dream and nothing more, I have no conscious memory of whatever I was to hear.

My wife and I awoke the next morning entwined in one

another's arms. I mention that ostensibly irrelevant domestic detail, because it has been the only time in our fifteen-year marriage that we have ever so awakened. We are both extremely active sleepers, constantly bumping into one another during the night, tug-o'-warring the covers, struggling for more than one's fair share of the too small queen-sized bed.

We opened our eyes at precisely the same moment. For me, time had not existed, and I looked wildly about for our bedroom invader. It was a bright summer morning. We were alone in our room. The children were beginning to stir.

I told my version of the previous evening's incident. Marilyn could remember taking me in her arms and comforting me, but she had no idea why she had done so. She thought that she could recall hearing a voice, but she was quite emphatic that it had not been her own.

The next evening I was once again awakened by the buzzing of the metallic bee. I felt a momentary jab of fear. I was lying on my stomach. I slid both elbows under me, banishing the annoying fear with an effort of will.

The peculiar buzzing sound was coming closer, becoming louder. The bedroom was once again being suffused by a greenish light. I looked over my shoulder, and a tiny orb of greenish light was moving toward our bed, making that eerie buzzing sound. It hovered over Marilyn's throat. Her mouth began to open. *I fell asleep!*

Such an act at such a moment is comparable to dozing off in the face of a cavalry charge. Our bedroom was being invaded by some incredible, unexplained something, and I fell asleep at extremely crucial moments on two successive nights.

I cannot explain such behavior on my part. Since I learned almost total control over my dreams in adolescence, I can easily count any discomforting dreams on the fingers of one hand. On that rare occasion when I have had a "nightmare," I have been an hour or more returning to sleep. For another thing, I function on very little sleep. I will often lie in bed all night thinking through a writing problem or simply listening to the night sounds in a relaxed state that is far removed from sleep. I am just not a drowsyhead, and nothing seems further from my characteristic behavior than to be awakened in the middle of the night by anything remotely indicative of a threat to me or my family—or an unusual phenomenon worthy of my attention and study—and to fall back to sleep under its very shadow.

I have never related this account to any but a few very close friends. One of my confidantes suggested that I was placed in a receptive trance state, rather than a sleep, so that certain materials and information might be transmitted to me. I have no evidence that such was the case. I have only sought to offer this account as straightforwardly as possible, knowing that even as I did so, readers who have their own biases would form their own interpretations.

A number of revelators and UFO contactees have since mentioned to me that just prior to the appearance of an entity they were aware of a strange buzzing sound. Witnesses of unexplained aerial phenomena have also referred to a buzzing or rushing sound shortly before the "flying saucer" appeared over them. I am also reminded that a great deal of poltergeist activity produces a preparatory "signal" of a buzzing, rasping, or winding noise. Could it possibly be that percipients of such paranormal activity are hearing some dimension-hopping entity "tuning in" to our frequency? Could the sounds and lights that seem so mysterious to us be simple electronic by-products?

Throughout the pages of this book, the reader has met revelators who have changed their names upon the instructions of their Source. Many of those who have retained their given names have admitted that they do have "spiritual names," which permit their Source to locate and identify them with greater facility.

"Every name has its own vibration," a revelator once told me, "and a person has to vibrate with his name to be truly whole and effective as a channel." Does the Divine Fire really need broadcast "call" letters to assist it in zeroing in on certain select revelators?

Some theologians hold that God's announcement of his name, Jahweh—more than the giving of a name so that man might appeal to his Creator by the human method of speaking directly to a Named Someone rather than an abstraction—was a direct self-revelation, since to Moses and his contemporaries the essence of a person or a thing lived in its name.

Joseph Jeffers, a former Baptist minister, insists that it is most imperative that one uses the Creator's true name whenever one addresses Him. "People always ask, 'What difference does it make?' " Dr. Jeffers admitted. "Well, my friend, it makes a lot of difference. If your name is Brad, you do not wish to be called Bob. A name has a vibration, and the name Yahweh vibrates to power! But perhaps the most important reason of all is that the oft-used terms of 'God' and 'Lord' are not names all, but titles. And in all Scriptural references, emphasis is made on the Divine Name, not a title."

Dr. Jeffers is convinced that people approaching the New Age must begin to use the Creator's true name. For twenty years of his life, Dr. Jeffers says, he was a "fervent Baptist pastor"; but this spiritual expression did not satisfy his "inner rebellion." He resigned his position in the Baptist Church as pastor and State Evangelist for the Baptist Executive Board of Dallas, Texas, and began a private quest for truth. Then he found Yahweh, and his "soul ceased to rebel."

"This is the Aquarian Age, the New Age, the age of light and logic," he reminds us. "Many hidden facts come to light when a new age dawns and an old age dies. I want to proclaim the Creator's True Name so that others might receive this great revelation."

When Dr. Jeffers rediscovered Yahweh, he claims that he also found the "secret to prophecy and the key to unlock it." Since 1936 Dr. Jeffers has been publishing his dreams and visions in such publications as *Kingdom Voice* magazine and *Yahweh Power Report* newsletter.

Dr. Jeffers claims that since he began to use the Creator's true name, he has correctly predicted the hour, day, and year Adolf Hitler would take power; World War II and the defeat and division of Germany; the value of gold being raised to $35 an ounce; the death of President Franklin D. Roosevelt; the discovery of the Dead Sea Scrolls; the nomination, election, and assassination of President John F. Kennedy; the untimely deaths of Senator Robert F. Kennedy and Rev. Martin Luther King.

"These can all be found documented in various issues of our publications, plus predictions for the future," Dr. Jeffers says.

"Why don't we have the secrets that men had four thousand years ago when they built the great pyramid of Gaza?" Dr. Jeffers asked me. "Those men who built the pyramids were more intimate with the Creator then we are today. Those men knew how to harness the power of the Creator and tap the unlimited resources of knowledge within their own spirits.

"The spirit is our life. It is Yahweh's breath, or that portion of Himself that He has given to us. In many foreign countries today, the Holy Spirit is translated 'Holy Breath.'

"Many people confuse the spirit and the soul. Our body is the house, the temple, a tabernacle, which houses the soul and the spirit. The soul is another surrounding for the spirit, an inside wall for our house. The spirit is a part of us that we call Yahweh.

"The reason we Ambassadors of Yahweh receive so many accurate prophecies is because we use the name of Yahweh, the Creator, and because we follow Yahweh's prescriptions, as it were, instructions as to how to get the messages. In Seattle in 1960, we asked Yahweh how, when, and who would be nominated and elected President of the United States. That night in a dream, Dr. Helen Jeffers, my former wife—whom I believe was the greatest woman psychic who ever lived—came to me in a dream and said, 'Jack Kennedy will be nominated and elected as President, but he will be assassinated during his first term.'

"When this didn't happen, in September of the last year, we asked her again, and she said his death would occur on the twenty-third. I didn't know what month. All I got that night was the twenty-third. I wrote to Mr. Kennedy and to his brother Robert. I have the letter from Attorney General Kennedy thanking us for the information that we gave him. We wrote him later that we had gotten October, then November; and we later published November in our paper and on radio and television.

"Yahweh is electricity—there's your Divine Fire for you! "Remember Elijah calling for fire from Heaven to prove that Yahweh was the Creator, and not Baal?

"When I was on the Marty Faye Show on Chicago's Channel 23, I called on Yahweh when lightning struck the city and seventy thousand homes were blacked out. The engineers said that we could not carry on the call-in portion of the program because the power was out. I said to them, 'Gentlemen, that's wonderful. This gives me a chance to prove that the power of Yahweh is electricity. They looked at me as though I were crazy. I clapped my hands three times and said: 'Yahweh, Yahweh, Yahweh! Lights, power, fire, as it was.' Suddenly all the lights came back on and the telephones began to ring, and we went right on with the program.

"Next year when we went back to Chicago to appear with Marty Faye, people called in to say that they remembered the night I turned the lights back on through the power of Yahweh.

"When we were on WGN radio with Irene Hughes and others, we gave another demonstration of this power. After the show the engineer played back the tape of the program as proof of the experiment. When I said, 'Yahweh, Yahweh, Yahweh' the lights went out and the station went dead, showing the power of Yahweh. When I clapped my hands again, the current came back on.

"Electrical shock has been given to mental patients to restore their minds to normal. Actually, the doctors were giving suffering humans a little dose of Yahweh."

# SIX

## Anima and Aumakua-Contacting the High Self

Although I tend to dismay a great many people when I persist in doing so, I cannot help mentioning the possibility that the Divine Fire—and its attendant spirit guides, angels, and Space Brothers—may be externalized projections of the revelator's own personality. Parapsychologists generally agree that the poltergeist, the "noisy ghost" that levitates objects and generally disrupts things, is not an autonomous being at all, but the externalized aggression of an emotionally disturbed youngster within the household. Psychology holds it as an axiom that whatever the conscious mind represses, the unconscious embodies in allegorical form, either in dreams or in conscious creative imagery. Demons, for instance, often serve as personifications of undesirable emotions, such as lust and hatred. If the Divine Fire seems to be breaking out more often these days, could it be simply the externalization of religious feelings that are increasingly denied expression in our secular world? Dr. Al Siebert, for one, has some reservations about the quality of revelatory material:

*Dr. Siebert*: Even in my own life I have sensed some intelligent existence that is beyond this world that has influenced my life and what has happened to me. In moments of jesting, it sometimes amuses me to think that we might be some college student's term project! As a general statement in regard to spirit guides and mediums, though, I will say that in any of the books I've looked at or any of the people that I've listened to in trance, there has not been one instance where I have experienced any material that was as sophisticated or as knowledgeable as my own. What I'm saying is, I'm not only a Ph.D. in psychology, I'm in Mensa and all sorts of things . . . at no time have I sensed a level of understanding or an intelligence beyond my own. So I always have to accept the least sensational hypothesis for an explanation, and that is usually that this may be another self, or another face, of the revelator's personality that is speaking in an attempt to get harmony, love, peace. I have spoken to entities who are supposed to be the Supreme Commander of the Seventh Ring of the Fourth Galaxy and that kind of stuff, yet the ideas coming through are the things I would expect from a college sophomore. Most of what comes through seems to be the same old words that people have been saying for a long time. It's just that it's coming through in an unusual and fascinating way.

*Dr. Walter Houston Clark*: I find psychical study most interesting, but the fact that so few of these revelations disclose truth useful to us on a spiritual or religious plane has prevented such study from monopolizing the center of my scholarly interests. I have learned things about myself and the mystical consciousness from visionary experience under the influence of psychedelic chemicals, as at an Indian peyote ceremony, for example. But any figures I have seen in such states I have always assumed to have been symbols created by my unconscious rather than coming from an intelligence in another plane of being. In the first chapter of *The Varieties of Religious Experience*, William James ventures his insight that often it is the nature sensitive enough to suffer mental illness which might be the best instrument for the reception of profound religious truth. It follows that such persons may often be mistaken in their perception of figures that appear to them to be bearing messages from another plane of existence. Nevertheless, those who have received messages from cowled figures, angels, or venerable men in dreams and visions and then find that these messages contain verifiable truths should treat these figures with respect, whatever their origin.

Dr. W. G. Roll is one of the mainstays of the Pyschical Research Foundation, Inc., Duke Station, Durham, North Carolina.

*Dr. Roll*: From my work in parapsychology and in areas that touch on it in one way or another, I cannot help but be aware of the vast ranges of the human mind and consciousness. These ranges are just barely tapped, even by parapsychologists, in my opinion. I would tend to view so-called experiences of revelation as perhaps, in some instances or maybe in all instances, an individual being brought or coming into contact with regions of his own self that he has not previously been in contact with.

Revelation is a sort of self-discovery, but since the self appears to be much more expansive than we tend to think and expands probably into the world of space-time, it is also sort of an outward journey. Inward and outward–it really becomes synonymous. The individual making an exploration of inner space makes it of outer space, as well.

"Do you think it's possible, then, for a person to receive a revelation from an entity, an intelligence, outside of himself?"

*Dr. Roll*: My thinking in this general area would be that the kind of things one is brought face to face with, the kind of things one experiences, are perhaps only superficially distinct from one, and that further exploration–either exploration into one's consciousness or using the tools of science–will indicate that many of these things that seem to come up, either in forms of theoretical hallucinations and encounters with so-called apparitions or visions of Mary and whatnot, are really expressions of something that is going on in the self.

Self, in the proper context, encompasses the world. I think this is where parapsychology is exciting, because indications suggest that there is no real distinction between certain levels of experience. There is no distinction between persons and between a person and his physical environment. These things are part of a sort of continuum, the sort of thing that physicists talk about, you know, space-time continuum. But this is not very interesting unless this continuum can be made the object of experience, and this again can happen as the result of any number of procedures, of which the ordinary ones would be meditation, prayer, and other attempts to reach beyond this more narrow ego, or self, that we live with almost every day of our lives.

Carl Jung (who also suggested that flying saucers were extensions of the perceiver's psyche) postulated that in every man's unconscious there exists an "anima," a personification of his repressed female attributes. (Conversely, every woman possesses an "animus.") In dreams, different aspects of the dreamer's personality are often represented by different people. Therefore, when a man reports a female "angel," it may be simply his Anima in disguise; and when a woman sees another female being, it may simply represent her "ideal" self, as the unconscious visualizes it.

"The Divine Fire that has burned in all of us for centuries is the Goddess of the Old Religion: Diana, Aradia, Demeter—call her what you will," Dr. Leo Louis Martello, an *Imago* (male witch), told me.

"Diana has always been the benefactress of the outcast, the lonely, the people of the night. It was not the Christian God that offered the runaway slave sanctuary and protection, but the Pagan Goddess. She has never cared what, or who, you are. Her standards have never been those of any given society. She has always helped all those who pay her homage.

"To this day," Dr. Martello went on, "there is a vast underground network of *streghe* [witches] throughout Italy, Sicily, with allies on Malta, including a few Roman Catholic priests, who accept the Blessed Virgin Mary because they know that she is just another incarnation of the Goddess Diana. One day we will once again have a public temple to the Goddess."

Some will say that the above is but another controversial statement by the colorful Dr. Martello, who seems always to be embroiled in one *cause célèbre* after another. On Halloween, 1970, he led the world's first "Witch-in" in New York City's Central Park; and, at the same time, won an initial civil rights victory for witches when he managed to obtain a permit from the City Parks Administration by threatening civil liberties action against them for discrimination toward a minority group. Others will say that since Martello is a witch, he would of course be prejudiced in his claim that the Divine Fire is an expression of the Female Principle in the Deity.

He is not, however, the first person who has observed that one of the failings in Christianity and Judaism has been their lack of feminine aspect within the Godhead. More than one observer of the mass conversions of the pagan populace of Europe during the Middle Ages has commented on the fact that the common folk simply went underground with their worship of Diana, or made the motions of giving reverence to the Virgin Mary, while secretly directing their true devotion to the Goddess. Martello has something to say about this, as well:

"While I was living in Tangier, Morocco, in 1964, I took a three-week trip to Sicily where I visited my relatives, *paisans* and local *streghe*. They knew at once that I was an *Imago*. We visited ancient temple sites, and they showed me how the Divine Fire of Sicilian witchcraft managed to burn underground for centuries. For example, close inspection of the Madonna and Child in the Cathedral at Monreale will reveal that the child Jesus is *female*!

"Christianization forced the Old Religionists underground in the twelfth century, but the sculptors paid tribute to their goddesses Demeter and Persephone by creating the Madonna and female Jesus. In ancient times people from all over the world worshiped at the Temple of Demeter in Enna, Sicily, where they celebrated her daughter Persephone's resurrection from the underworld to become Goddess of souls and immortality. To this day the Sicilians worship the female deity more than the male, and every city has its sainted patroness. The year that I spent in

North Africa in 1964, and my trip to Sicily, was a spiritual voyage to *myself*."

If it is true that the great masses of people have been hungering to give spiritual expression to a Mother, as well as a Father, deity, one wonders if the many reported appearances of the Virgin Mary in the last five hundred years might not be the result of a kind of psychic compensation for an orthodox, ecclesiastical emphasis on a "male chauvinist" Trinity.

Visions of the Madonna, it seems, nearly always appear to women. Could it be that subconsciously women have felt cheated of a more active role in the Church? A member of the Roman Catholic priesthood is addressed as "Father." His female counterpart is relegated to the role of Sister, differentiated from other women because she has surrendered her individuality to become a Bride of Christ. Only within the last few years have the major Protestant churches permitted more than a token number of female pastors and ministers.

The most thoroughly documented series of appearances of the Virgin Mary in recent years occured in Garabandal, Spain, from 1961 to 1965. Among the image's numerous utterances, which were repeated by the four children who witnessed the apparitions, was the following message: "Mary is very approachable. She seems to want to close the gap between herself and those on Earth."

Mrs. Maria C. Saraco of Brockton, Massachusetts, has chosen to devote the rest of her life to "making the message of Garabandal known to the world." Mrs. Saraco has traveled across much of the United States with her slides and lecture program and on-the-spot slides of the visionaries, who are now twenty-two-year-old peasant women.

According to Mrs. Saraco, the vision told the four girls that "... mankind must do penance and make many sacrifices or suffer the wrath of God. Many priests are on the road to perdition, and with them they are bringing many souls. We must avoid God's anger by our efforts of amendment. The Virgin Mary has promised a miracle in Garabandal so that all may believe the apparitions and be obedient to the message."

Mrs. Janet Bord of London, England, has been making an

extensive study of the appearance of religious apparitions throughout the world. Through correspondence, I asked her which religious figures seemed to materialize the most often.

In her reply, Mrs. Bord stated: "So far in my research, the Virgin Mary seems to appear the most often, or rather, the female figure is identified as her. Other traditional saints also appear. However, I think that the identification of the visionary person depends very much on the witness, and the entity materializing takes the form he or she would be expected to take. I feel they do this in order to be more acceptable to the witness."

Many people believe that the frequent appearances of the Virgin Mary over the past one hundred and fifty years have to do with the Second Coming of Jesus, or, as the less orthodox might phrase it, the giving of Cosmic Consciousness to the entire human race. St. Louis Mary de Montfort, a Catholic scholar and writer of the eighteenth century, said: "In the second coming of Jesus, Mary has to be made known and revealed by the Holy Ghost, in order that, through her, Jesus Christ may be known, loved, and served."

Nada-Yolanda, the well-known medium of Miami, Florida, was quoted in the November-December 1971 issus of *Chimes* as saying that Mary had come "through" her channeling to reveal the following:

> As in the story of the birth of Jesus, I am the teacher, the example from which the seed [the message] comes forth. Therefore, manifestations of my work and teachings have to come forth prior to the teachings of the Son of God . . . I have demonstrated fertility and willingness in the minds of men to receive the message of the Second Coming . . . .The Second Coming is literal, as well as spiritual, for the individual as well as for the race.

On another occasion, Nada-Yolanda's ascended "master" brought forth this additional message:

> Mary represents the subconscious or the mold in which all things are gestated . . . She is the mother in which the seed does grow. She represents that aspect of the God consciousness, as Jesus represents the male, or the active, force. . . . She represents the

> nourishing part of God's seed, always remembering that each one is a representative and a part of the whole, serving each other part of the whole.*
>
> Her role at this time is the same as it was during the life of Jesus. She nurtured the seed for nine months—and many years, of course, after his birth—as the physical mother. But she also is nurturing the seed of mankind by her special work in the etheric for the last two thousand years; and will continue until all men are brought into Christ-conscious awareness.

In the above, one can surely detect a less than subtle attempt to make Mary more than a simple little Jewish girl who became the mother of a great teacher—or even a virtuous woman honored above all women who was visited by the Holy Spirit and impregnated with the Son of God. And as though devout Roman Catholics might not be offended enough by the thought of the Holy Lady speaking through a spirit medium, the anonymous author of the article in *Chimes* calls her "an ascended master, expressing universal consciousness and divine love . . . no respecter of historical times, individual positions, personal honor or glory, specific religions, races or nationalities . . . her appearances and messages are given to peasants, priests, working men, children, journalists and prophets among Muslims, Christians and Jews."

In the October-November 1971 issue of *Cosmos*, an editorial writer introduced a profile of a New Age minister, Rev. Betsy Chattaway, with the comment that in the Aquarian Age, woman would be returning to her role of leader in religions, only now she will be called "reverend," rather than "priestess."

"There have been many civilizations in the past where woman guided mankind's homage to God," the article states:

> "In Christianity, woman has always been relegated to the back seat. The Catholic Church has its Madonnas and St. Theresas—woman could bring forth the Christ Child and become a saint, but she could not lead or direct. The best she could do was to become

*There is an occult tradition that Jesus and Mary were "twin souls" who had a long history of previous simultaneous incarnations.

> a Mother Superior in a convent, but she was subject to a masculine heirarchy. The Protestant Reformation and Puritan concepts did not permit any more freedom of expression. The only proper calling was of minister's wife and helper. . . .

The article goes on to say that the Aquarian Age will recognize and comprehend that all people have within them characteristics of both male and female. There will be a new understanding for the active woman and the passive man. "Androgynous humans, so suppressed before, are being allowed to let their creative energies flow. They truly will prove to be mankind's saviors. Mortals will be led by androgynics into a fuller expression of themselves as they are taught to be what they really are—supernatural."

During the course of my interviews with revelators, I made the acquaintance of a remarkable woman in her early forties, who believes that the Christ vibration will reincarnate in the New Age as a woman; moreover, she feels that she herself may be that female aspect, that female incarnation of the "Duality of the Word." Louise Zimmerman is attractive, pleasant, and surprisingly low-key. Our conversation began with a general discussion of why there had been so many appearances of the Divine Fire in the last few years.

*Miss Zimmerman*: I believe that there is a vibration one step up from the Jesus vibration which is now existing.

"Are you saying that a truer picture of who Jesus was is now being revealed?"

*Miss Zimmerman*: Yes, I feel that we have to tie in astrology. A person just doesn't incarnate without a reason. Even the crucifixion took place at a time when there was the ultimate climactic culmination in this individual's life. I feel that there are certain individuals who incarnate to be leaders. Each leader draws certain people into his ashram. He becomes a focal point for this group. Jesus left in the last era hanging up on a cross. Now he has all these people who are in his ashram. He has to reincarnate. He is still responsible to them.

"Do you think that Jesus will reincarnate in this era?"

*Miss Zimmerman*: He will never again be recognized as Jesus Christ. We can all tap in on the Jesus vibration. This is possible for everyone.

I believe that there are people who emit an energy that is incredibly faster than the speed of light. I believe that these people are the predestined focal points for uplifting people. For the most part, they are probably unknown, only recognized by individuals on a high level of development.

When I had that vibration hit me, I had so much energy flowing through me that the ends of my fingers were burned. They didn't have feelings for about three days.

"What precipitated this experience for you?"

*Miss Zimmerman*: At that particular time, I more or less related to Jesus as an abstract deity. I didn't know anything about astrology, nothing about mysticism. I was not the kind of person who dealt in spiritualism. I had always been a very practical, realistic person.

On this particular evening, May 5, 1966, I felt a need to be praying. I think there was a full moon. Then this fantastic sensation happened to me. It didn't last very long. It must have been something like St. Paul went into. After I reached this level, there was a force field of energy around my bed.

"You compared your experience to that of St. Paul's. Did you see a bright light?"

*Miss Zimmerman*: No, it was more of a glory feeling. I made a petition to the Cosmic. I didn't know what was happening then, but I have received insight into my experience since that time.

The planetary lineup of May 5, 1966, combined with my personal chart, caused my time to come. In other words, the apex point of my personal incarnation took place, which brought about the highest vibration, or positive polarity, possible for my lifetime. My astral body traveled to its higher source—how many light years away, I do not know—but I briefly attained unity with my higher self. This glorified state lasted for only a few seconds, and as my astral body descended in a highly positive state, it attracted a negative entity. As I lay in bed, highly polarized and very powerful, an entity, or a projection of my higher self, appeared beside me and warned that I must expect an attack from a negative being that had been attracted to me because of my positive vibrations.

It took three days for that negative entity to find a human body to work through, but he came to me through a personal attack in the night. The individual who attacked me was found, burned beyond recognition. I have since been informed that negative entities always destroy the bodies they use. However, it is my belief that the extreme, positive energy which was on my aura at that particular time came into contact with my attacker's opposite negative energy and destroyed him, not by some abstract force, but merely by the fact that the vibrations of his electromagnetic field were such that they drew destruction to him.

After weathering the two diametrically opposed experiences, Louise Zimmerman told me that her vibration was "highly erratic and extremely fluctuating." She felt that she had the "consciousness of Eve." She felt herself to be to Eve what Christ was to Adam.

"Except for the fact that I was living," she recalled, "I had an idea of what the crucifixion must have been like." As a result of the May 5, 1966, experience, she began to produce fragments of "scripture" through automatic writing. Here are two samples of this inspired writing that became especially meaningful to her:

> Oh, the day of the Lord; Oh, the hour of the Lord;
> That hour shall be darkness.
> I beheld Satan as a thief in the night, a robber of flesh, an enemy of God.
> He appeared to forestall the dawn, but he could not,
> For his end was the hour of the Lord.
> Hence my flesh has gone to the Fire with him; together we were destroyed; yet do I live, body and soul, not wholly of Heaven,
> Not wholly of Earth, but in that realm between, wherein the bridge is formed, whereunder the water shall flow.
> Fire is the judgment; Flesh is the victor.
> God is the redeemer, and the weapon is the word.

As the word formed the world, so has the word power to destroy.
This I know, for I was born of the word,
Lived by the word,
Destroyed Satan by the word,
And therein do I have life eternal.

*Proverbs of the Remnant*

As men belong on Earth, so do saints belong in Heaven;
And it is a happy and contented soul that knows its place.
There is a place of knowledge and a limit of truth to each seeker,
But no man may abide at one level forever. As a healthy tree
Reaches to Heaven, so does the heart of the wise and prudent.
There are clouds that roll black and fierce from which no rain falls,
Yet have bright days brought a flood.
The world is filled with itself, but a godly man is filled with love.
Though a man be shackled and bound with weights, yet can his mind be free.
A fool speads his own snare and encompasses himself daily,
But the righteous are assisted by seven angels.

"After the shock of the traumatic encounter," Louise told me, "I felt a desperate and compelling need to go to California. As I arrived, I noticed hundreds of kids coming in and gathering in the same locale. I did not associate this movement with myself, nor, in 1966, did I think that I was a focal point for this group. I was still suffering from erratic vibrations—something like the erratic music that stemmed out of 1966—and I felt that God had contacted me and the Devil had raped me.

"Those unstable children, those self-styled hippies, many of whom died from dope and other dreaded causes, have now formed a central core group on their ascent to the current Jesus Consciousness. It is interesting to note that so many of these people were born between 1930 and 1949, when the outer planets were in extremely hard aspects, such as being at ninety-degree angles to each other, causing a very negative polarity. But this is what made it possible for these First Resurrection children to incarnate.

"During that period, 1930-1949 and following, souls from the Lost Tribes, which the Mormons prophesied would appear in the Last Days—the murdered Indians, the crucified Christians, and, as I said before, the children of the First Resurrection—began to incarnate for the New Age."

Her pilgrimage to California completed, Louise Zimmerman returned to her home in Chalmette, Louisiana, where she began to publish a newsletter which gave expression to her "Eve" consciousness. At the present time, Miss Zimmerman writes a newspaper column and directs the Psychic Group Center (P.O. Box 1183, Chalmette, Louisiana 70043).

And what of Miss Zimmerman's specific role in the New Age? "I believe that I am the female aspect of the Christ Vibration who must represent the revelation of Jesus Christ.

"We must remember that Jesus himself, who was under Neptune vibrations, as all saviors are, is responsible to the mass of people whom he affected by his promises and by his creation of the highest vibration ever to hit this planet. Since he died to put out this first energy, he must come back again to complete his own incurred Karma to these individuals. Thus he has returned in the form of an individual who cannot add to his glory, nor take away from it, but merely reveal the new teaching to the entire Christian population for whom he is responsible."

Max Freedom Long was the recipient of quite a different kind of revelatory insight. After years of research, Long managed to break the secret code of the Kahunas, the magician-priests of Hawaii, who in his opinion had developed a workable system of magic for everyone who would follow its precepts.

Max Freedom Long came to the Hawaiian Islands as a schoolteacher in 1917. From the first he was intrigued by the outlawed Huna sect and the native priests, the Kahunas, the "Keepers of the Secret," but when he sought to study the original religion of the Islands, he met with rebuffs on every level. His greatest advance came when he fell heir to the materials that Dr. William Tufts Brigham, curator of the Bishop Museum, had collected over a forty-year period; and he set to work earnestly, seeking some clue that would reveal the central mystery of the Huna code. The code had been passed only from parent to child under vows of inviolable secrecy, and the few remaining Kahunas had learned by past unfortunate experience to shun all whites, whatever their avowed motives might be.

In 1931, shortly before he left the islands, Max Freedom

Long was awakened one night by having the mosquito netting which surrounded his bed flooded with a light so strong and so brilliant that it was quite unlike anything that he had ever experienced.

"There was no sound to go with it, just the night silence. But I had a strange feeling that I was being subjected to some initiation or other. I just sat up in bed and stared and waited. In a matter of a few moments the light slowly faded and all was as before in the room . . . except that I was greatly impressed and set wondering."

It was after he returned to the mainland and was living in California in 1935 that Max Long was again awakened in the middle of the night by another manifestation of the Light and provided with a clue that would lead to his breaking the enigma of Huna. It was suddenly given to him that since the Kahunas must have had names for the elements in their lore, these words would be found in the dictionary of Hawaiian-English that had begun to be formulated in 1820. Since the Hawaiian language is made up of words constructed from short root words, a translation of the root usually gives the original meaning of a word. If he were to derive the roots of the words used by the Kahunas in the recorded chants and prayers that had been collected by Dr. Brigham, he would be able to obtain a fresh translation which would disclose secrets that had been overlooked by disinterested missionaries.

Long recalled the Huna teaching that man possessed two souls, the *uhane* and the *unihipili*, that work as a team, relying each on the functions of the other, each needing the physical medium of the body. By examining the meaning for these words in the old dictionary, he was able to determine that *uhane* could be translated as a weak, animal-like spirit that could talk, and that *unihipili* could be understood as a secretive spirit that adheres to, and sometimes hides, another spirit. In other terms, Long had discovered the Kahuna idea of the conscious and the subconscious, a pair of spirits closely joined in a body which is controlled by the subconscious and used to cover and hide them both.

The conscious spirit (*uhane*) is more human and possesses the ability to speak. The unconscious spirit (*unihipili*) does its work in secret, but it is stubborn and disposed to refuse to obey when it holds a fixation that a certain action will bring about punishment. It blends with the conscious spirit in order to give the impression of being one with it.

Long's most important discovery was that of the *Aumakua*, the older, parental, androgynous spirit that has both the low self (*unihipili*) and the middle self (*uhane*) under its guidance and protection. The *Aumakua* occupies the level of consciousness immediately above our own conscious level and may be considered the "god" within each of us–an older, parental, utterly trustworthy spirit that incorporates both the male and the female essence. On one level the *Aumakua* may correspond to the superconscious in psychology; but to the Kahuna, it is the High Self, the highest "god" with whom man can deal. The Kahuna believes in a supreme creative force, but he does not believe that he can pray to it. The Huna system maintains that man's only contact with the Creator can be through connection with the High Self. After he had broken the Huna code, Long learned that the symbol and code word for the High Self is "Light," not just the sun, which was worshiped in so many religions as the Light and the Supreme Deity, but an actual mystical experience which comes to those who work to develop contact with the High Self in order that they might live the good life and be opened to Higher Intelligence.

"Given this certainty that the Kahunas had known for thousands of years all the psychology we had come to know in the last few years," Max Freedom Long said, "I became quite certain that their ability to perform feats of magic stemmed from their knowledge of important psychological factors not yet discovered by us." Huna works as a system because it contains a form of consciousness that directs the magical processes; a force utilized by the consciousness that provides the necessary power; and a substance, visible or invisible, through which the force can act. And the Kahunas believed all these elements to be inherent in each individual.

According to Huna belief, the three spirits are surrounded by three shadowy, "etheric" bodies. These amorphous bodies are made up of *aka*, which may perhaps be likened to the "ectoplasm" of Western occultists. Each body of man has its own supply of *mana*, vital force. The low self uses simple *mana*; the middle self operates on a higher-voltage *mana-mana*; and the High Self employs *mana-loa*. Low *mana* may be likened to body waves and *mana-mana* to brain waves, both of which may be scientifically recorded. Science has not yet provided us with a counterpart to *mana-loa*.

The most essential element in the successful practice of Huna magic is contact with the High Self. It is on this level, above our own conscious level, that the power is sufficient to perform miracles.

According to Huna, the conscious, or middle self, cannot of itself approach the High Self. Only the subconscious part of man can reach the *Aumakua*, provided there is no blockage. The role of the middle self is to instruct the low self to accumulate an extra supply of *mana* to be held in readiness until the next steps have been taken. Then the subconscious, acting under the orders of the middle self, reaches up the connecting *aka* cord and makes contact with the High Self. It is the High Self that brings about the desired conditions expressed in prayer, although prayer itself is brought about only by the integrated efforts of the three composite selves.

The Kahunas taught that there was an ideal condition to which the individual might aspire, in which the aid and guidance of the High Self could be requested, received, and then acted upon. The one rule of life that must be obeyed is that no man should do anything that might hurt another. For the more advanced Kahunas, the rule included loving service.

The practitioners of Huna often demonstrated their ability to foresee the future of an individual and to gain the aid of the High Self to change it for the better. It was believed, however, that the High Self could not interfere if the middle self was creating thought forms of ill will toward others. The High Self cannot violate the entity's free will, nor can it render assistance until it has been properly asked. In no case will the High Self perpetrate injustice or cause injury.

Huna also holds the concept of union between all High

Selves. The unit responds as a whole, but is also capable of responding to a part. It is both universal and individual.

"If the High Selves working in a union or a oneness quite beyond our comprehension take the deeds and thoughts and desires of the world of middle and low self humanity, and, averaging all these, produce the pattern of the future, then that pattern is visible on the High Self plane of consciousness and set, insofar as the main pattern of the future is concerned," Max Freedom Long wrote.

"The Kahunas believed that the great events of the future were set and could be foreseen far ahead. World or national events might be seen hundreds or even thousands of years ahead. The future of the individual, because of the shortness of a human life span, could be seen only months or years ahead."

Long suggested the intriguing hypothesis that since the Kahunas had often demonstrated their ability to change the future of an individual through contact with the High Self, an appeal to the collective High Selves might bring about changes that could affect the entire world.

"I believe that the future of entire nations might also be foreseen and changed for the better by a concerted effort if we were sufficiently enlightened," he said. "Today when we consider the possible use of the atom bomb as a weapon, or the hydrogen or cobalt bomb, we might, if greed did not rule the world, still be able to alter what appears to our eyes to be inevitable disaster. Love can unite men and enable them to do great works for the good of all. Hate and fear can unite men only for war and destruction."

As Max Freedom Long followed the Light of his own revealing High Self in an ever-expanding examination of the Huna code, he became convinced that the system of "magic" practiced by the Kahunas may well have been the best preserved expression of the Divine Fire's universal revelation extant in the world. Set apart from civilization and its myriad theologies and philosophies, the Islanders may have been better able to guard against the distortions and abuses that come with organization, ritualization, and the dogmatic interpretations of an ecclesiastical establishment.

The Kahunas had no temples or shrines. They had no dogmas that demanded the achievement of salvation. They did not believe that the Higher Beings could be injured by man. They did not believe that man could sin against a Higher Being. The Huna system held that God was too high and too all-powerful for any human being to hurt by any mortal act. "I cannot sin against God: I am too small." the Kahunas would protest to the Christian missionaries. In Huna, the one recognized sin is to hurt a fellow human being.

The Huna system believes that after death there is a continuation of growth and progression, the low self reincarnating as a middle self in due time, and the middle self eventually progressing to the level of the High Self, becoming the "utterly trustworthy parental spirit." This process of graduation is accomplished after death, during a period of inactivity resembling a long sleep, such as the caterpillar that becomes a pupa, lies dormant for a time, then bursts forth as a butterfly.

"I have elected to call Huna a psycho-religious system for the reason that it includes so much that has always been considered a part of religion," Max Freedom Long said. "However, I consider Huna a science in the strictest sense of the word. The Kahunas knew nothing about gods. They admitted freely that it was probable that there were such Beings, but they were honest in saying that they were convinced that the human mind would never be able to do more than imagine them–invent them in terms of lower humans. The basic urge of other religions to appease gods or gain favors from them (religion plus magic) is replaced in Huna by the purely magical operation of prayer to the High Self for the purpose of gaining favors in the way of healing or bettering one's circumstances through a change in the predictable future."

Some would argue that Huna is a primitive system with little revelance for an age of moon landings and mass communications. But primitive man is also basic man, and the eternal truths remain unaltered and ever contemporary.

In his *Psychology and Folk-Lore*, Dr. R. R. Marett wrote that he felt the moral of the history of primitive religion to be:

> . . . that religion is all along vital to man as a striving and progressive being . . . There is a real sameness, felt all along, if expressed with no great clearness at first, in the characteristic manifestations of the religious consciousness at all times and in all places. It is the common experience of man that he can draw on a power that makes for, and in its most typical form wills, righteousness, the sole condition being that a certain fear, a certain shyness and humility, accompany the effort so to do. That such a universal belief exists amongst all mankind, and that it is no less universally helpful in the highest degree, is the abiding impression left on my mind by the study of religion in its historico-scientific aspect.

A "common experience of man that he can draw on a power" if a certain "fear, shyness and humility accompany the effort so to do" remains "vital to man as a striving and progressive being" whether he commutes by jet airplane or by dugout canoe.

Emile Durkheim's study of primitive man (*Elementary Forms of Religious Life*) lead him to comment on what I would maintain is one of the principal responses of any man or woman, primitive or twentieth-century-civilized, who has been touched by the Divine Fire:

> The believer, who has communicated with his god, is not merely a man who sees new truths of which the unbeliever is ignorant; he is a man who is *stronger*. He feels within him more force, either to endure the trials of existence or to conquer them. It is as though he were raised above the miseries of the world, because he is raised above his condition as mere man. . . .

As Olof Jonsson, the great mystic-clairvoyant, has said:

"The utilization of the powers, the 'sparks of divinity,' within each of us, should never tempt the wise to make a religion out of spiritual blessings that have been dispensed to all men. Rather, an awareness of the powers within should serve to equip the interested and the receptive with a brilliant searchlight on the path to Cosmic Harmony.

"It is in one's own home, in his own little chamber, in

moments of quiet meditation that a stream of the great light of Cosmos is best able to reach in and enrich the soul and open the eyes to the magnificent and tranquil gardens that lie beyond the borders of the Unknown. That which governs a man's life is neither chemistry nor physics nor anything material, but the proper spiritual linkup with the powers within his own psyche and the blessed Harmony that governs the Universe."

Perhaps that is what our messengers for a God who hides himself—whether they be independent spiritual entities or projections of our own High Selves—have been repeating to us these many centuries: it is in man's soul that he will find all that is necessary to express his freedom and to realize his dignity.

# SEVEN

## *Angels, Guides, and Other Messengers for a God Who Hides Himself*

Helen Hoag came into my office in Decorah, Iowa, an enthusiastic vibration of good cheer and great personal warmth. She readily admitted to being "a senior citizen," and she said that she had come from the Awarenesss Research Foundation, Incorporated, in North Miami, Florida. Miss Hoag was traveling around the country in search of Jesus' reincarnated Apostles. Of course his name was not really Jesus, and all the apostles are women in this incarnation.

"Let me see your fingers," Miss Hoag requested. When I complied, she studied my fingernails briefly, then emitted a delighted chuckle, "Oh, you're an angel, too!"

My associate, David Macmaster, entered the office and was put to the same test. To her explosive pleasure, it was obvious that he, too, was of angelic origin, and as an added bonus, she learned that David and I had lived on the same planet in another incarnation.

How does one tell whether or not he is an angel? By an examination of the cuticles. If your cuticles are nice and rounded, you are an angel. If they are rather pointed, you are of Luciferian heritage, which is not quite the same as being a devil, but nothing to brag about. If your cuticles are rather square, straight across at the bottom, you are nothing exotic at all. You are simply of Earthman stock.

In order to present a complete portrait of contemporary mysticism and revelation, we would be remiss, indeed, if we omitted an examination of that esoteric philosophy that speaks of a strata of other planetary worlds, a hierarchy of heavenly kingdoms, and a multitude of Lords to govern their respective galaxies and celestial domains.

*Helen Hoag*: I've found James, Andrew, and Jude, who wrote the Book of Jude. In this life they are all girls, who are rather young, in their teens or early twenties. I've also located Mark, who wrote the Book of Mark. And the man who furnished the donkey cart and the donkeys for Mary and Joseph to take Jesus into Egypt. You can find out who *I* am by reading the chapter of John, verses forty-six to the end of the chapter. I was the nobleman from Capernaum whose son was ill of a high fever. My name was Samuel ben Joab. I was a man then, a woman now, because we must change sex so that we may become as balanced as the Creator.

After Jesus–we call him Sananda, his spiritual name–cured my son of the high fever, I took a ten-camel caravan to Jerusalem. Sananda came along as tutor to my son. He also brought John Mark along. At that time he was just a boy of ten.

"How do you see these things, Helen? By entering a light trance?"

*Miss Hoag*: No, not by trance, but by conscious projection. I use a technique to open the Akashic records. Everything that has ever happened and every word that has ever been spoken throughout all creation since the beginning of time are in the Akashic records.

In your mind's eye, visualize a really dark night. Then recall a bright, sunny day. Do this several times and give yourself an instruction. I send my people up to the Temple of the Lords on the twelfth plane and ask them to go to a conference room and find a Lord there and ask him whatever questions they want to. I also send my people to the Central Universe to talk to the Creator Himself. As far as I know, outside of Awareness, there is no one else who can send their people up there.

The Creator's name is Sacrana. When Sacrana created you or me or anyone else, He took a part of His own spirit–the Bible says I am in ye; ye are in me–and he set it out as one single, spiritual atom. He said, "Go and know my Universes and return then unto me."

Each spiritual atom goes to the mineral kingdom, the plant kingdom, the animal kingdom and the human kingdom. From then on, you go on up to become a seventh-plane angel, a twelfth-plane angel, seraphim, cherubim, and so forth. Just as you go to school and complete various courses of study.

"I've always thought of the angels as a race apart from man."

*Miss Hoag*: No, man evolves into angels. The angels who were present before the creation of man came from another creation to help out here with this one. They have previously gone through an evolutionary process.

After you become a twelfth-plane angel, the next step is *Manu*–that is like getting your Master's degree. When you do more advanced spiritual work, you graduate to become a Lord, or a Son of the Creator. Then you have come full circle. You are back up to your Creator. You say, "Father, I have now experienced all your kingdoms, and here I am. I am now ready to do your bidding."

The Central Universe where the Creator lives is a sphere, and he has created satellite creations, twelve of them. We are in the seventh plane of the twelfth creation.

Sacrana says that He does not care what people call him–the One, the Eternal, Allah, Zeus–he is still Sacrana and it is his creation. Each of the planets has twelve planes: mineral, plant, human, and so forth, up "Jacob's Ladder." And each soul has consciousness on every one of those planes.

"And each soul must experience all twelve planes before it returns to Earth to be reincarnated?"

*Miss Hoag*: The Karmic board decides that. They know how much Karma each soul has to pay, so each soul is sent where it can best prepare for its next life. In my previous life I had not learned the value of money. In this life my father was a lawyer and my mother a schoolteacher, and believe you me, we did not have any more money than we could just barely get along on. I had to work my way through the university to get my Master's degree at Ohio State and some courses on the Ph.D. level at the University of Miami.

About three or four years ago I was asked if I had learned the value of money. I said it wasn't worth a damn! So the guys upstairs said that I had learned my lesson and now I could be allowed to do what I wanted to do. I was very ill at that time. I almost died. I said that I wanted to teach people if they would let me live. They kept their end of the bargain, and I'm trying to keep mine. I'm going around teaching people that there is no such thing as death: it is merely a change of energy.

"Are all the planets habitable, but merely in various stages of evolution?"

*Miss Hoag*: Every planet I've seen is habitable, and they are all higher than this. This is the lowest planet in creation.

Luciferia was also low, but it was blown up. Satania is trying to evolve itself on a higher level. There were three other planets that were also experimental–Kondon, Fachia, and Suran in an adjoining solar system–but they have been taken off the experimental stage because Lord Michael, who is Lord of the Seventh Universe, got a bright idea. He thought he would block people's memories from the time they were born and see how long it would take for them to find their way back to the Creator.

"Is Lord Michael the creator of our planet?"

*Miss Hoag*: No, the Elohim created it. That's in the Bible. Every constellation has a Lord over it. Every solar system has a Lord. Every plane has a Lord.

The Elohim work, I believe, directly under the Creator. You might say that they are minor gods. If you want to go one step higher than a Lord, you become a god with a little "g" by creating something new that will be of value to all persons on all planets and all the solar systems throughout all creation. There is a way where you can become a little god, and then you can work up from there to become a god of your own creation the way Sacrana did.

"Are you saying that there is a god over Sacrana?"

*Miss Hoag*: I'm not saying that there is someone over him now, but I know that there are other creations with other gods who have equal stature; but that's a little too much to give to people when they don't even know about life on other planets, much less another creation. People just go blank and get headaches. I'm not out to give people headaches—I want to take their headaches away!

"Did Sananda sacrifice himself on the cross as Jesus?"

*Miss Hoag*: Yes, he was supposed to have lived longer, but the Luciferian element wouldn't allow it. He projected himself out of the body so he would not have to bear the pain of the torture. He appeared dead, but when the soldiers laid him in the tomb and rolled the stone in place, a spacecraft hovering overhead disintegrated his body and reassembled it in another location. Then, later, the spacecraft picked him up. When he went up in a cloud, it was really a spacecraft. And the Bible says he is coming back the way he left, and that means he is returning in a spacecraft.

There will be those who say that, at best, what the Awareness Research Foundation offers its members is another way of dealing with reality, a way of dismissing life's disillusionments and disappointments and placing them at the feet of an immediately accessible "Lord" who will quickly dispose of them. Sacrana, the Creator, may be spoken to, even scolded, as friend more than Father. Sananda, his son, is a brother, yet a most high Lord, who came to this world from another to set an example for confused humanity. The opportunity to relive past lives provides the recipient of these "memories" with a bit of vicarious glory and dignity from man's spiritual past. Or might we still see the basic, essential sparkings of the Divine Fire glowing behind such confusing bits and pieces of age-old occult philosophies?

The following report came to me from one of my correspondents, Don Worley, who stated that his informant, Pfc. E. M., is a young man of twenty-one, whom he has known all his life. "He has no interest or knowledge of the paranormal," Worley said in his report. "He has never heard of such a thing as this before in his life. He is a reliable observer, and he swears this event is true."

In August 1969 a group of Marines were on a defensive perimeter near Danang, Vietnam.

*Pfc. E. M.*: There were three of us sitting on top of the bunker, looking west at our part of the perimeter. It was about 1:30 A.M. There was a half-moon in the sky. Visibility was good, and there were no limiting factors except darkness.

All of a sudden, I don't know why, we looked up in the sky and saw this figure coming toward us. It had a kind of glow, and we couldn't make out for sure what it was at first. It looked like a gigantic bat. After it got close enough so we could see what it was, it looked like a woman, a naked, black woman with big wings and a kind of greenish cast to her. She glowed and threw off a radiance.

It looked like her arms didn't have any bones in them or anything, because they were so limber. And when she flapped her wings, there was no noise. When she got over our heads, she was maybe six or seven feet above us.

We just froze. We couldn't believe it, because we had never seen anything like this before in our lives. When she was maybe ten feet away from us, we started hearing her wings flap. The total time we watched her until we lost sight of her must have been between three and four minutes.

*Don Worley*: Did you report this to anyone?

*Pfc. E. M.*: We told everybody! Of course we told our lieutenant and junior execs, and they kind of looked at us like we had been on dope or something.

*Worley*: Was this winged lady solid?

*Pfc. E. M.*: Definitely! She was a well-developed woman! She was completely naked, but there was a kind of down or fur covering her body. She glowed a greenish color, and even though her skin seemed to be black, her hair was straight like a Caucasian's rather than curly like a Negro's.

It may be easy to conceptualize three Marines on guard duty fantasizing a well-developed woman visiting their lonely post at night, but it is hard to imagine why they would visualize her coming equipped with wings to keep herself out of their reach. Such tales may be born out of difficult-to-fathom fantasy; however, I have within my files accounts of winged entities coming to warn of impending tragedy, arriving to escort the souls of the deceased to another dimension, and providing desperately needed money, the equivalent of manna. But we are concerned in this present volume with accounts of men and women who received direct communication from angels and spirit guides.

In the Bible Moses is warned that any mortal that looks upon the face of God is killed by the sheer glory of the Creator. The same idea—that a deity's unmasked radiance can have fatal results—appears in legends and scriptures of other cultures. Perhaps Supreme Intelligence shows itself to the revelator in an appropriate human form so that the revelator may receive the revelation in a manner most meaningful to him rather than having his psychic receptors "burned out" by an overload of Divine Energy.

Guardian angels, spirit guides, etheric masters—whatever man chooses to call them—the concept of ultraphysical beings who materialize to aid man in times of crises appears to be universal. Generally these teaching, preaching entities function in precisely the manner that the name "angel" implies, as messengers of God, intermediaries who deliver personal or group messages. In other instances they serve as rather militant entities who protect the spiritually vulnerable from the forces of disharmony. In the opinion of the skeptic, of course, the whole matter of otherworldly beings smacks of fairy tales and regressive behavior; but I think that a careful examination of the accounts in this chapter will indicate that our angels and guides are more firm and purposeful than whimsy and fantasy.

Actress Dyan Cannon told William Peter Blatty for *On View* magazine that she had seen an angel on two occasions. She said that she had been alone in her hotel room in Chicago, depressed, just sitting there, when suddenly the angel had appeared.

> The "angel" was a woman, an apparition clad in white with long blonde hair flowing over her shoulders; she did not speak but somehow communicated with Dyan—"not words or ideas but—well—feelings. She sort of—made gestures with her hands, moves with her hands. I really don't know how long it lasted. It seemed like a minute or two," she said quietly. . . . "Then they melted away—I mean, my problems—I relaxed. Then she was gone."
>
> "Why do you say it was an angel?"
>
> "I don't know. I just knew that's what she was."
>
> The phenomenon recurred a few months later. The conditions were practically identical, except that the apparition was not the same woman.

J. D. M. of Baltimore told me that when he was six years old, a dangerous case of diphtheria left him with violent headaches. At these times he would see a woman dressed in garb reminiscent of Biblical times standing beside his bed.

"Everything about her seemed real," J. D. M. attests. "Her long white gown with a girdle at the waist, her mantle of blue, all moved as she did, and she seemed to be about twenty-eight years old. She was beautiful."

A bit of childish delirium? J. D. M., now a mature man, says that this entity has appeared to him from time to time in his life: "About eight years ago was her last appearance to me. At this time I asked her who she was and what she wanted me to do. She answered, 'When the time is right, I will tell you who I am and what I want you to do.' "

Mrs. Helen Hadsell of Dallas, Texas, told me that in 1956, when she was sixteen years old, she was confined to bed for three months due to rheumatic fever. At that time, medical science had little to offer a person who had this serious, and sometimes fatal, disease. Helen had received an extremely strict Roman Catholic religious instruction. "Just the thought of having a mortal sin and the possibility of going to hell or purgatory sent me into hysterics," she remembers.

After three months of suffering and no improvement in her condition, Helen overheard the doctor tell her mother that he could do very little more for her. That night she mustered up her courage and announced out loud that she was ready to die. She was tired of dragging out her pain. Then, according to Mrs. Hadsell, it appeared that someone must have heard her:

"As soon as I had made the demand to die, there appeared at my bedside a rather serene looking man. I was positive that he was not Jesus, but he did have a rather bright yellow glow about him. He reminded me of the holy pictures of the saints which I was given by the Nuns when I made good grades in school. He had such an air of peace and love radiating from him. I had no fear of his presence.

"'What makes you think that you're going to die, little girl?' he said. 'You have too much to live for and too much to do.'

"I know that he was real, or so it seemed to my mind's eye. I was still determined to die, so I asked him what I could do tied to a bed.

"He smiled and said, 'You are healed. You will return to your studies. Later in life, you will be inspired to write many experiences so that many will learn from you. This is the purpose for your life, and you will be guided when the time comes.' Then he seemed to fade away, as if disappearing into the wall.

"I was one excited teen-ager. I yelled for my mother to come quickly. She took my temperature and it was normal! She made me promise never to tell anyone about my 'visitor,' thinking it was only a strange dream; but the next morning my feet touched the floor for the first time in three months. Within a week I joined my family at the dinner table, and the following week I was back in school."

Helen told me that the serene young man reappeared for the second time in her life in 1971, when she sat at her typewriter. "Once again he appeared as a young man, gentle, calm, serene, with outstretched arms and eyes turned toward the sky. The floodgates of memory were opened, and the recognition of this vision rushed toward my conscious mind."

When the vision returned on the following night, Mrs. Hadsell made a hurried sketch of her mysterious visitor. Although she disclaims any real artistic ability, she set about painting a likeness of her "angel," and in three nights she had completed the portrait. Since Mrs. Hadsell was kind enough to send me a color photograph of her otherdimensional visitor, I can only comment that her portrait is as compelling as her story.

The remarkable Contesa Gypsy Amaya of Santurce, Puerto Rico, told me that when she was a little girl traveling with her parents in the circus, she would often communicate with "young, lovely ladies," who smiled and assured her that they would always be near to take care of her.

"Many times my angels came to me," Gypsy remembered. "And although I was born nearly blind, they continued to work with me until I could see. The doctors were very puzzled by this, because they had said that I would never be able to see well.

"The time the angels really helped me was when I was on the USO tour with the singer Jane Froman in 1943. As we were landing in Lisbon, Portugal, our *Yankee Clipper* crashed into the Tagus River. I had never learned to swim, but I felt my angels supporting me in the water. I had a broken shoulder, a broken collarbone, and I was bleeding very, very badly. I had thoughts that if there were sharks in the water, they would smell the blood and would surely take me. It was very frightening. But then I had my visions of the lovely angels telling me that everything would be all right. These beautiful people stilled my terror.

"Then out of nowhere came a light, and after being in the water for one hour, some fishermen found us. Out of the thirty-nine people on board, twenty-four lost their lives.

"On Christmas Eve, 1945, I was again with a group of USO entertainers in Kobe, Japan. I had just gone to bed, and I was in a kind of semisleep, when I saw this beautiful lady standing beside my bed.

"She told me to get up, and she held out her hand to pull me out of bed. Her hand was very solid. I started to dress and she handed me my clothes. Then I noticed the chandelier begin to swing. The whole building started to shake. I had no sooner got out of my room when the ceiling collapsed. I ran through the streets, following the beautiful lady. I ran from one place to another. All around me things were falling down and being demolished. Finally we reached a doorway where she told me to stay. Then she disappeared.

"I stood there, safe, completely clothed against the cold, but I had forgotten to put on any shoes! I developed pneumonia, and I was taken to Tokyo General Hospital. General Douglas MacArthur came to see me and called me the "indestructible Gypsy." But I know that it has been my angels that have made me so indestructible!"

In July 1971 an article in the Vatican's daily newspaper defended the concept that each human being has a "guardian angel" to assist him in leading a good life. According to the Associated Press:

> Controversy over the existence of angels has swirled up in the Roman Catholic Church in recent years since the famed Dutch catechism declined to include them as part of essential Church teaching.
>
> In the article, the Rev. Carl Boyer cited references to angels in both Old and New Testament and wrote: "More wonderful than the visible universe, there exists the invisible world of the angels."
>
> He went on to uphold "the doctrine of guardian angels," saying it was "based on the word of Jesus." And he quoted Matthew 18:10: "See that you do not despise one of these little ones, for I tell you, their angels in heaven always behold the face of My Father in Heaven."

Although the orthodox are somehow able to dissociate their saints and guardian angels from the mystical concept of spiritual guides, masters, and teachers, it is clearly a matter of semantics and religious-cultural background which determines the appellation one assigns to those otherdimensional beings who, for some reason, concern themselves with the activities of mortal men. Buddhism has its bodhisattvas, beings who have earned Nirvana but who stay behind to help suffering humanity. And, of course, there are the "familiars" of witchcraft, the "loas" of voodoo.

Christianity has no monopoly on guides, as the following account illustrates.

I am fortunate to have as a friend and adviser a very wise man named Fay Clark. If it were not for the pioneers in this field, devoted men and women such as Fay, it may not have been possible for me to write such a book as this today. Fay had a direction given to his life when, as a young boy living in the Black River Falls area of Wisconsin, he was adopted by Michael Red Cloud, chief of the Winnebagos.

*Fay Clark*: His wife's name was Hattie, and they had no children. He went to my folks and asked if he could adopt me. I lived with them for the better part of two years. Michael Red Cloud told me that since I was his son, I should learn all of the things of his people. This was the first summer I stayed with him, and he convinced me to participate in the Indian puberty rite.

"How old were you?"

*Clark*: I wouldn't have been quite thirteen. We were given preliminary tutoring for several weeks on what to expect and what was expected of us. Then we were asked to go out into the woods and pick a spot where there was a stream. We were told that we must not bring food or seek out berries or any kind of food. We were also told that we must not seek shelter, but must remain exposed to the elements, to the rain or to the sun. We were to weaken our bodies and to continue praying at least three times a day for our guide.

"To what deity did you pray?"

*Clark*: We prayed to Manitou, the Supreme Being. The main thought behind the rite is to completely exhaust the body as quickly as possible. One of the exercises the Winnebagos suggested was to find a place where there were rocks, so that we might pick them up and run with them from one place to another. Make a pile one place, then pick them up and carry them back again, repeating the process again and again. You see, this exercise enabled one to busy his conscious mind with a monotonous physical activity while the subconscious mind was concentrating on the attainment of one's guide.

After a while, one would begin to see wildlife that would seemingly become friendlier. After a time, some creature would approach, as if to offer itself as totem, or guide. It could be a bird, a chipmunk, a gopher, a badger. If the boy were very hungry, and if he were afraid of staying out in the wilderness alone, he could accept the first creature that approached and say that he had found his guide. But we were taught that if we could endure, Manitou or one of his representatives in human form would appear and talk to us.

I spent twelve days fasting and awaiting my guide. I had many creatures, including a beautiful deer, come up to me and allow me to pet them. The deer, especially, wanted to stay. But I had been told that if I did not want to accept a form of life that offered itself to me, I should thank it for coming, tell it of its beauty, its strength, its intelligence, but tell it also that I was seeking one greater.

On the twelfth day, an illuminated form appeared before me. Although it seemed composed primarily of light, it did have features and was clothed in a long robe. "You I have waited for," I said.

And it replied: "You have sought me, and you I have sought." Then it faded away. But it had appeared before me as real as you are, Brad.

On the evening that each boy was required to come before the Winnebago council to tell of his experience, my guide was accepted as genuine. And I don't think there is any way that any young boy could have fooled that tribal council. They knew when he had had a real experience and when he had used something as an excuse to get back to the reservation and get something to eat.

One thing we were taught is that we must never call upon our guides until we had exhausted every bit of physical energy and mental resource possible. Then, after we had employed every last ounce of our own reserve, we might call upon our guide and it would appear.

"Have you had those crisis periods when you have called upon your guide?"

*Clark*: Yes, and it has appeared twice when I have not asked for it. One time my wife and I were going to bed early in a motel in Klamath Falls, Oregon. We planned to arise early the next morning and search for the lava tubes in the Mount Shasta area which they say go clear to the West Coast. My wife was washing out a few items in the sink and I was talking to her, when things just blanked out.

The room became filled with a peculiar light, so white that it nearly blinded me, and yet it was soft. I turned my head because something seemed to be directing me.

The west wall of the motel disappeared, as far as my sight was concerned, and here was my guide coming down at an angle and into the room. "If you love this woman, you will get her out of here now!" he said to me. Then he was gone without any explanation. I told my wife that I knew it sounded crazy, but we must leave at once. She said that she had had a peculiar feeling about the motel and that she would be happy to leave. We started driving until the sensation of pursuit left us, then we found another motel.

"And had the first motel then burst into flames?"

*Clark*: Neither my wife nor I ever found out why my guide appeared to me that night. Possibly it was just as a test to see if I would obey.

The second time my guide appeared to me without any apparent reason was down on Cozumel Island off the coast of Yucatan. My wife and I were sleeping in an old Spanish jail that someone was attempting to convert into a hotel. Again, things just faded out—my wife, the room, everything. And the same individual was standing before me, this time in a different dress. I knew, though, that it was the same guide because of his face, his eyes.

"I know that you cannot identify your guide, but can you say whether or not he was an Indian?"

*Clark*: No, he was not an Indian, even though the first time that I saw him was in an Indian rite. He had long, flowing hair, and there was nothing to identify him with any race of people. When he appeared in Klamath Falls, he wore a brown robe with a rope tied around his middle and a cowl over his head. He definitely appeared to be some kind of monk of indeterminate nationality, except that his skin was brown.

The first time that I saw him, his face was so surrounded by light that I could not comment on his skin color, but I would say that it was white.

On Cozumel he wore very little clothing, just some type of shirt that reached just below his shoulders and some kind of apron that went around his middle like a pair of shorts. I know he was barefooted and seemed brown-skinned.

"Come," he said, "you will go with me." I told him mentally that I would, and then I seemed to blank out.

When I was once again conscious of my surroundings, I saw a group of people seated in a circle. The one who brought me was not the leader, but he seemed to have quite a bit of authority.

My guide took me to the one who apparently had the most authority and said: "I told you he would come. He came of his own accord. I did not bring him. Therefore I insist that he has the right to return, because he will come when the time is right."

The next thing I knew, I was back sitting on the edge of the bed.

"It seems as though you might have passed another test situation."

*Clark*: All I know is that to me these things are real, and I have spent thirty-five years of my life trying to help other people to see the greater reality. These experiences have changed my life from thinking about making that dollar to trying to help other people *know*, not believe. The pastor gets up in church to talk about God, Heaven, and salvation. Does he really believe it, or does he just hope he believes it? He may not even be certain that there is a life after death, but these experiences have taught me to know that these truths are valid.

I can still recall the time in my childhood when I lay in my bed and watched out of the window in fascination as a rather smallish man with a conical hat stood on his tiptoes to another window and watched my parents as they moved about in the kitchen of our farmhouse. After several moments of seemingly enthralled observation on both of our parts, the little man must have felt an uncomfortable sensation of someone watching him. He turned to look at me over his shoulder, and I got a good look at his tiny, pinched features in the light from the kitchen window. He smiled, shook his head; and then I am not sure what happened, but it seemed that he simply disappeared. At the time, I was convinced that I had seen a brownie or an elf. In my later years I had regarded the episode as the single most vivid dream of my childhood.

I began to reassess the memory, however, when I learned that there were mature men and women who would admit to having seen "little people" when they were children.

Hermann Hesse, author of such novels as *Siddhartha* and *Steppenwolf*, says in his *Autobiographical Writings*:

> . . . I do not know when I saw him for the first time: I think he was always there, that he came into the world with me. The little man was a tiny, gray, shadowy being, a spirit or goblin, angel or demon, who at times walked in front of me in my dreams as well as during my waking hours, and whom I had to obey, more than my father, more than my mother, more than reason, yes, often more than fear.

In her biography, *Know the Future Today*, the well-known psychic sensitive Irene F. Hughes tells of seeing a mysterious little woman in the attic of her childhood home:

> She was no larger than Irene and she never stopped smiling. Her clothing was nothing more than wisps and puffs of some kind of shiny material. A sparkling tiara rested upon her golden blond hair.
>
> "You're a fairy queen, aren't you?" the excited four-year-old asked. "I've always known you were around. I could feel you."
>
> . . . "Of course you could. You have the ability to feel many strange and wonderful things."

Little Irene was told that she would receive some pretty beads and a doll, gifts that seemed impossible to hope for in her home, where money was hard to come by. These gifts did materialize, but one wonders what even greater, even more "impossible" gifts were granted to that child without her slightest cognizance of transferral.

Another great contemporary mystic who had unusual "playmates" as a child is the remarkable sensitive Olof Jonsson. In the *Psychic Feats of Olof Jonsson* I was able to relate his adult impressions of these entities:

> "They may have been the same entities that so often represent themselves to small children as fairies and wood sprites . . . But, somehow, on occasion, I believe that I was able to see them as they really were. They were taller than I, but not nearly as tall as my parents. They were, perhaps, just under—or just over—five feet tall. They had much larger heads and proportionately much smaller bodies than an adult human. Their skin color varied from bluish-green to golden brown to a shade of gray. It was they who began to tell me wonderful things about the universe and Cosmic harmony. . . . I felt that they were friends, that they wanted to teach me and to help me. . . . I am still convinced that they are friendly and intend to help man as much as they can without interfering in his own development and free will."

It does seem significant that "little people" are seen most often by children, whose own small stature makes it easier to accept an "elf" than a stern "adult" angel.

The poet Edward Arlington Robinson once observed that the world was like a vast, spiritual kindergarten where everyone was trying to spell "God" with different blocks.

According to Harold Schroeppel, "One of the troubles with this whole business is that God and spirits and ghosts and a whole lot of other things are some kind of force or electronic structure. To try to read them out in 'people terms' is like trying to describe the magnetic field of the Earth."

"Do you accept the existence of other intelligences, from another plane of existence?"

*Lasca Schroeppel*: Oh, certainly. Sometimes I've seen them as

Indian masters, sometimes as Western people who weren't stylized—they just looked like real people.

*Harold*: They exist on a number of levels. Some of them may have been human, but others certainly were not.

For myself, when I need information, I find that I can tap a network with as many as five hundred intelligences in it. Information can be tapped from the lowest level exterior to people on the physical plane; and from there, if I need more information, I can go "upstairs" to other levels.

But, to me, these intelligences would not be "read out" as humans or anything like that, but, rather, "intending forces," forces or pressures that have a definite intention to bring about something, to cause something. Now how a given individual would perceive this we are able to see with our students. Most of our students see lights. However, if you were a spiritualist, chances are that whatever agency brings you messages will probably look like an Indian with feathers, because this is what you will expect to see.

I think these things are forces, or force patterns, and that the individual uses that "read out" that is acceptable to him. In other words, if he expects to see an Indian, that is what he gets. If he is Jewish, the mechanism probably appears as Father Abraham. If he is Catholic, his revelation probably comes from Mary—but Mary had better be dressed in a very particular way, because the Church knows what she is supposed to look like and they do not publicize it, nor do they paint it, but it is a flat matter of record that they have a way of checking if what a revelator really saw or envisioned was the real thing.

*Dr. Bruce Wrightsman*: I don't like to use the word "angel," because that calls to mind images of blue-eyed, blond-haired, Nordic-looking creatures with wings. It's clear that in the first century Christians believed in the existence of angels. They were operating in a Neoplatonic world view which had an established hierarchy of beings from God on down; so the powers and principalities, dominions, and princes of utter darkness that Paul talks about—the elemental powers of the universe which Christ triumphed over—were very real to him. They're not real to me; nevertheless, I have known people very close to me who have had experiences that suggest that this is possible. I would be the last person to say that such things are a lot of nonsense.

I believe that God can use any vehicle as a medium of transmitting himself, revealing himself. He used clouds, fiery pillars, oases on mountaintops, Balaam's ass, and the still, small voice within Elijah. God can use any of these vehicles, but none of them are to be identified as God. God always transcends the means of his own revelation, even Jesus.

We never see God face to face. Moses insisted on seeing God's face, but God told him if he looked into His face, he would die. So Moses said, "Let me see your back." God told him to hide in a cleft in a rock and look at Him as He went, but Moses could only see the back of God. That is very much a part of my theology, and I think it is consistent with the Old and New Testament and consistent with my own experience. But I'll always leave the door open to the possibility of such beings as angels.

Emanuel Swedenborg, who lived from 1688 to 1772, was perhaps the last of the Renaissance men—he was fluent in nine languages, wrote 150 works in seventeen sciences, was expert in numerous crafts, was a musician, a politician, and an inventor with dozens of major contributions attributed to his fertile brain. But if his name is remembered today, it is usually as a Swedish mystic who courted angels and cursed demons. Swedenborg claimed daily communication with the inhabitants of the unseen world, and his manifestations of remarkable psi phenomena are well documented.

In the Winter 1970-71 number of the *Psychedelic Review*, Dr. Wilson Van Dusen presented a fascinating study, "Hallucinations as the World of Spirits."

Dr. Van Dusen writes that by "an extraordinary series of circumstances a confirmation appears to have been found for one of Emanuel Swedenborg's most unusual doctrines—that man's life depends on his relationship to a hierarchy of spirits." Since Dr. Van Dusen is a clinical psychologist in a state mental hospital, he set out to describe as faithfully as possible his patients' hallucinations. Although he noticed similarities between the descriptions given by his mental patients and Swedenborg's discussions of the relationships of man to spirits, it was not until three years after Dr. Van Dusen had collected all his major findings that he discovered the "striking similarity" between what his twentieth-century patients had told him and what the eighteenth-century Swedenborg described in his accounts.

"I found that Swedenborg's system not only is an almost perfect fit with patients' experiences, but even more impressively, accounts for otherwise quite puzzling aspects of hallucinations," Dr. Van Dusen writes.

After dealing with hundreds of hallucinating chronic schizophrenics, alcoholics, brain-damaged, and senile persons, Dr. Van Dusen discovered that "it was possible to speak with their hallucinations." He began to look for patients who were able to distinguish between their own thoughts and the products of their hallucinations. Dr. Van Dusen told the patients only that he wished to gain as accurate a description of their experiences as possible. He promised no special reward and offered no hope for recovery. Some patients, he learned, were embarrassed by what they heard or saw. In other instances the hallucinations were frightened of the psychologist. Once he had reassured the patient and his hallucination, Dr. Van Dusen attempted to establish a relationship with both his seen and unseen interviewees.

According to Dr. Van Dusen:

> I would question these other persons directly, and instruct the patient to give a word-for-word account of what the voices answered or what was seen. In this way, I could hold long dialogues with a patient's hallucinations and record both my questions and their answers. My method is that of phenomenology. My only purpose was to come to as accurate a description as possible of the patient's experiences. The reader may notice I treat the hallucinations as realities because that is what they are to the patient.

On numerous occasions Dr. Van Dusen found that he was engaged in dialogues with hallucinations that were above the patient's comprehension. He found this to be especially true when he contacted the higher order of hallucinations, which he discovered to be "symbolically rich beyond the patient's own understanding." The psychologist also learned that in most cases the hallucinations had come upon the patients very suddenly. A consistent finding was that the patients believed that they had communion with "another world or order of beings."

"All objected to the term hallucination. Each coined his own term such as The Other Order, the Eavesdroppers, etc." The voices had the qualities of real voices, and on occasion could assume a specific known person's voice quality in order to deceive the patient. Such pranks and the shouting of vile and obscene messages and threats were the work of the "lower order":

> They will suggest lewd acts and then scold the patient for considering them. They find a weak point of conscience and work on it interminably. . . . The lower order can work for a long time to possess some part of the patient's body. Several worked on the ear and the patient seemed to grow deafer. One voice worked two years to capture a patient's eye which visibly went out of alignment. . . . They invade every nook and cranny of privacy, work on every weakness and credibility, claim awesome powers, lie, make promises and then undermine the patients' will. They never have a personal identity though they accept most names or identities given them.

Dr. Van Dusen found the lower order consistently antireligious, and some actively obstructed the patient's religious practices. Occasionally they would refer to themselves as demons and speak of hell.

The higher order of hallucinations stand in direct contrast to such demonic manifestations, but Dr. Van Dusen found that they made up only a fifth or less of the patient's experiences. The higher order respects the patient's freedom and does not work against his will. While the lower order prattles on endlessly, the higher order seldoms speaks. According to Dr. Van Dusen:

> The higher order is much more likely to be symbolic, religious, supportive, genuinely instructive, and communicate directly with the inner feelings of the patient. . . . In general the higher order is richer than the patient's normal experience. . . . It looks most like

> Carl Jung's archetypes, whereas the lower order looks like Freud's id. In contrast to the lower order it thinks in something like universal ideas in ways that are richer and more complex than the patient's own mode of thought. It can be very powerful emotionally and carry with it an almost inexpressible ring of truth. The higher order tends to enlarge a patient's values, something like a very wise and considerate instructor.

After intensive study, Dr. Van Dusen concludes that there are a number of points which make the similarity between Swedenborg's description of a spiritual hierarchy and the psychologist's own findings "impressive":

> My patients acted independently of each other and yet gave similar accounts. They also agree on every particular I could find with Swedenborg's account. My own findings were established years before I really examined Swedenborg's position in this matter. . . . It seems remarkable to me that, over two centuries of time, men of very different cultures working under entirely different circumstances on quite different people could come to such similar findings. . . . Because of this I am inclined to speculate that we are looking at a process which transcends cultures and remains stable over time.
>
> Then I wonder whether hallucinations, often thought of as detached pieces of the unconscious, and hallucinations as spiritual possession might not simply be two ways of describing the same process. Are they really spirits or pieces of one's own unconscious? . . . .
>
> It is curious to reflect that, as Swedenborg has indicated, our lives may be the little free space at the confluence of giant higher and lower spiritual hierarchies. . . . There is some kind of lesson in this—man freely poised between good and evil, under the influence of cosmic forces he usually doesn't know exist. Man, thinking he chooses, may be the resultant of other forces.

Robert Shell told me that he, with his adherence to the Ordo Templi Orientis, would be considered blasphemous if he did not believe in entities and in beings that exist on other planes.

"I personally refer to them as the Secret Chiefs, who could

just as easily be called angels, masters, guides, or even gods, who operate from another plane of being to influence mankind's development and to influence it in directions that are not always comprehensible to the people influenced. The overall goals of these beings may be incomprehensible to us, or from a human and very limited point of view, may seem to be evil. Human value judgments really don't apply on these levels."

It is Bob's opinion that at our present level of understanding, it is rather pointless to speculate very heavily on the purposes of these entities. "Except that if we accept that they exist, we must also accept that they are a natural development of the universe and that they exist with as much validity as we do."

Bob went on: "There is a very nice line in C. S. Lewis' *Screwtape Letters*. The gist of it is that a demon is speaking, saying that once mankind has produced the true materialist magician, the man who worships what he calls Forces without acknowledging the existence of *consciousness* behind these Forces, the demons may consider the eternal battle won.

"Too many modern materialistic scientists fit this description. I think it is frightening that a scientist can spend years running rats through mazes, and as a result of an atheistic philosophy, come to the conclusion that man must renounce his dignity and his freedom in order to exist. My personal belief is precisely the opposite. I think man is man because of his freedom and his human dignity."

# EIGHT

## *From Outer Space, With Love*

In the fall of 1956 one of the engineers at a major electronics firm in Cedar Rapids, Iowa, called Fay Clark and asked if he might bring a tape to his home that had been recorded the evening before.

"It appears that they were having their scanning device going to see if they could pick up any signals from outer space," Fay recalled for me. "While they were tuned in, a voice started talking that appeared to be emanating from an indeterminate point thousands of miles away from Earth. As I understood the engineer, it would have been impossible for this voice to have come from this planet, but it had talked on for nearly two hours.

"I listened to the tape for at least thirty minutes. The voice appeared to be sexless. It sounded almost mechanical. The material it was relaying was good, very worthwhile, but I did not recognize the source for any of it. From time to time it sounded like something one would expect to find in the *Upanishads*, either poetry or prose that sounded like a cross between Kahlil Gibran and the *Bhagavad-Gita* . . . what one might term universal truths, free of any one particular Earth philosophy.

"A few nights later I once again received a call from the electronics firm. The engineer told me the voice was back and said that I should look at approximately two o'clock in the north sky. I have a pair of night binoculars which brings up the stars and moon very well. I went out and looked up, and there was an object moving perfectly horizontal from east to west across the sky. It appeared to be about one-third the size of the moon.

"It would move across the horizon, stop, remain stationary for a bit, then drop down a little lower, back up rapidly, and move once again across the horizon. It reminded me of a kind of cosmic typewriter moving across the sky, returning the carriage, dropping down a line, and typing another sentence. . . . It repeated this back-and-forth process six times before it accelerated speed terrifically fast and moved out of sight.

"The next morning the radio and papers said that the night before an erratic meteor had caused thousands of telephone problems. The Cedar Rapids electronics firm had a track on it, and so did stations in Omaha and Davenport. Apparently, as far as they were able to determine, the erratic 'meteor' was about three thousand miles distant from Earth. What they did not publish, of course, was that the erratic meteor was also a talking, metaphysical meteor."

Just as Arthur C. Clarke postulated mental beings from Jupiter who assumed a bit more than an academic interest in the cultural development of Earth's man-apes, perhaps we might conjecture soul beings from other dimensions who assumed an interest in man's spiritual development. When the Old Testament speaks of the *Elohim* creating man in their image, we might speculate that these Higher Intelligences were really more concerned with presenting man a spiritual, rather than a physical, pattern for development. Whereas Clarke imagined his interplanetary tutors planting monoliths to probe the man-apes' minds, map their bodies, study their reactions, and evaluate their potentials so that they might one day evolve to explore the stars, we might imagine cosmic missionaries seeing to the implantation of spiritual truths in "human monoliths" so that man might one day evolve to a New Age, spiritually equipped to explore new dimensions, new frequencies of being.

As I have stated repeatedly in this book, *Someone* has been broadcasting certain essential universal truths ever since man became man. Certain human receptors, that is, prophets and revelators, have been tuning into these cosmic frequencies for centuries, because for some indeterminate reason, they have been able to receive the channels with greater clarity than their more distracted or disinterested brethren. In the last century, however, we have developed artificial extensions of our own sensory apparatus so that now we have mechanical, as well as human, receptors of the Big Cosmic Broadcast.

John A. Keel has written (*Saga,* November 1968):

> Radio signals of undetermined origin have been flooding our atmosphere since 1899. Two generations of scientists and astronomers have argued indecisively about their possible meaning and purpose, even though dozens of carefully worded and very explicit messages from some mysterious source have been received all over our muddled little planet. Those messages . . . too "far out" to be accepted by either the scientific establishment or the press . . . are allegedly from some alien group in outer space. . . .
>
> There is now abundant evidence that somebody . . . aparently a very foreign somebody . . . has developed a technique for broadcasting not only to HAM operators, but to civilian band radios, car radios, cheap walkie-talkies, and even other telephones. Television sets have also begun to chatter in strange voices and Morse-code-like signals everywhere. The activity is now almost universal—and is largely unnoticed. . . .

Here again is a situation in which one may argue at great length about "which came first." Did a mysterious *somebody* recently develop a technique for interjecting messages into all these various frequencies, or have our mechanical extensions of our own sensory apparatus been picking up these impulses quite by accident?

Keel states that when the voices are not received as run-together gibberish or nonsensical chatter, the most commonly received messages have to do with friendly warnings to stop nuclear testing and to cease hostile and warlike attitudes toward one another. Keel writes:

> . . . On August 3, 1958, HAM radio operators throughout the U.S. reportedly picked up a strange broadcast on the 75-meter international band. A male voice purporting to be "Necoma from the planet Jupiter" warned his listeners that the American atomic bomb tests could lead the world to disaster. He spoke for *two and a half hours* in English, German, Norwegian, and his own language which was described as a kind of "musical jibberish."
>
> "It was the most powerful signal ever picked up," one account said. "There was plenty of time during the broadcast for hundreds to listen in, and radio operators called in friends and neighbors and phoned long distance to relatives in other states."
>
> The F.C.C. later denied any knowledge of the broadcast. . . .

Another point of speculation is whether or not our world technology with its sudden mass production of radios, television sets, telephones, and a plethora of electromagnetic devices will jumble the Big Cosmic Broadcast and cause faulty reception. We do not yet know what effect all of our electromagnetic transmissions will have upon the human organism. We do know that intense magnetic fields can produce hallucinations and speech changes, but how our psyches have been reacting to twenty-four-hour-a-day bombardment by radio, television, and telephone may not be known for another one or two generations. The reader may be interested in the following item which appeared in *Pulse*, January 21, 1966:

> A common hallucination of schizophrenics is that they feel "influences," "electromagnetic waves," and so on. Are they right after all?
>
> Possibly, says Professor Hans Neuberger, Professor of Meteorology

at Pennsylvania State University. Today there is a vast amount of electromagnetic radiation emanating from television, radio, radar and other electronic equipment, and this may cause malaise, he thinks. "The general unrest among people may well be a direct result of electromagnetic insults of their nervous system."

Charles' face began to contort; his eyes opened wide in a strange, fixed stare.

*"I am Ishkomar."*

The tone was deep, vibrant, almost as if it came from some kind of echo chamber. The voice came from Charles' mouth, but the inflections and vocabulary were no more his than was the bizarre expression on his face.

*"I bring you greetings and good tidings from beyond the stars."*

This time Lois was ready, the tape recorder at her side. She would not sit in stunned confusion as she did that first time on October 1, 1966.

Lois summoned her courage, interrupted the entity who had usurped her husband's body. "I . . . I'm sorry," she began hesitantly. "But the first time you gave your message, I had no tape recorder. I asked you to repeat the message when you came on the following night, but when I played the tape back, it had such a loud hum on it that I couldn't understand a word you said. Would you, I mean if this is really important, would you please repeat your message a third time?"

"I speak to you via a tensor-vector beam," the entity told Lois. "It is a light beam similar to a laser. Vector is a beam that carries a message or thought. I did not have the beam yet in perfect adjustment. It affected the magnetic field of your recorder. I have made the correct adjustments. There will be no hum on your tape this time. It is important that you record this communication of our intent for the inhabitants of your planet."

Charles is a blue-collar worker of modest education who lives in Phoenix, Arizona. I have tape recordings of the Ishkomar material in my files. I have received details of the revelatory experience from a woman who was a neighbor and friend of Charles and Lois. The woman, whose true identity is known to me, was told by Ishkomar to change her name to "Tana Marue." Here is the text of the first message from Ishkomar:

"I will explain to you briefly who and what we are and what I am. You have named some of our craft that move through your atmosphere 'flying saucers.' I am now recorded in one of these.

"The craft that contains the instrument in which I am recorded is four and three-tenths miles in length—by your method of measurement—and two and one-tenth miles in circumference. This craft also contains others of us who are in human form. I have passed the phase of human form. My knowledge and mind processes were long ago recorded into an instrument you would liken to a computer.

"I was brought to the vicinity of this planet approximately thirty thousand years ago, by your method of time measurement. Your planet and the living forms upon it have a specific value to us. Your form of life has a particular value to us.

"For this reason, at about the time I was brought to the vicinity of your world, we interfered with the natural development of the species of man that inhabited this planet. Our purpose was to shorten the cycle of development necessary for the human inhabitants of this planet to be of use to us.

"We have worked patiently with you for over thirty thousand years. The development brought about would have taken, by normal cycles, over two hundred and fifty thousand years. Our intent, however, is not to control or to rule over you. Intergalactic law within our group forbids this. We are, however, permitted to guide you. Your acceptance of us is by your own choice.

"Those in human form inhabiting our craft have ceased to reproduce. This condition makes it necessary to choose one of two courses when it becomes necessary to dispose of the human vessel—whether to be recorded in a device and stored, as I was, or whether to be recorded into another suitable human form. We have been unable to manufacture successful and suitable human-type forms by synthetic means. This, therefore, makes it necessary to find planets young enough where new man beings are being born, yet old enough for the human form to be developed to a point that will provide suitable bodies with sufficient brain capacity to receive our knowledge.

"By mutual agreement between a planetary dweller and an inhabitant of our craft, the knowledge and the memory of one of us may be blended with the planetary inhabitant without the loss of the receiver's identity. The one from our group adds only his knowledge to the planetary dweller, and the abandoned body is disseminated. This blending may not take place without mutual agreement between the beings involved, and the planetary dweller must fully agree and desire this blending. We seek, therefore, not to take, but to give.

"We, however, are not alone in our interests in your world. There is in existence with us another group. Their interests are not necessarily harmful toward you, yet their methods are in direct opposition to ours. They also have interfered with the development of your planet. They wish to reach their ends, not be cooperation, but by control and domination. . . .

"You must reach a high level of mental development and knowledge to be able to understand our purposes. We have attempted to gain your cooperation for thousands of years. We have been vigorously opposed by the other group. We must achieve our goal by guidance of your kind, but you must desire guidance for us to be of assistance to you.

"Our work is beyond your present level of understanding, and yet you will eventually be of great assistance to us by cooperating with us in the study of life forms and conditions on your planet. The results of these studies will be intercorrelated with other studies being conducted on other worlds; and they will benefit your own planet, our people, and the inhabitants of other worlds.

"We also have limitations which make it necessary to adhere to certain conditions that are difficult for you to rationalize at this time. The inhabitants of your world have repeatedly been told of these, and they always have converted them into spiritual ideals. It is an understandable thought process to attempt to understand the unknown by measuring it with the known. We do not condemn you for this. But to those of you who will follow certain steps, we may be able to help reach a higher understanding, thereby improving man's opportunities for survival on his world, while, at the same time, assisting us in our endeavors.

"The man whose body and mind I am using to speak to you is being used by his own full cooperation. Had he not reached out, I would not have been beamed to him in answer. Yet all who reach out are not answered, for all do not reach out in honesty of purpose. Some wish to acquire some personal gratification of the moment; therefore, they do not reach a point of open acceptance necessary to receive me. I am beamed to many on your world. This man is not unique.

"We are using many methods at this time to inform your people of our presence and our immediate purposes. The time is quite near for cooperation between us to begin. Your next step upward will soon begin.

"Full knowledge of our presence will soon be known to your people. There will be, at that time, great upheavals on your planet. We regret this cannot in any way be avoided. We knew this from the beginning. We, therefore, have warned man repeatedly to prepare for these events, both mentally and physically. Those who take not the trouble to prepare themselves are of little value. We do not intend any evacuation of your planet on any scale. You are of no use to us in the Outer Reaches. Our craft are now adequately manned.

"Our need of your cooperation involves habitation of your world by your own people—under more suitable conditions than you now realize. Following the climatic upheavals on your world, we will provide guidance to bring about the desired conditions of your, and our, mutual benefit.

"Seek us and you will find us. We only await your call. Peace be with you. I am Ishkomar."

We can imagine the questions that must have set Lois' mind to boiling after the successful recording of Ishkomar's message. Why had Charles been selected to be a voice box for an intelligence from some other world? When had he indicated his desire to cooperate with an alien race?

In 1956, when they were still living in Michigan, they had sighted a UFO over their home—a slow-moving, red light that seemed momentarily to hover above them as they stood in the driveway and watched it.

"I'm just a little guy," Charles had said, speaking to the UFO. "But I'm friendly. I would like to be your friend."

Lois had laughed at her husband as he continued his

monologue to the strange red light. Even after she had grown weary of observing the phenomenon slowly traversing the night sky, Charles had remained on the driveway, his head tilted upward, speaking seriously of his desire to be friends with the Unknown. Had his overtures of peace really been heard?

Then, later that summer, one night when he had been out fishing, the lake suddenly became eerily quiet, and a strange curtain of wispy light had settled down about him. He had rowed for shore in a panic, but later he told Lois that he wished he would have kept his wits about him and remained to examine the indescribable beauty of the light. That had been nearly ten years ago. Still, a year to someone on Earth might be but a day to someone from another space, another time.

And what of the implications inherent in the visitation of such an intelligence? Ishkomar spoke of his "group" having, from time to time, "blended" with the dwellers of this planet in order to guide and assist them. Could such activity explain the process of revelation throughout man's recorded history? And what of this "other group" that Ishkomar mentioned? Could they, with their desire to control and dominate Earth dwellers, be considered the "devils" that had appeared to subvert mankind's physical and spiritual development? When Ishkomar returned several nights later, Lois had a list of queries ready:

*Who sees flying saucers?*

"This is restricted to no primary group of any kind. It only happens by chance. It is not that we allow or disallow any being to see our vessels."

*What planet did you inhabit?*

"We reach throughout the galaxy and beyond. We explore."

*Then you are interested in more planets than Earth.*

"That is correct. To you, your Earth stands alone. This is your home. We extend throughout this galaxy. Your planet is of little significance, yet it has a prime importance."

*But you aren't the only travelers in the universe. You said there was another group that was up to no good.*

"I would not say that their purpose is not good. It conflicts with *our* purpose. This does not mean that their intentions are not good or honorable."

*But they want to control the Earth.*

"That is correct. We guide; they wish to control."

*Is your group of travelers recorded knowledge—as you are—or do others have physical form?*

"There are those of us who have been committed to what you would recognize as a computer system. Our mental processes have been recorded into a device that is other than human form.

"There are others on our vessels who must carry out menial tasks. They are in human form. There are men upon your planet who have developed because of our physical-form beings. This was done by what you would term artificial insemination. This occurred often in a recent age with a primary type that inhabited your planet. From this development, there were intermediate races as by-products to reach a higher form more near our human form. These are nearest to the form who inhabit our vessels."

*Was Jesus Christ of such a birth?*

"He was."

*And Buddha?*

"No. He consisted of an Earth body and beamed knowledge. On your planet today there are thousands of men who could be termed Buddhas."

The question-and-answer period went by rapidly; but once again, Ishkomar terminated his appearance with a warning of approaching cataclysms and the intriguing statement that the Earth dwellers were very important to the "work" of his group. When Ishkomar next appeared, he would not deign to answer questions. In an authoritative voice he presented a teaching on the sovereignty of the individual.

"The man beings of your planet are engaged in turmoil to decide which grouping of man beings should own your planet.

"Many of you who are aware of us call to us to help you slay and destroy those whom you believe to be your enemies. Those who do so do not understand that among the ones that they call their enemies are man beings who are also aware of us and request the same task of us. Are we then to accept these calls and destroy *all* of you?

"The inhabitants of your world have always searched beyond themselves for others to solve their problems for them, individually and as groups. You refuse to accept the fact that your world belongs to all the man beings that inhabit your planet, equally, yet combined as one mind, complete and sovereign.

"There can be no ultimate solution to your problems as an individual being or as a sovereign world until you have eliminated the complex barriers you have placed between yourselves.

"Each of you, singly, is a sovereign being and could be likened to a universe complete unto yourselves. You coinhabit your world with other beings who are equally sovereign to themselves.

"There is no question of right to this state of existence. It is the ultimate fact. Not one of you, or all of us, have the right or power to own a sovereign being. To trespass upon that sovereignty in any action or thought is a grave and most serious action. The complexities you have created for yourselves through lack of knowledge of this first principle of existence has wreaked untellable havoc in your world.

"The combined goal of all man beings on your world should have but one end result toward which to expend all effort. Care for your planet. Preserve it. Improve it by balancing its imbalances. Garden it, for it is your home. It is necessary for your place of habitat.

"You yourself are responsible to your world as a whole. Every thought and action that disregards your responsibility to the well-being of the coinhabitants of your world constitutes an irreversible seed of destruction that will ultimately grow to add its branch to the tree that now blights your world.

"Only the combined total of the beings who inhabit your world may bring into bloom the Tree of Life. We will assist none of you to destroy. We *will* assist you to gain the principles by which you might build. We only await your call. Peace be with you.

*"I am Ishkomar!"*

Lois studied the elements contained in the message with a great deal of care. Could her husband, a man with only a seventh-grade education, produce, either consciously or subconsciously, a dissertation of this kind on the subject of man's individual sovereignty?

Lois contacted Bill Finch, a Phoenix writer with a strong

interest in psychical research, briefly explained the series of experiences that her husband had undergone, and invited him to listen to the tapes. Finch was impressed with the material after an initial session, and it was not long before he, too, had an opportunity to ask questions of Ishkomar. Within a short period of time Finch had written a number of newspaper columns about the mysterious "voice from space," and certain of Ishkomar's words began to receive public exposure in the Southwest.

"On one occasion," Tana Marue told me, "Ishkomar was scheduled to speak on the radio. He had not been informed that these arrangements had been made by the writer, so when Charles called him and Ishkomar transmitted down, he refused to speak on the telephone hookup that Bill Finch had set up. Bill tried to talk Ishkomar into going through with the broadcast, but Ishkomar was dead set against it. Then, in order to settle the argument, Ishkomar said that he would take the radio station *off the air.*

"Just a few minutes before the program announcer was to call Ishkomar, the station lost its power. Ishkomar did talk to the announcer over the phone, and he explained that he would not answer questions from the public over the radio because it would take too long to give adequate answers; therefore, he would speak briefly off the air.

"The instant the conversation was over and the announcer hung up," Tana Marue continued, "the radio station came back on the air. The radio station was flooded from listeners who had tuned in to hear Ishkomar and had received nothing but dead air. "I called the station to ask if they knew why they had had a power failure at that precise moment. They said it was a mystery, because after the conversation, they had full power again, just as though nothing had happened. They admitted to being mystified; however, they could not admit that they believed Ishkomar had been responsible, even if they did think so."

As incredible as this incident may seem, I have heard the tape recording made of the flustered and frustrated announcer attempting to explain to his listeners why the radio station went off the air at the precise moment that the interview with Ishkomar was to begin.

Ishkomar gave instructions to the small group that gathered for lessons, messages, and question-and-answer sessions, stating in no uncertain terms the need to keep Charles' true identity a secret. "None of us will break our pledge to Ishkomar," Tana Marue told me. "He told us Charles' life would be in danger if ever we made his real identity public."

Literally dozens of revelators throughout the world claim to be receiving direct communications from entities who identify themselves as beings from other worlds. In UFO research there is the phenomenon of the "contactee," one who claims special knowledge through direct communication with the occupants of what he is told is an extraterrestrial spacecraft. Again, we may be observing the evidence of an intelligence that presents itself to percipients in a manner that they will find most acceptable.

Their alleged communion with the UFOnauts has definitely touched the "missionary" element within certain of the UFO contactees, and they have received many of the same communications as those revelators who have seen themselves touched by the more familiar Divine Fire. The contactees are told, for example, that man is not alone in the solar system and that higher intelligences have come to teach, that man must raise himself to higher levels of vibration in preparation for elevation to new dimensions, that man stands now in the transitional period before the dawn of a New Age.

As in the illumination experience of the mystics, the contactee is often confronted with a blinding light—that, in this case, appears to be emanating from a strange craft either on the ground or directly overhead. The contactee communicates with either an attractive "Space Brother" or a "voice inside his head." He is very often told that he has been selected because he is someone very special. The criteria for his uniqueness range from his being the reincarnation of a notable world figure of the past to his being a cosmic "seedling" who was planted on Earth as a very small child. After the initial visitation, the contactee experiences several days and nights of restlessness; then, after a period of a week to several months, he finds that he can no longer contain the burning fire in his heart and he prepares to spread the Space Brothers' message to the world. The contactees are barely heedful for their own personal welfare or the needs of their families, and those closest to the contactee report that he has become literally a changed and different person.

Dr. Bucke would probably be offended at my mentioning UFOs in the same breath as Cosmic Consciousness. He implies that the individual who receives Cosmic Consciousness has, in a very real sense, been preparing himself for such an experience by the life that he has been leading. In the case of the UFO contactee, the blinding light strikes without any kind of religious or moral preparation and at any age. No doubt some process of selectivity may be involved, but it is too subtle and on too deep a psychic level to be easily apparent.

I cannot help questioning whether the Space Brothers might not be angels, spirit guides, and other messengers hiding themselves in more contemporary, and thereby more acceptable, personae. Of course, the central question remains whether we truly have Higher Intelligences adapting themselves to roles which the contactee may readily assimilate on the psychic level or whether we have Supreme Intelligence itself sparking out in humanoid fashion in order to prevent the percipient from seeing the face of God. And I must also suggest that such information and such entities may come from the channeler's own High Self, rather than from any separate and distinct outside intelligence. I have often and freely stated, however, that I can no longer doubt that the contactee phenomenon is taking place on a global scale, with an increasing number of recipients of the Celestial Gospel joining the ranks each day.

Miss Marianne Francis, "Telethought Channeler" of the Solar Light Center (7700 Avenue of the Sun, Central Point, Oregon), receives her principal information from the Space Brother "Sut-ko," whom she describes as a "highly evolved being from the planet Saturn."

*Miss Francis*: My first contact must have been in Santa Barbara in the summer of 1958. I had been interested in UFOs since 1947, and on this night I was aware that I was being mentally impressed with thoughts that were not my own. I spoke these thoughts to my ex-husband, who had the insight to say that they made sense to him.

I said, "Well, apparently I have made some kind of contact with them." At first the communications came in just a few sentences and a couple of paragraphs. Then they must have assumed that I was ready for extensive channeling.

"How do you distinguish between your thoughts and the thoughts of another intelligence, since both are taking place inside *your* head?"

*Miss Francis*: The Space Brothers' thoughts always come in a very clear framework, very often about things I am not particularly connected with, and I can distinguish them from my own consciousness and my own mental impressions. I don't analyze or think about the material as it comes in to me. I do analyze it afterward, though. . . . I am convinced that they are not discarnate entities, and I am convinced that they do not come from any mind on this planet.

"What about their place of origin being another dimension which coexists with our own?"

*Miss Francis*: I feel that life on many other planets exists at what they term a physical-etheric, rather than a physical dense level, so there is a question of other dimensions existing. But I don't feel that I'm receiving from other dimensions here.

"Do you think that your Space Brothers may be what other mediums call spirit guides?"

*Miss Francis*: No, I have had a great deal of experience in the past as a reporter in the psychic field, and I do not feel that Space Intelligences are the same as spirit guides. Spirit guides do one thing, usually a very good thing, at one level; but Space Intelligences are something very different again. I have what is termed clairsentience, rather than clairvoyance or clairaudience, and this is the thing that has guided me in my work for a long time.

"Do you feel that these beings, these Space Brothers, have been interacting with us for many centuries?"

*Miss Francis*: Oh, . . . very definitely, at least according to what degree they have interacted with us in recent times. I think in ancient times there were comings and goings between other planets and us.

"What is the Space Brothers' purpose at the present time?"

*Miss Francis*: I think they are greatly concerned about man's misuse of atomic energy and the fact that he can, and will, destroy the planet if this misuse continues unchecked. If man should destroy Earth, the balance of other nearby planets in the solar system would be upset. . . .

I don't think they have ever regarded us as dupes or pawns. All those whom I have contacted consider themselves our elder brothers, who have much to offer us. They say constantly, "We don't think of ourselves as being so far beyond you. We think of you as also aspiring toward the same goals of spirituality.

I think that today there is a tremendous search for awareness, and I believe this has to do with the fact that we are moving into a new age, a new cycle, and man has to develop his spiritual capabilities or perish.

"I am awake when my contact talks to me or shows me things," says Joan Howard of Toronto, Ontario. "We talk any time of the day or night, but it is easier in the middle of the night when things are quiet. The visions and things I receive come better when I can close my eyes. I have also met him several times on astral trips. He has black hair, white-golden skin, long, slightly slanting eyes, which can sometimes send out light rays. He is about five feet, eight inches tall."

Mrs. Howard, an ex-service woman, who served her country for five years, says she knows enough about physics and psychology to suspect that she was witnessing an invasion by aliens of unknown origin. "I took nothing for granted about them," she told me. "I shot questions at them, real fancy ones, like about how, if they were 'physical beings,' could they travel so far in so short a time. I told them, 'Don't you dare lie to me, as I don't believe you, anyway.' I made it good and hard for them, believe me!"

But today Joan Howard publishes a mimeographed journal entitled *Eternity Calling* that features material from her "inter-dimensional Space Contacts, Thoth, Zio, Motag, and Thrishna." Mrs. Howard also offers a mimeographed book, *Genesis to*

*Eternity,* on which, she says, "Zio and the boys worked darned hard to put together."

Ted Owens, from Cape Charles, Virginia, claims that he alone is the Earth's principal intermediary for Space Intelligences. He has become extremely controversial, because in addition to claiming to do nice things like demolish hurricanes, end droughts, and rescue villages from volcanic lava, Owens says his "SI's" can also do nasty things like mangle professional football players, sink the boats of seal hunters, and threaten with "psychokinetic" vengeance almost everybody who arouses his ire.

Ted Owens has said that his brain became "modified" by the SI's one night in 1965 while he was living in Fort Worth, Texas. He and his daughter were driving in the country when a cigar-shaped UFO suddenly appeared and came floating toward their automobile. He can remember no Space Brother stepping out to declare himself, but he writes in his book, *How to Contact Space People,* that "from that day on, my life changed radically." Owens endears himself to psychic sensitives by telling them that they are but babes-in-arms compared with the power he can command from Space Intelligences, and he frightens readers of the prediction annual I have edited for the past two years by providing me with material intended to "shock, horrify, and/or infuriate your readers."

The May 3, 1970, issue of *Sports Illustrated* was at last forced to take official notice of Ted Owens in their "People" section:

> . . . back in February, Owens decided to cast a spell upon the Baltimore Colts. And charge $100,000 to unhex them. Now, was it Owens' fault that Johnny Unitas tore his Achilles' tendon, Tom Matte got appendicitis and Sam Havrilak sprained his ankle? Well, when a Philadelphia writer challenged Owens to "prove you can do something" the PK man announced he would hex Tom Woodeshick of the Eagles, and within 15 minutes, Woodeshick was ejected from the game for fighting. . . .

Shortly before the 1971 football season, Owens told me he would remove Joe Namath for the season. And, whether by coincidence or not, poor Broadway Joe got tacked up in a freak accident in a preseason exhibition game with the Detroit Lions.

"I picked up the game on my powerful, shortwave radio and I threw my mental force at Namath," Owens observed coolly. "I sent him a copy of George McClelland's [Sports Editor of *The Virginian Pilot*] article, 'If Owens Speaks, Listen,' in which George wrote that I had said that Namath wouldn't last half the season. Namath should have read that article and paid attention to it.

"Several years ago, I knocked Norm Snead of the Eagles out for the season with a broken leg in the first play of the first exhibition game in Philadelphia. With Snead, there was no doubt about the mysteriousness of it. Not one soul was near him when he went down as if pole-axed. I was in the stands at the time, using my mind on Snead. Stan Hochman of the [Philadelphia] *Daily News* told me he was there on the sidelines taking pictures of Snead when it happened. He couldn't believe his eyes, because no one approached or hit Snead."

Thankfully, Ted assures me that he is far more interested in helping, rather than hurting, people, but sometimes he cannot resist a challenge. Ted believes that there have been select "Hu-Si's" (hybrids of human and Space Intelligence matings) who have assisted mankind throughout the centuries.

"It takes me only a few seconds or minutes to implant creative, helpful, healing psi force in a human. Yet when this power begins to grow within the human, it is so great and powerful in its results that nothing can compare with it. It is only necessary to flash a picture into my mind, which alerts the UFO intelligences who monitor me, then flash another picture or combination of symbols covering the project I wish to 'PK.' From that point on, the miracle comes to pass.

"This is what Jesus was talking about. He was trying to tell his disciples that PK force grows. For instance, when I saved Brenda Sue P. from dying–after the doctors had given up–I 'planted' an angel on her head as she lay in bed. This is a rainbow effect which is projected mentally by my mind. This is a form of healing SI force. As the days went by, the rainbow effect pulsated and grew larger and larger until it filled the entire room.

Psi force grows and expands with time. The amount of PK power can also be regulated when applied by a disciple or a special human.

"My several hundred miracles are documented and on record. Should you balk at the thought of UFOs being involved in all of this, then be reminded that millions of human beings have seen UFOs."

Dr. Wolfgang John Weilgart met beings who wished to teach him and guide him in helping others toward the ways of peace and understanding. Although he has doctoral degrees in linguistics and psychology from the universities at Vienna and Heidelberg, in a single mystic moment he was given *aUI*, a new language for a new brotherhood of man.

When he was a child of five in his native Austria, Dr. Weilgart had his first cosmic experience. A stranger in a star-strewn mantle appeared to him and said: "Thou must die, Wolfgang."

The child answered firmly: "I am ready." From this moment on he felt a new cosmic life-stream had entered him, as if his former life had been dissolved, as if his former self had died. Wolfgang dictated to his older sister a drama *SaradUris* (which, in the Language of Space, means that "good light" which comes "through the Spirit"). SaradUris is a spaceman savior who comes to the earth to guide mankind away from its wars and to bring peace through understanding. The rules of peace revealed in this drama are not only derived from sentimental love, but also from a justice which is based on the status quo as well as on a program of survival for those who are worthy to survive and can survive. "Creative Spirit, lives on still/ Destroyers perish, while they kill."

Dr. Weilgart relates his most crucial cosmic experience in poetic form as an introduction to his book *aUI, the Language of Space.*" The boy "Johnny", seated at a mountain creek, is alerted to an alien presence by a strange flutelike sound. There is a mysterious being, a butterfly with green leafy wings and rootlike legs.

It circled and sat down on my knee.
The sounds it made were piped through its flute-like body,
and yet they wafted from far away.

And then I knew that this thing must have
come from somewhere else.
And I began to understand that it was talking to me.
Could we be friends?
It showed strange signs,
and put them together,
and they made sense.
And what I heard was from another place.
I learnt
The language of Space.

Johnny learns that the Being has come from a distant star, from where it had watched Earthmen fight against the dragons of the sagas. "But now when nature's foes lie defeated at his feet, man turns his weapons against his brethren, and his rallying cry is still the slogan of hate, the word of conventional language."

Your words give murder a beautiful name,
and call a killer a hero.
So if I gave you the gold of my wisdom
wrapped in the burlap bags of your words,
You would use it to club each other to death. . . .

When Wolfgang told his parents of his experience, they sent him to a psychiatrist, who, however, found the six-year-old child's only abnormality to be the fact that he could solve the problems of a thirteen-year-old. His Binet IQ tested above 200. (Recently, IQ tests were repeated on Dr. Weilgart, and he was made a member of the American Mensa, the world's highest IQ society.) The psychiatrist warned the child that in Western society, uncommon experiences may be told only as dreams or in poems.

Dr. Weilgart wrote his first doctoral dissertation on "Creation and Contemplation." It was one of the few outspoken pacifist statements against Hitler and the whole Nazi ideology of aggressive action: "In horizontal collective action man resembles a swarming ant. But man's contemplative eye comprises the cosmic universe. Horizontal action leads to reaction and clashes in war and ultimately annihilation. But in creation and contemplation, man rises vertically up to the Spirit."

His father, Dr. Hofrat Weilgartner, had worked for the *Anschluss* (the annexation of Austria by Germany), and so the Nazis expected similar cooperation from the son. But John Wolfgang had another of his cosmic communications. He spent an afternoon and evening wrapped in contemplation. In a cosmic insight of peace, his father's dreams of the glory of the German Reich and his mother's entreaties faded into nothingness.

The Nazis had offered him a high position in their secret service because of his dozen languages, his knowledge of psychology, and his friendship with the underground, against whom they wished him to be an informer. Although this "intelligence" position would have been the only way to rehabilitate himself in the eyes of the Nazis, whom he had offended by his dissertation, Dr. Weilgart refused.

His cosmic voice told him to flee to Holland. He had few friends whom he could trust, and no connections with practical helpers. His parents had filled his pockets with money, but so much money was a sign of flight. Following his inner voice, he gave his funds, together with the address of his parents, to a man near the border. The man sent all the money back to his parents. Most people would have suspected flight and would have kept the money or even betrayed the refugee to the Gestapo, whose border patrols searched every suspect. Dr. Weilgart was in fact stopped by such a patrol, but the inner voice took over, and to his surprise Dr. Weilgart heard himself command the patrol to another mission. Strangely, the patrol obeyed, as if Dr. Weilgart had been in the uniform of a higher officer.

Soon Holland was being rapidly invaded by the Nazis, who would have executed Weilgart as a deserter. The young mystic's inner voice brought him to the Dutch Governor of Java, who happened to be in The Hague, and he wrote an American visa for Weilgart and gave him a ship ticket. In the meantime somebody had sent Weilgart's poems to Thomas Mann, who, as Nobel prize winner and honorary Doctor of the University of California, gave him a postdoctoral research fellowship there to write his book *Shakespeare Psychognostic.*

Weilgart, as a disciple of Albert Schweitzer, followed the inner voice, which told him that in a generation the blacks' problems would engulf America. From 1945 to 1950, he served as Professor at Xavier University for Tropians and Indians. ("Tropians", for the race originating in tropic climates, and "Caucasians" are terms Dr. Weilgart prefers to "blacks" and "whites," which make the contrast too harsh. Also, "black" in Western languages has a negative connotation. In *aUI,* the language of space, a Negro is called *iau,* "sun-space man"–a man adapted to sunny regions.) Then he received a United Nations' research grant, finished his second doctoral degree in psychology and psychotherapy at the Universities of Heidelberg and Zurich, became a psychotherapist for the U.N., and invented the WERT (Weilgart-Ethos-Rhyme-Test), not only for crime and suicide prevention, but for personality development. Chand & Company of New Delhi, India, published Dr. Weilgart's *Language of Space,* which is available through the Cosmic Communication Company, Decorah, Iowa 52101. The Language of Space makes man immune against the slavery of slogans and the idolatry of ideologies, for it makes language a communication of transparent truth.

"For millennia–ever since the confusion of tongues–prophets had to speak their messages in a Babel of conventional languages," Dr. Weilgart says. "And their message has been misunderstood, as it was distorted into slogans of hate. Even Jesus' use of the word 'faith' was distorted. Jesus said: You must believe in me, you must believe my word of love, so that you will follow me and do as I do; love God and your neighbor. But then 'faith' was used as a belief in certain scholastic dogmas, and whoever was not a dogmatic believer became an infidel or heretic to be burnt at the stake without any Christian love. *Auto da fé* [act of faith] got to mean a most hateful torture and execution.

"There is no danger of malignant men misusing the Language of Space. For it is the Language of Peace through Understanding, and the Logos of health. [The introduction by the Academy of Science calls it a logotherapy of mental health.] Logic, wisdom and loving goodness coincide in the Language of Space, for in the atomic age it is finally wise to be good. Only the wisdom of love can survive."

A housewife in Colorado, whom we shall call Melanie,

suddenly began to recall a life on another world. At the same time, she began to go into trance to predict coming Earth changes. I was sent a tape on which Melanie uttered brief snatches of her "native tongue" during a trance session. I was told that linguists at a number of universities in Canada and the United States had been unable to determine the root of the supposed language.

I asked Dr. Weilgart if he would listen to the tape and see if he could offer any clues to the origins of the strange language. Dr. Weilgart found Melanie's dialect unknown to him in any language other than in the logos of *aUI,* which had been revealed to him as a small boy.

Once before, when he was a young psychotherapist, Dr. Weilgart received a shock when he encountered a young boy in a mental hospital who addressed him in *aUI.* Dr. Weilgart learned that the lad had been placed in the hospital because he insisted on speaking only in this language, which was unintelligible to his parents, teachers, and physicians. The young psychotherapist went to the director of the hospital and told him that the boy was not sick, that his language made sense. The director ignored Dr. Weilgart and ordered electro-shock treatment for the boy.

The boy resisted the electroshock as much as he could. He told Dr. Weilgart that he feared the treatments would make him forget what he had learned on the "other star." In his struggle the boy died, but with his dying words he said to the psychotherapist: "You believe in me. You tell others about the Language of Space!"

Now Dr. Weilgart was listening to a woman from Colorado, who one day was a busy housewife and mother, the next, after touching the Cosmos, a revelator who spoke often in an unidentified language. The psychotherapist was cautious. He pointed out that the woman's unconscious might have retained bits and pieces of overheard Amerindian dialects, and now, years later, was reassembling them and uttering them as a language from another world. But he wrote down *aUI* symbols as Melanie's voice uttered the sounds again and again from the tape recorder.

Because Melanie spoke very rapidly, Dr. Weilgart was not able to hear all of her words, but he transcribed the following phrases which he plucked from the strange speech: "way of movement around space" . . . "from life above space" . . . "to move for a light-existence" . . . "a good existence in a dimension above space."

In my *Aquarian Revelations* I presented a distillation of the Outer Space Apocrypha which would seem to contain the basic concepts presented to the world by all those whom the Space Brothers select to preach the Cosmic Gospel:

*Man is not alone in the solar system. He has "Space Brothers" and they have come to Earth to reach him and teach him.

*The Space Brothers have advanced information which they wish to impart to their weaker brethren. The Space Brothers want man to join an intergalactic spiritual federation.

*The Space Brothers are here to teach, to help awaken man's spirit, to help man rise to higher levels of vibration so that he may be ready to enter new dimensions. According to the Outer Space Apocrypha, such a goal was precisely what Jesus, the prophets, Confucius, and the leaders of the great religions have tried to teach man.

*Man stands now in the transitional period before the dawn of a New Age. With peace, love, understanding, and brotherhood on man's part, he will see a great new era begin to dawn.

*If man should not raise his vibratory rate within a set period of time, severe earth changes and major cataclysms will take place. Such disasters will not end the world, but shall serve as cataclysmic crucibles to burn off the dross of unreceptive humanity. Those who die in such dreadful purgings will be allowed to reincarnate on higher levels of development so that their salvation will be more readily accomplished.

During one of the last sessions Tana Marue attended in Phoenix, Ishkomar was asked if his group ever prayed. The entity replied that they prayed to the Father Creator, although he, who had thousands of years before been recorded into a machine, no longer prayed.

"Were I to be rerecorded into a human vessel, however, I would then be capable of prayer," Ishkomar said.

Someone in the group said that he would like to hear the manner in which Ishkomar would pray if he were using a human vessel once again, instead of a machine. Several months later, Ishkomar gave them this prayer:

"My thoughts are now directed to the Father Creator of all that is, ever was, or ever shall be, whose in-going and out-going thought force gives form and being to all that exists in the Universe.

"I am, within myself, thankful that I have been created and given the opportunity to live. Within my own being lies the awareness of my individuality, yet also my oneness with all that is, ever was, or ever shall be.

"You have given me a oneness as a sovereign being, and I have created my own kingdom of inner worlds and outer worlds. With responsible attitude, I have accepted my place in time and existence, and by so doing, I have brought peace to my inner worlds and order to my outer worlds.

"My self-appointed task is to bring peace and order to all I may reach in your universe. Not by yoke and forceful domination, but by persuasive reason.

"I cannot judge another sovereign being, but I can help that being to expand its awareness so it may judge itself.

"With honorable purpose, I express my willingness to justify each moment I exist in usefulness to the universal whole, that the universal whole may also justify my existence.

"I stand in a moment of time between the Eternal Past and the Eternal Future, content that, for me, all that was before and all that will be cannot exist for me, and yet I exist because all that was before me gave me my moment in time, and I will share the responsibility for all that will exist in the Eternal Future.

"I recognize the Adversary, the Destroyer, the Deceiver of Worlds—wild, uncontrolled fear that can grow in the intellect of all thinking beings. I know that caution is a progressive thought form from which fear grows. When ungoverned by reason and understanding, it becomes the author of confusion and the enemy of all that is.

"I dedicate my moment in time to the task of bringing peace and order to all beings wherever I may be permitted to touch their intellects with my presence, that in their self-created kingdoms they may establish peace to their own inner worlds and order to their outer worlds by denying fear to exist, thereby committing it to an endless void of eternal disuse.

"Father Creator, your kingdom is mine, for I am aware of it. My kingdom is yours, for because of you, I created it.

"I am *Ishkomar.*"

# NINE

## Our Sons and Daughters Shall Prophesy

*And it shall come to pass in the last days, saith God, I will pour out of my Spirit upon all flesh: and your sons and your daughters shall prophesy, and your young men shall see visions, and your old men shall dream dreams: And on my servants and on my handmaidens I will pour out in those days of my Spirit; and they shall prophesy.*

*Acts 2: 17, 18*

Many claim that this prophecy is being fulfilled now and that the Divine Fire is stepping up its activity. The wife of a Florida evangelist, who was asked to comment upon the Jesus People, the God Squad youth, and their participation in what many have called the most profound spiritual revolution of modern times, replied: "Right now there is a great outpouring of the Holy Spirit." During the course of my research I asked a number of theologians, psychologists, and revelators whether they agreed.

"I really believe," David Anderson told me, "that we are in the midst of a great spiritual awakening, and it is a demonstration that Christianity is not dead, that certainly God is not dead, and that the great Gospel message that has been proclaimed for two thousand years is becoming more real than in probably any other time in the past."

*Dr. Conrad Baars*: I believe that the Holy Spirit has always been pouring out during all the past ages, and I don't believe that our generation is more of a recipient than other generations have been. Maybe there is a greater interest, maybe there is a greater receptivity, and maybe there is a much larger percent of pseudo-outpourings claiming to be real outpourings of the Holy Spirit.

*Dr. Walter Houston Clark*: When one asks why there should be a spiritual awakening at this time, I must reply that there may well be sources of it beyond my understanding to which astrology may yield some clue. But I think the best explanation is the obvious starvation of man's nonrational needs over many decades. Materialism, competition, power politics, and human exploitation can be endured only so long before they begin to make nonsense to sensitive natures jaded by the persistent denial of their essential longing, the longing for a living God and vital religious experience. Just as a spiritual and artistic awakening suddenly emerged out of darkness in the twelfth century, so is a similar awakening, whether on a smaller or larger scale, occurring today.

*Dr. Bruce Wrightsman*: I think "profound spiritual revolution" is saying too much, because it presupposes that the Holy Spirit has been idle in the past. I think it is claiming somehow that God has been sitting around doing nothing, or that revelation stopped with the closing of the canon in the first century, that He's been sort of floating since then, or that He only occasionally forays from Heaven to stir things up. That's too interventionist for me. I like to think about God as omnipresent in the human situation. The Spirit of God is always working, trying to open doors, confronting people, energizing them, enlivening, creating human beings out of Homo sapiens, human in the sense that Jesus was human with a humane, compassionate consciousness. I don't think there's been a recent "outpouring of the Holy Spirit." That's always been going on. But there has been a tremendous *effectiveness* of the Holy Spirit in recent years.

A Lutheran pastor remarked: "There is a kind of awareness coming about with regard to the barriers that exist between man and man, man and God. Maybe the Holy Spirit is finding a way of communicating directly, and man is realizing that religious denominations cannot monopolize the channels."

*Lasca Schroeppel*: I feel that the real spiritual revolution is happening in the new vigor of the youth, working with others across the old, standard barriers of religious differences. The medical students I deal with seem to have emerged out of this honesty that was coincident with the so-called hippie revolution. I like these young people.

*Harold Scroeppel*: I personally notice that there are a great many more of what I would call "baby telepaths"—people who have psychic or spiritual ability, who either don't have any training or who don't have any idea of what the blazes is going on. They have been born into the world like the Fool and the Pharoah [Tarot cards], and they are in the same stage. As far as your "profound revolution," well, something is changing. There is a lot more psychic and spiritual awareness. The Age of Secrets is about dead.

*Diane Kennedy Pike*: My personal conviction for the reason that we are entering into this new phase of spiritual consciousness is that we are in an age of transition from one astrological age to another. From studying the period in which Jesus and the early Christians lived, it turns out that the Dead Sea Scrolls, and the people who wrote the Dead Sea Scrolls and the Apocalyptic material, relied very much on their understanding of astrology to help them understand what was happening in their period. They had a tremendous awareness that they were at the end of an age, and this, astrologically speaking, was the end of the Age of Aries and the beginning of the Age of Pisces. At that time they began to have experiences of the outpouring of the Holy Spirit, which they called the Holy Spirit or the Spirit of Holiness; and they had the sense that everything was coming to a tremendous climax, the end of an age. And, therefore, those who wanted to enter the New Age would have to make a conscious choice about that and would have to change their ways of thinking and their ways of living in order to enter the New Age. Astrologically speaking, we today are in the same kind of transition. We're at the end of the Age of Pisces and the beginning of the Age of Aquarius, and it seems to me that the persons who are privileged to live in such an age of transition, though it is a difficult time in which to live, do have the opportunities that the people had at the time that Jesus lived and at the time that his disciples were preaching of entering a whole new level of spiritual consciousness, or awareness. It is, in a sense, because of the forces of nature that this peculiar opportunity is available to us.

"According to astrology," Dr. John Paul Gibson said, "the term 'Procession of the Equinoxes' implies that every two thousand years brings a new era of life, a new culture, and a new religion. Therefore, according to this theory, we are now approaching the end of the Piscean era and entering the Aquarian era.

"Jesus was born in the beginning of the Piscean era," Dr. Gibson went on, "and the sign of Pisces represents religion. The world has experienced religious turmoil ever since Jesus was elevated to God at the Council of Nicaea in A.D. 325 and the Christian Church became the state church. Anyone who did not agree with the Nicene Creed was tortured, imprisoned, or put to death, both Christians and Pagans.

"Now that we have moved into the cusp of the Aquarian Age, religious changes are taking place that are quite noticeable throughout the world. Under the sign of Aquarius, there is a higher rate of vibration between the spirit world and the earth plane, so that communication is possible today, just as it was in Bible times."

Many people express less than keen enthusiasm and less than complete confidence in astrology. I asked Dr. James T. Hayes, a professor at Murray State University in Kentucky, to provide me with a statement regarding revelation through astrology:

"Genesis 4:14 (And God said, 'Let there be lights in the firmament of the heavens to separate the day from the night; and let them be for signs. . . .') points clearly to the divinity of revelation through astrology. Man's task since he first became aware of his own presence in his environment has been to determine through a study of celestial motions and configurations the order that was divinely established with the creation.

"Very simply, earliest man brought into existence the science of astrology when he sought the answers to his primitive questions about why part of his time was light and part dark, why part of his time was warm and part cold. He looked to the heavens and found the solutions—interplanetary relationships. Through methodical observations and inductive reasoning, then, man began developing the science of synchroniticity—astrology.

"And this precisely is what astrology is—a timing device. Contrary to popular belief, astrology is not a fortune-telling system or a cause-and-effect study. It is in its purest form man's attempt to find revelation through an insight into the meanings of an infinite number of planetary configurations.

"Hence, as a timing device, astrology does not show *why* something is true; it simply points to the *when*, the *where*, and the *how* of an event, a condition or an act. If, for example, man should wish to time the seismic activity, he would, through a careful study of horoscopic charts for past earthquakes, determine the one or more celestial conditions common to all charts. He would then conclude that these in-common conditions reveal the timing of earthquake activity. Revelation, then, would come through an orderly study of the 'signs' identified in Genesis 4:14.

"In his quest for attunement to the cosmic or universal mind, man labors constantly. One of his best sources for revelation of truth, however, is indeed astrology. Henry Van Duke was keenly aware of the validity of man's oldest science, psychology, and religion when he said, 'The highest of all learning is the knowledge of the stars. To trace their course is to untangle the threads of the mystery of life from the beginning to the end. If we could follow them perfectly, nothing would be hidden from us.' "

Astrologer Rod Chase explained that oft-heard phrase, "the dawning of the Age of Aquarius" to me in this way:

"To put it very briefly, there is a new age every two thousand years. Four thousand years ago was the dawning of the Age of Aries, which was the time of the Old Testament. Aries is the sign of the ram, and the Old Testament is filled with Aries symbolism. God is referred to as the Great Shepherd, and the people are referred to as the sheep. As a matter of fact, the great prophets Moses, Abraham, and Joseph were shepherds.

"John the Baptist and Jesus ushered in the Age of Pisces and a lot of fish symbolism. Many of the disciples were fishermen, and Jesus referred to his followers as 'fishers of men.' They got away from the Aries rituals of burnt offerings and circumcisions, and in came baptism, immersion in water. Pisces is, of course, a water sign. The New Testament is just filled with Piscean symbolism.

"Now we are entering a new age. This does not contradict the past ages; it will simply be a new way of looking at things. Aquarius is the sign of the water carrier or the gardener. The vital prayers of the New Age will be like planting seeds. I think a lot of the new prophets will come out of the communes. Aquarius is the sign of the communes, and a lot of the most exciting young people are going to live in communes.

"Jesus' first miracle was changing water into wine. In the new Age of Aquarius, the kids smoke grass, because they smoke it through the air; and it is practically always a group activity—you know, they pass the joint around in a circle. That's very Aquarian. I'm not trying to justify it; I'm just saying that it is happening.

"Astrologers disagree about when it starts. Edgar Cayce said that the Age of Aquarius began in 1932. Some astrologers think that it is hundreds of years away; however, I think we are already well into it. In any case, we've been in the transition period for at least a couple of hundred years."

*Reverend Kingdon Brown*: Basically, what is happening is that there is a vibratory change going on, whereby everything is increasing its vibratory rate, and in the process some things and individuals will be left behind and some will advance into a new dimension.

"I've heard that from several revelators."

*Rev. Brown*: I talked to Colonel Burks a few weeks ago, and he is aware of this, too. He feels that about 1965, something clicked whereby everything advanced. He refers to it in terms of time, whereby everything accelerated in pace very suddenly.

"That is interesting. I've heard other revelators refer to 1965 as being a key year. Why do you think that is?"

*Rev. Brown*: Colonel Burks seems to feel that everyone with whom he's discussed the matter went through a major change at that time, and although it wasn't evident from a social, economic, and so forth, point of view, things began to happen to people on a very personal level.

Col. Arthur J. Burks (U.S. Marine Corps, Retired) is a popular lecturer in the field of metaphysics, whose specialty is the exploration of Akashic Records of past lives. I was able to ask Col. Burks about the matter of "1965" when we were among the speakers at the Aquarian Age International Conference in Honolulu, Hawaii, February 2-9, 1972.

*Col. Arthur J. Burks*: This is a peculiar thing, and I think a number of people have taken note of it. In February and March 1965, I began to get little ideas from people who came in for study. People would come in with the notion that things were moving faster. I came to the conclusion that about February or March 1965 it was as if each person in the world had started to take a step forward, and he stepped across a period of years from 1965 to 1995. Since everybody did it, nobody noticed it. And it became evident in the studies I did for people that spirit was taken by surprise. After a period of time, I found a reading by Edgar Cayce (I think the guy is infallible. I didn't know him, but Mrs. Burks did and had readings by him), who said in 1912, that there would be a collapse of time, some interference with time, that would cover a period of years near the end of the century. It seemed to me that these words of Cayce offered some sort of confirmation on this giant move ahead.

"You're saying, then, that in 1965 everyone took a step into the future."

*Col. Burks*: Everybody stepped across thirty years on the

spiritual plane . It is confusing, because in spirit there is no time. I've notice another strange thing. When I made a prediction before 1965, I would be within a couple of days of being right on target. But now I have discovered–and I hear that others have, too–that a prediction will work out all right, but it will be realized faster than predicted. If I say something will work out in June, it may happen in February. In other words, everything seems to be stepped up.

According to Dr. Richard L. Rubenstein, Professor of Psychology of Religion, Florida State University in Tallahassee, our extraordinary technological revolution is manifesting itself in shifts in religious attitudes.

"I think society has become far more organized and to a certain extent stratified as a result of the complex kinds of products which society now needs in order to maintain itself," Dr. Rubenstein explained. "I am thinking of jet planes, computers, television cameras and television receiving sets, and the whole realm of services which support such tools. I am also thinking of the vast expansion of the industry of education which has been taking place in the last ten or fifteen years.

"This has required new elements, new ways of apprehending reality as a result of the opportunities made available by the new techniques. Our reality is not the same with a color television set as it was in the world in which one went home in the evening and read by candlelight. Our reality is not the same in a world where almost instantaneously we can be transported to other lands, as it was when such trips took thirty days to complete. Furthermore, the complexity of the machine is matched by a complexity in the social organization required to manufacture and distribute these machines. This has changed our lives in an extraordinary number of ways, and as people's lives have changed, as the reality they apprehend is changed, their religious lives are inevitably changed with it.

"You see, as a professor of religion, I am aware of the fact that there is what I would call a contextual relationship in what people do and the class in which they find themselves and in the kind of religion which they accept. It is no accident, for example, that upper-class native Americans tend frequently to be members of the Episcopal Church. It is no accident that some churches, like the Seventh-Day Adventist or some of the Pentecostal churches, tend to attract people of a very different social class and background. Throughout history there has been a corollation between the community and the class that a person comes from and the kind of religious belief that he has manifested.

"Now, specifically, there has been a rise in Pentecostal and charismatic movements in the last five years, and I believe that the rise in these movements is in some sense linked to a phenomenon in religion which I call the collapse of transcendence. When all of the traditional ways of seeing reality as ultimately guided by a Divine Destiny no longer work, people are not going to be satisfied with living in a world in which God is not present in any sense. The world is capped and in some sense completed by the presence of God or the presence of Jesus. This need to experience God or to experience Jesus becomes very important.

"Once you have the 'Death of God' theologians who speak of the absence of God and once it becomes difficult intellectually to argue against such people, then the next step is liable to be: 'Well, I can't argue intellectually with those who say I can't argue intellectually, but I *have* experienced God in my life.' This, therefore, is a shift from the intellect to experience.

"I have had no such experience, but I would never say to a person who says that he has experienced God or he's experienced Jesus in some sense that he was wrong. All I can say is that I have had no such experience and that I don't know what such a person is talking about, because the only way to know what such a person is talking about is to have the experience that he has experienced."

Robert Shell of Roanoke, Virginia, an occultist, a disciple of Aleister Crowley, a member of the Ordo Templi Orientis, says: "I've always thought that it was an extreme shame that Carl Jung became a psychologist rather than a mystic. He had so much in terms of mysticism, religion, occultism, he could have risen to really great heights as a magician."

In his *Memories, Dreams, Reflections*, Dr. Jung wrote:

> From the beginning, I had a sense of destiny, as though my life was assigned to me by fate and had to be fulfilled. This gave me an inner sense of security, and though I could never prove it to myself, it proved itself to me. I did not have this certainty, *it* had me. Nobody could rob me of the conviction that it was enjoined upon me to do what God wanted and not what I wanted. That gave me strength to go on my own way. Often I had the feeling that in all decisive matters I was no longer among men, but was alone with God . . . outside time; I belonged to the centuries; and He who then gave answer was He who had always been . . . He who always is there. These talks with the *Other* were my profoundest experiences: on the one hand a bloody struggle, on the other, supreme ecstasy."

In his *Flying Saucers: A Modern Myth of Things Seen in the Skies*, Jung ventured that such things as signs in the skies and personal revelations represented "changes in the constellation of psychic dominants, or the archetypes, or 'gods' as they used to be called, which bring about, or accompany, long-lasting transformations of the collective psyche." Jung maintained that such transformations began within the historical tradition, first in the transition from the Age of Taurus to the Age of Aries, then from Aries to Pisces, which was coincident with the advent of Christianity. The psychiatrist said: "I am, to be frank, concerned for all those who are caught unprepared by the events in question and disconcerted by their incomprehensible nature."

Was Dr. Jung only concerned for the intensely rational who might not be able to cope with spiritual revolution? Or did he feel that the New Age was to be approached with a certain caution? I asked a number of my interviewees to offer their own comments of how one might best prepare for the New Age:

*Dr. Richard Rubenstein*: I would agree with Dr. Jung that the world that we are entering is largely an uncharted planet as far as we are concerned and to be unprepared for it spiritually is to invite danger psychologically. Nevertheless, I see the problems more in sociological terms . . . I believe changes in mankind's spiritual life . . . will reflect the changes in mankind's sociology.

As far as changes in the constellation of psychic dominants, there again I feel that we simply apprehend the world in radically different ways than men have ever apprehended it before, and in that sense there has been a change in the constellation of pyschic dominants. Dr. Jung was not really a *believer* in the sense that some of the people who participate in Charismatic or Pentecostal movements are believers. He tended to see changes as shifts in psychology, shifts in the collective unconscious of mankind, and I think he was essentially correct in this. I would stress the fact that these changes are not only psychological but sociological, . . . rooted in the changes in the tools we use and changes in the structure of society, which must be organized in order to create and to manufacture and distribute these tools. . . .

Because there is so much more to reality than common sense can make available to us, my fear—one that I apparently share with Dr. Jung—is that people will not become aware of their own depths and the way these depths are operative, not only in relationship to others, but also the way they are operative in society as a whole. We will either find ways to be in contact with our own depths, or we will find ourselves being overwhelmed as by a tidal wave by these depths.

*Dr. Walter Houston Clark:* [Jung] may have meant that the mystical state of consciousness is so different from ordinary consciousness that those who unexpectedly have such experiences either think they are going crazy or become very lonely, feeling that nobody will understand what has happened to them. Such feelings can make them schizoid or even develop into full-blown schizophrenic states, particularly since the average psychiatrist is not equipped to distinguish between mental illness and superior, sensitive creativity.

I think the best way to prepare for such an eventuality is to talk with those who can describe such states or do reading in books like William James' *The Varieties of Religious Experience* or my *Chemical Ecstasy*. After they are convinced of the reality and possibility of attaining such states . . . then they should seek some of that reality for themselves through pursuing what to them seems the most appropriate and congenial discipline.

*Diane Kennedy Pike*: It is not only the intensely rational who will be unable to cope with the New Age. Again, we have New Testament precedence for this . . . the people who lived in that period were going through the same thing. You remember Jesus talked about people who would be caught unprepared, "... and woe to them who will be out in the fields working when the hour comes."

My personal conviction is that the Age of Aquarius has to do with our developing a large overview of how things are related. It's my hope and expectation that this ... will be integrating the various levels of our consciousness–physical, emotional, mental, and spiritual–in one world view and one vocabulary and one way of talking so that we won't have the split that we've had for so many years, where we think that science and religion are talking about separate things ... We need a language in which we can talk about the spiritual forces and energies the way we are learning to talk about other natural energy in the universe. The language of physics probably offers more potential at this stage than any other language, because they're talking in universal terms about energies and vibrations and forces and force fields and so forth, all of which I think are applicable to the spiritual life.

I think we are now in a stage wherein mass consciousness can evolve to the spiritual level, and ... it is at that level where there can be a reunification of religion and science. I don't think such a unification diminishes the spiritual nature. On the contrary, I think the physicists are ... discovering the vast, endless potential in the unseen realms, and that is why I believe that a merging of the languages of science and religion will be one of the keys to the universality characteristic of the Aquarian Age. Science speaks a universal language, but religious language has always been very exclusive in its whole frame of reference.

*Dr. Bruce Wrightsman*: I think what Jung is saying is that the whole universe is in a state of cosmic evolution. We are going on to something else, and ... the world, or God, is evolving in another state of existence that we can call mind or spirit, a new form of consciousness ... Many people today, with their sensual, genital definition of manhood, are going to be completely ill-equipped to enter this new state of existence.

It means that the day of the warrior, of the gladiator, is gone. We can see this in a massive aversion to war, which has never hit the general population as it has now. I saw also in Russia a tremendous aversion to armed conflict among the young people ... For the first time in history, man has the means to destroy himself with war, and that means that global responsibility of going to war is correspondingly magnified. Survival will depend upon evolving men of such consciousness that the ideal of the gladiator, the warrior, the competitor will have to go. I think young people are anticipating this in their styles of life and hair and dress and communal styles of living.

What this leads to, then, is something very simple that Jesus said a long time ago, that the meek will inherit the Earth in the most literal fashion possible, because only they, by their consciousness, have conferred upon themselves the advantage in the struggle for existence. The strong will destroy themselves, and a lot of other people along the way. But the meek will survive to inherit the Earth.

*Robert Shell*: I'm also somewhat motivated by the same fear Jung had, because I do think that this coming period of change ... is going to catch a large number of people totally unprepared and may be a very violent, turbulent era. Kenneth Grant, the British head of the Ordo Templi Orientis and also a friend of mine, has speculated that these beings referred to as "those on high" [occupants of UFOs] are the same beings that Aleister Crowley always referred to as the Secret Chiefs, and the Egyptians deified into their many god forms. These beings are, in the ultimate settling, the true rulers and true owners of this planet, and we humans are only vaguely aware of them most of the time. Our petty interests and concerns are so far beneath their level of interest that they very rarely show themselves or interfere with humanity. I do think, however, if humanity ever got to the point of having a full-scale atomic war ... these beings would intervene for the sake of the planet, rather than for the sake of man, and stop things before they were carried too far—not necessarily saving mankind in the process, but saving the planet for themselves.

The spiritual revolution is just beginning. As time and events go on, we're going to see more and more escalation of the process involved. This revolution is probably going to be very frightening to a large number of people, because they're so totally bound to material goals and ideals that when spiritual things happen to them, they're completely unprepared to cope with them. They have no belief in their minds that such things happen. Miracles are okay as long as they're kept at a safe distance–such as two thousand years ago. If, for example, someone walked across the water in New York harbor today, almost no one would be prepared to cope with it. It would probably be written off as a mass hallucination, as so many modern miracles have been.

I think there really is a basic, cosmic truth to the idea of the Age of Aquarius; however, I think that the terminology used by Aleister Crowley, in referring to it as the Age of Horus, the Age of the Child–child crowned and conquering–is probably more accurate than the idea of the Aquarian Age that you pick up from rock musicals.

I do think the New Age is to be approached with caution and joy, because it is going to be something different from anything that has ever existed within recorded human history. I'm not a Utopian. I don't think that we're going to have perfection on the face of the earth or that angelic beings are going to come down with manna from heaven, but I do think that a vast improvement is going to be seen.

*Rev. Kingdon Brown*: The new spiritual awareness which is becoming evident is a sign that mankind is attempting to understand change in light of the Total Cosmic Plan. We are searching for our complete selfhood by looking at our eternal evolution in the Universe. The New Age represents the increased "vibratory change" which appears to be taking place as each individual alters his consciousness to be in attunement with the Total Cosmic Plan for the Universe. This is accomplished by allowing oneself to be guided and directed by the Infinite Plan as it is received and understood, not by the conscious mind, but by the soul.

Each soul has a position in the New Age as it progresses toward the Light of God. Each religion may view the New Age differently, but the end result is the same: Government of man by God; guidance of man by Spirit; awareness by man of the Law which changes all manifestation.

The New Age is a fundamental awakening of man's capacity

to understand the nature of change within himself, within others, within the Universe. Knowing the Universal Truth of change, man can adjust himself to it and thus manifest his total spiritual potential in this lifetime and in succeeding states of being.

I think the ecological question is the most obvious one with respect to this matter, but the basic issue is not really one of ecology. It is really a matter of how we conceive of ourselves. I think that as long as we continue to exploit each other, we're destroying each other. The nitty gritty is probably in the answer to the question, what are we, really? Are we just this body, or are we this mind or these feelings? Are we here temporarily or many times?

"You obviously feel that man is much more than body?"

*Rev. Brown*: We are primarily spiritual beings, and we are evolving so that we may all be instruments. I believe when people function naturally, they receive guidance. Perhaps this is what caused primitive man to find water and to produce children, I don't know; but most men seem to have lost that extra sense.

I think the revelations being received now are designed to prepare us for new ways of perceiving ourselves. If there is a crisis inherent in the New Age, it will be a crisis between those who will understand, and those who will not. This, in effect, is what Manta Ru told me.

"Why should this awareness be occuring now, at this time?"

*Lasca Schroeppel*: It has been coming on us. We have conquered so much of the vast, material world that we are now becoming impatient about bridging into the spiritual. When you can see everything at once, big and small, you naturally want to know what is next. I saw this in instrumentation. The physiologist almost always apologetically says that the very thing one is measuring is always distorted by the instrument of measurement:

I think we have to be honest, because, ultimately, we ourselves are the instrument of measurement. I feel that this soul searching will grow where we will explore ourselves more deeply as instruments of measurement, because the physical world, while it does have challenges, certainly has shown us what its limits are. People are going to know more about themselves as the observer; and this, inevitably, is where we will go to the more spiritual, the more subtle.

I have seen distance and time traversed. I have seen things that are far more subtle and far more precise than things ordinarily seen with the five senses. I feel the communication base is inevitable, and if one person with ability meets another, the spiritual revolution will continue to grow. It has a lot to do with the honesty that bridges across lines or organized religion, thanks to our youth and all others who want to communicate with new ideas. The inevitable outpouring of revelatory experience is the next logical step. The basic, cosmic truths being revealed are not going to be given in words or symbols, but they will be seen directly, and more and more people are going to know the difference between seeing directly and receiving secondhand impressions. As people raise themselves through more subtle, and vaster, levels of perception, they will know themselves as a very subtle vehicle with many domains.

"It has nothing to do with anything we might have deserved, then, or evolved toward?"

*Diane Kennedy Pike*: I was just talking to some friends about that. We would need, I should think, a much larger perspective in order to say whether those of us who are living in this age have merited living in this age, or whether that's more circumstantial. I don't really believe that anything is purely circumstantial. In one sense, then, I would say that those who are in this age are here because we are able to take advantage of it.

*Deon Frey*: I think that the young people today have come into life with less Karma than we older people have. They are more ready to receive spiritual things and to become spiritual. They're not so wrapped up in materialism. I feel that with their knowledge and their expression of truth they're sending out a purer light to the people of today, because so many of them really seem to love each other and to be more truthful with each other than we as a group used to be. Even though their language may seem different, it is a pure language, because to them it is the language of love, and they express it in their voices and in their faces.

"Would you go so far as to say that it may be something Karmic?

*Diane Kennedy Pike*: It might be. I think more and more that the whole concept of reincarnation makes sense out of a lot of things that don't make sense otherwise.

One of the things that people who talk about reincarnation say is that when we reincarnate, we need to find opportunities or circumstances that will enable us to either work through the things that we have left over from past lives or to learn new lessons that we need to learn now. It would seem to me that there would be particular opportunities in an age of transition, like we're living in now, that might not be available at other times—or at least not for another two thousand years or so. Therefore, if there were those of us who missed the boat the last time such an opportunity was available, for whatever reason, we might have come back now and have another chance, a really unique chance.

I don't mean to say, though, that it would not have been possible for people to have received the Spirit in the two-thousand year interval. But I think in the cultural sense we are all aware that there is something very dramatic going on in our culture right now, and it has both its negative and its positive aspects. Its positive aspect is that it offers a fantastic opening up to the whole spiritual realm. This is happening to a lot of people, just as in New Testament times. It's happening to a lot of people who don't even have a religious background.

In the Book of Acts we have the story of Peter being called to the house of Cornelius. Cornelius and his whole family had received the gift of the Spirit, and they were Gentiles and had no background of study, which is why they called Peter to them to explain what was going on.

This is happening again in our age. It's one of the things that causes a great many people to become what we might call even mentally disturbed because of spiritual experiences that they've had. Because of their previous mental orientation or their lack of understanding of religious matters, they don't have any frame of reference. So what happens to them? They receive this tremendous power, but nobody ever told them that such a thing was possible!

Suffice it to say at this point that regardless of one's position on the "New Pentecost," everyone seems to agree that there is some kind of spiritual awakening process at work, and a good many observers feel that this growing mystical consciousness may have something to do with the "last days." In the revelations presented in this book, the reader will no doubt notice the sense of urgency with which most of them were relayed. A wide range of prophetic voices tell us that the increase in revelatory experience, the outpouring of the Holy Spirit, has been accelerated due to the inescapable fact that our age is drawing to a close. Nearly all the revelators sense coming earth changes, a time of fire and destruction. But whereas some revelators see this "End-Time" as only the transition period between ages, others see it as a Day of Judgment prefacing the end of our world.

In apocalyptic visions, prophets see ahead to the End-Time. Man's salvation lies in the future, and the meaning of the present is obscured in the chaos of survival on the earth plane. In apocalyptic thought, the present is a time of trial and tribulation, and its meaning will only be made clear in the eschatological birth of the New Age. In primitive Christianity, mankind's destiny is viewed as steadily unfolding according to a great design of God. Apocalyptic thought presupposes a universal history in which the Divine Author of that history will reveal and manifest His secrets in a dramatic End-Time that with finality will establish Jahweh, the God of Israel, as the one true God. Placing the ultimate revelaton of God at the End-Time seems to imply a history for God, as well as for his creation—or at least an evolution, or translation, from one sphere of activity to another.

To most orthodox Christians, the profound meaning of the New Testament is that Jesus Christ previews not only the Last Days, but the resurrection of the dead. Although man continues to live in anticipation of a Second Coming, the resurrection of Christ has already completed history.

In his *Doctrine of Revelation*, Wolfhard Pannenberg writes:

> It is through the resurrection that the God of Israel has substantiated his deity in an ultimate way and is now manifest as the God of all men. It is only the eschatological character of the Christ event that established that there will be no further self-manifestation of God beyond this event. Thus, the end of the

> world will be on a cosmic scale what has already happened in Jesus. It is the eschatological character of the Christ event as the anticipation of the end of all things that alone can establish this development so that from now on the non-Jew can acknowledge the God of Israel as the one true God, the one whom Greek philosophy sought and the only one who could be acknowledged as the one God from that time on. This is a point of view quite distinct from the self-vindication of Jahweh through the giving of the promised land to Israel. This acknowledgment, and the accompanying ratification of the universal revelation of God in the fate of Jesus, is itself a fact that became a part of world history through the absorption of the classical world into the ancient church.

The apocalyptic messages that have been so very much a part of man's interpretation of the revelatory experience may be the result of the echo of the inevitable death of our planet, which, for us, lies somewhere in the undetermined future. If during the ecstasy of communion with the Divine Fire (the reception of this continual transmission of universal truths), one may rise to the consciousness of the Eternal Now where he can see all of history as a whole, then one's heightened perspective may enable him to see the demise of our planet as an event that affects everyone who has ever lived. All of mankind shares in the loss of Earth's art, music, literature, sculpture, architecture, and philosophy. These man-stamped tangible and intangible artifacts comprise the unclaimed legacy left to the unborn in A.D. 70 as well as to the unborn in that unnamed day when the sun dies. If history is truly cyclical, then the end will never be far from the beginning, regardless of the centuries in between.

*Dr. Wrightsman*: Working out of a Christian perspective, we must remember that the heart of the Gospel is eschatological, end-oriented. The whole theme of Jesus and the Apostles is that the last stage of history, the end-time, was being entered into with his appearance. It doesn't mean that the old age has stopped abruptly. There is a kind of overlap going on, and we live, as it were, between the ages. We live in the new time, if we share that consciousness, that style of life that Jesus calls us to. But we also live in the old age, where law and sin and evil are still a real part of daily existence, so we feel the tension.

"Do you see a literal Judgment Day?"

*Dr. Wrightsman*: Not a day in which all men are going to have to stand before the great court of God. In Matthew 25 we are told that the judgment had already taken place. "In as much as you did or did not do it to the least of these, you did not do it unto me." And that's where the decision was made. The confirmation, the formal confirmation of that judgment, takes place, perhaps, after death; but that simply confirms what is, in fact, already the reality of judgment.

Many of the Biblical prophecies were subjunctive and conditional. "If you continue to do this, *then* the Lord will do this"—The kind of thing that a prophetic figure like Martin Luther King would say today: "If America continues to do this, then this will surely happen." That sort of prophecy is based upon the knowledge of God and what he is about in history, and it is always political, which is to say that it is always about something that happens down here on Earth.

God is not an inflexible principle of destiny that is inexorably going to carry out Its will, so that prophets can only forewarn people to prepare for the inevitable doom. With God it is always subjunctive. Jonah got angry because God did not destroy Nineveh after the prophet said that He would. "You can't do that," Jonah protested. "I can forgive them, but you can't!" And that's the uniqueness of Biblical prophecy. There is always that "if."

If people do have authentic revelations today and do make them in the name of God, this may be the reason why the prophecies do not turn out; because they may not have heard the conditional character of them. Prophecies generally speak a word relevant to their own time for the purposes of bringing people to recognition of their plight and to repentance *now*. The purpose of prophecy is not just to forestall disaster, but to restore men and women to God and to the kind of covenant of light that God intended for them in the first place, usually through justice and righteousness and peace in the land.

Nobody gave the Old Testament prophets a magical vision of the coming of Jesus. The Jews were looking for a Messiah, a king, a ruler, who would be just and fair. King David was their model.

He was a scoundrel at times, but at least he was God's kind of man. He knew his place before God and he was capable of repentance. Jesus came to show them that "God's kind of man" is not necessarily a glorified military leader, but may be a man who can embody certain of these characteristics in a nonpolitical kingdom. *My kingdom is not of this world,* he kept telling his contemporaries: "It's not the kind of kingdom you usually think about."

This concept may bring the Biblical prophets down to a different level. Some people think it makes them less than what they are; but to me, the whole nature of prophecy is basically political rather than apocalyptic and otherworldly.

The light of God is always in the world, and it always brings judgment upon whatever is darkness or evil. I think that the special social, political, economic conditions of history convey the impression of the apocalyptic moment. During moments when everything is coming loose, we look around and then begin perceiving crisis. But I think it is always there.

When an ego in an excited, emotional state attempts to convey a contact with the Divine Fire in finite terms, the poor human brain simply must put some kind of contemporary, historical limits to the universal truths realized in the communion. Our finite brain with its compulsion to limit, its desire to conceive of a beginning and an ending to everything, seeks to trap an Infinite Intelligence, free of Time and Space, into man's marking of history. It is our obsession with sunrises and sunsets, springs and winters, that gives birth to rituals, theologies, and the denouement of the Judgment Day.

Throughout all time, prophets have received the blast of the Divine Fire and have filtered this vibration through the injustice of the social ills they see around them. In the loneliness of their convictions, they have identified strongly with their concept of God—a Perfect Being—and the disgust that they believe He must feel as He beholds imperfect beings wallowing in sin, filth, and degradation. Translated through their psyches, the Eternal promises that the Kingdom of God is at hand become fiery condemnations, and the Divine Fire becomes Hell Fire.

As John Keel has said: "Each generation is, from their singular viewpoint, the 'last generation.' Each generation is given the same information and the same warnings, and each restructures these so they appear pertinent to their own contemporary problems. History itself follows repetitious and somewhat predictable patterns. The prophecies of 520 B.C., or A.D. 1970, could be effectively applied to *any* epoch. You can be sure that there will be people in A.D. 2070 who will be receiving the same signal and applying it to their period."

The Apostles of A.D. 30 believed that they were living in the Last Days, that Jesus would soon return and take them to live with him in Heaven. The early Christians were advised to be watchful, to be ever prepared for the final hour. But obviously, the world did not end with a bang, but continued to whimper along to the next sunrise. If there really is no End-Time, but only periodic transition times, the whole area of Apocalyptic revelation has little, or no, meaning. Prophets will always proclaim their age as the final one, and their contemporaries will always suffer their admonitions to repent for the Judgment Day that is always at hand, but never on schedule.

There have been many physical, group "Judgment Days." Each old age terminates with a period of purgation which purifies those humans who live during the transition between ages so that they might be better prepared for the New Age. These "Judgment Days" occur, according to some Cosmic Calendar, approximately every two thousand years. Our age is experiencing no false alarm. It is no coincidence that the Divine Fire has begun to touch the souls of an increasingly large number of men and women. Another two thousand years have run their course on the Cosmic Calendar. Our time closely parallels those days of unrest in the Apostolic era. Another Judgment Day is at hand.

Once again, many recipients of the Divine Fire are not interpreting the news as an exciting summons to reach out and touch God. The Divine Fire tells us that we are the children of God, that peace and harmony await us, that we have but to prepare ourselves properly to ask so that we might receive. If we can keep ego and personal concerns out of the way, we can translate these messages as the eternal truths that they really are.

The crisis moment is always with us on the physical plane; but so, too, is the Divine Fire always with us. We live always in the Day of Decision. The Kingdom of God is always at hand. The Spirit of God has always been upon all flesh. The sons and daughters of men have always been able to attain higher levels of consciousness and obtain the gift of prophecy. Young men have always been able to see visions, old men have always talked to God in their dreams. There has never been a time without the Spirit of God, but the Divine Fire showers more and brighter sparks when it is time for the sons and daughters of men to make transition from one age to another: for each progression from age to age requires a higher level of consciousness, a more intense awareness, a more complete understanding.

In John Keel's words: "The great adventure ahead of us will be the proper, accurate interpretation of the 'signal.' We will suddenly, and for the first time, realize the true purpose of mankind and the true nature of the Cosmos. This is already beginning with the mass illumination of young people worldwide. It will lead very soon–within thirty years–to the collapse of organized religion and all the nonsense theology has thrust down our throats for two thousand years."

I quite agree with Keel that the "great adventure" ahead of us will be the proper, accurate interpretation of the "signal" that the Intelligence that we have called God has been continuously transmitting through the Divine Fire of His thought patterns, but I see a great, universal, timeless relevance in these repetitious broadcasts.

The message of the Divine Fire is that the great spiritual truths exist in the Eternal Now, valid for all ages, available to everyone, free of all finite boundaries, aloof from all man-imagined beginnings and endings.

# TEN

## The Ageless Message of Revelation

In *Divinity and Experience* Dr. Godfrey Lienhardt, Lecturer in African Sociology at Oxford, related the details of his extensive study of the Dinka tribe of the Southern Sudan which led him to observe that there is a common religious experience and tradition:

> Divinity is thus everywhere, and everywhere the same. The different names by which different peoples know it are matters only of different languages. So in Divinity, the Dinka image their experience of the ways in which human beings everywhere resemble each other, and in a sense form a single community with one original ancestor created by one Creator.

Dr. Martin Marty told me: "When the revelator is speaking in tongues, he is not imparting any information; he is not being gnostic. He is expressive of a revelational experience without having a substance that is being revealed. Our press [University of Chicago] is going to be publishing a book soon in which the author has gone around the world with tapes and phonetic translations and has decided that glossolalia is an anthropological, general experience—that is, there are no special colorings to the syllables and sounds just because they occur in the Christian West or in Africa. You can't tell the history of the religion by the sounds."

My friend John A. Keel researched revelations given to various recipients throughout the centuries. As Keel told me: "During my research I located and studied many old and rare books (mostly privately published) from the nineteenth century and the 1920's, and I was nonplussed to find that those earlier percipients were not only undergoing the classic experiences, but they were receiving messages almost identical to the modern messages. It seems to me as if all these people, widely separated by time, have been getting communications which are being broadcast over and over again by some giant phonograph in the sky. The slight alterations probably are made in the percipients' minds to tailor the messages to contemporary situations. There is a storage factor. Perhaps the original signal is stored in the collective unconscious, or perhaps there is some mechanism beyond our space-time continuum which is repeating an endless 'tape.'

"This phonograph factor was a keystone to my negative hypothesis. If all percipients in all ages have been receiving the same signals, then the actual transmission is not especially pertinent to any given period. The same source and process which inspired the Book of Revelations is at work in modern revelators."

Why is it that so many of the thoughts and basic ideas of so many revelators are essentially the same, whether they claim their source as Space Intelligences or angels, or spirit guides? The answer seems intimately related to the nature of the whole revelatory experience.

"The basic, genuine true discovery of revelation *has* to be the same," Father Ed Cleary, a Roman Catholic priest, told me. "The essence of revelation is the revealment of Soul as Reality for the individual, Spirit as Reality for the All, God as Ultimate Reality."

*Dr. Bruce Wrightsman:* The significance of revelations being essentially the same is that it's the same God that is revealing these things to man. He hasn't changed His will, His intention, His conception of what it means to be a man, what it means to be in this world. There is also the consistency and identity of what it means to be God. The same thing is true in other religions that claim revelation. When I test them out, as I am wont to do, by my own understanding and experience of revelation, then I find a lot of things very revelatory of God—things not inconsistent or in conflict with what Christianity and Judaism teach.

*Miss Marianne Francis:* I think the point is that Truth does not change; and if man is not yet living the ancient truths, such as the simple things that Christ taught, what point would there be in giving man something more advanced? I think that the things that Christ taught in all simplicity, and which were later so distorted by the Church, are very much the same things that the Space Brothers are saying.

Numerous comparative religion scholars have noted that in the millennium before the historical Jesus, a new spiritual enlightenment came to all the civilized peoples of Earth. Its influence was first felt in Asia, but it is best known to those of us in the West because of its high development in Greece and Southern Italy in the sixth and fifth centuries B.C. This spiritual cosmology recognized an unseen world of eternal values existing behind the material world apprehended by the senses. Pythagoras embraced this mystical faith, and Plato gave it such a full and firm expression that it passed into the theology of the Christian Church during the Roman Empire's revival of Neoplatonism.

Was it in that millennium before Jesus that a Higher Intelligence began to transmit its basic messages?

Peggy Townsend of Harrisburg, Pennsylvania, received a dramatic vision when she lay in an illness that she thought might be her last. She was told that she had God's work to do and that she would live to do it. Now, for the past two years, Peggy has "completely established links with spirit helpers." She feels that she is able to call on spirit help whenever she meets people who need healing or who need spiritual, as well as physical, aid.

What is the source of such revelation and such spirit helpers? "I would say they come from a higher plane," Peggy replied. "This one teacher came through to me and he said, 'I have been bidden by the Teachers of the Universe to come to you from a mountain beyond your knowledge!'"

Just a few days before I spoke to Peggy Townsend, she had received some writing from that "mountain beyond our knowledge."

"No, it's not automatic writing," she clarified. "I'm fully aware of what I'm doing. The thoughts come into my mind, and I just start putting them down." Here, with Peggy Townsend's permission, is an example of the inspirational thoughts which she has recently received:

GOD IS

Each tiny grain of sand becomes a mountain when it is placed under a microscope. So do we become to God when we let His light and love shine onto others of our kind. . . . We are each a separate entity, but like the sand, a complexity beyond comprehension. The creation of God does not disregard the needs of His people, nor do His creatures suffer.

Now is the time of God. Awaken! O Mortal man, lift your eyes from the clay of which you were created and look for your Creator.

To each of us is given responsibility. The first is to ourselves, then to our neighbor. If one should hear the teachings of the Masters, let him share it with another. If the other does not listen, know that the seed has been sown and weep not that it has fallen on stone, but look for fertile ground.

Open the doors to the Universe and let the stars rain down, bringing light into the darkness of man's mind. Each tiny speck of light will, and must, intensify until it shines forth. Man will speak of these things, and in the saying add more than has already been said, and the knowledge will grow. The words are of God and for God. To learn the way is not easy. Trials and tests are given to us

**all. We must learn to be humble and to accept this—not as a burden to be borne, but as a gift to teach us to grow.**

**God holds out His hands to us. We have bitterness on the one hand, joy on the other; but one cannot have the joy without the pain. We are as a woman giving birth—there is pain, but then the joy is complete.**

**When man asks, "Where are you God? Are you in the clouds, the trees, that clump of bushes, or perhaps in that animal or this?" God answers, "Yes!" But know beyond any doubt that you and I can find God at any time, under any circumstances, and that He is within each of us. We need look no further than our own hearts, for He is there.**

**I was with Him in the clouds. He opened His hand and said, "look."**

**I saw clouds below me, around me, above me. I was in the Heavens He had designed. The sun was setting and everything was clean and quiet. God shook His fingers and the stars fled before them, only to return to their place as before.**

**He pointed His finger at the dark clouds below me, and lightning flashed and played, showing me that even in the darkness there is light—and in the light there is hope if one will but look.**

**I reached out to touch Him, but in the reaching, felt His arms around me and knew that the love I felt for Him was returned and multiplied.**

**Then He said: "Go down into the towns and cities and tell them of my love. Let each one you tell, tell another, and in the telling, the word and the love will grow."**

**My heart was filled to overflowing, for one had come to me and had told me of the things that I would do and the things I must do. The plan was already underway. In the towns they listened and were happy. God showed them the words were true. They spoke to one another and the words spread to the cities. Thank you, God!**

**He smiles . . . the clouds open . . . and I know in my heart the song I hear is the song of the quiet.**

Dr. Thelma Moss, of the Neuropsychiatric Institute, UCLA Center for the Health Sciences, Los Angeles, California, wrote that she agreed with my contention that "... revelation is a vital and continuing process, and that it utilizes the same—whatever it is—among all people, everywhere."

Dr. Moss said that she did strive, in her ordinary life, to "... attain the state which has been described as 'cosmic consciousness,'" but she went on to say that she believed "that each person's experience is colored by his own individual personality; and that the experience by its very nature is an ineffable one. That is only what I believe—because I don't really think that I have experienced the phenomenon."

Dr. Moss wished me success in what, in her opinion, was "... a deeply important but vastly difficult area."

With minor alterations to adapt the messages to contemporary situations, have the revelators throughout the ages have been receiving essentially the same basic revelations?

*Lasca Schroeppel*: I think the basic messages have been the same. I do think that the "readouts" are different. I don't think that, in 1970, we are going to allow the distortions that occurred before people had so much access to communications media. Yes, it is the same Force, but a different "readout" and a different age.

*Harold Schroeppel*: Now this depends on what you mean by revelation. We have one man here in Chicago who had an understanding of how the world was put together. All he did was walk out his front door and turn left, and he had a whole mystical experience.

Dr. Richard Rubenstein told me that he believed that the basic function of religion is to make us aware of the reality of what he would call the "unmanifest."

According to Dr. Rubenstein: "There is a manifest common-sense reality which we face all the time, then there is what I would call the unmanifest unconscious reality. The difference between me and the people who claim revelation experiences is that what they regard as revelatory experiences I regard as revelations of the personal unconscious of the individual to begin with, and then, to a certain extent, the collective unconscious of the race. I believe that these revelatory experiences are attempts at psychic integration, attempts at psychic wholeness. One wishes to be at one with his whole being, and this is impossible unless one is first of all aware not only of the day-to-day practical world, but also of one's own unconscious, and, finally, the unconscious of the race."

Dr. Walter Houston Clark has observed that the fact that revelatory experiences often come to the nonreligious—or even the antireligious—first of all testifies to the fact that we are all basically religious, whether we acknowledge it or not.

"I have known five or six convinced atheists who have 'experienced God' or become religious through drug-released revelatory experiences," Dr. Clark said. "As a matter of fact, conventional religious beliefs may actually militate against such experiences through closing minds and fostering repressions by dogmatic theological beliefs. Such beliefs form the background for many ecclesiastical institutions, perhaps all of them. In our theological institutions religion is studied rationally and externally. The theological and ecclesiastical mind, therefore, becomes exceedingly critical and suspicious of nonrational perceptions and tends to approach religion exclusively in an external way. The nonrational, revelatory experience becomes a threat, because it is not understood and cannot be controlled. While I would not banish the rational approach to religion, or even religious institutions, for I think they have their place, I think they have achieved entirely too much prominence. In doing so, they have almost forgotten the roots of religion, which are mystical, eccstatic, and revelatory in nature. To the extent that this last sentence is true, I think it can be said that there is nothing that the churches fear as much as they do religion!

"It is the common ordinary man and sometimes the humble religious believer who is open-minded enough to be unfettered by such restrictions and so is free to experience revelation. Paradoxically, it has also been some of our greatest and most sophisticated thinkers who have gone through such ecstatic changes—Socrates, Pascal, Carlyle, Swedenborg, Bertrand Russell, and Arthur Koestler, to mention but a few, while it was none other than St. Thomas Aquinas who, after a religious experience toward the end of his career, said it made all of his writings 'like straw!' Presumably part of the greatness of any great mind is its open-mindedness and humility. This helps to explain why so many great mathematicians and scientists have also been mystics."

In his classic work, *The Varieties of Religious Experience*, William James writes:

> This overcoming of all the usual barriers between the individual and the Absolute is the great mystic achievement. In mystic states we both become one with the Absolute and we become aware of our oneness. This is the everlasting and triumphant mystical tradition, hardly altered by differences of clime or creed. In Hinduism, in Neoplatonism, in Sufism, in Christian mysticism, in Whitmanism, we find the same recurring note, so that there is about mystical utterances an eternal unanimity which ought to make a critic stop and think, and which brings it about that the mystical classics have, as has been said, neither birthday nor native land. Perpetually telling of the unity of man with God, their speech antedates language, and they do not grow old.

Dr. Walter Houston Clark told me that the kind of revelation experience that has impressed him in recent years has been that which has sprung from greatly deepened religious sensitivity of a mystical nature. In Dr. Clark's opinion, such a sensitivity leads often to a greatly lessened valuation on external and material values in exchange for a strengthened valuation of the non-rational and a heightened compassion with its concern for others and for nature.

"On the basis of the knowledge of, and respect for, the mystical consciousness, which has been growing on me now for fifty years," Dr. Clark said, "I fully agree with William James' statement in his *Varieties of Religious Experience* to the effect that personal religion has its origin in the mystical consciousness. Succinctly, James expressed my position for me when he wrote in a letter to a friend: 'The mother sea and fountainhead of all religions lie in the mystical experiences of the individual, taking the word mystical in a very wide sense. All theologies and all ecclesiasticisms are secondary growths superimposed.'

"I believe that all people are potential mystics, just as each one of us is a potential poet, artist, or ecstatic," Dr. Clark continued. "This hunger for the expression of the nonrational is sleeping within all of us. It goes beyond those valid needs of food, clothing, and shelter that keep our bodies alive. Nonrational and intangible values keep us alive by giving meaning to life, and whether consciously or unconsciously and though suppressed by the priority of material needs in our society, a sensitivity to them always has the possibility of being awakened by the proper stimuli. The longer this sensitivity is neglected or starved, the more spontaneous and forcefully it is expressed when it surfaces."

Reverend John Scudder of Homewood, Illinois, shared the following thoughts with me:

"The revelations of the prophets have been the same from Genesis to Revelations, even before there was a Genesis. In order to understand the Divine Fire that has guided man through these centuries, we must first understand its spirit.

"Spirit has no dimension. Spirit has no weight. Spirit is not subject to distance, and spirit is not subject to time. Spirit always has been and always will be. It is that divine substance which is light. It is that divine substance which is man. Even though we see it encased in a house of clay, commonly called the body, spirit still exists as that part of God in man.

"It was not the divine plan that man should be separated from God. It was the divine plan that man should be a part of God, aware of God, and able to call upon divine knowledge and strength whenever necessary. We have paid a high price in pain, suffering, and ignorance, because we became crystallized in matter and grew further and further away from God.

"Divine Revelation has always been, and it always will be. There will always be great mystics and holy men who have not become crystallized in matter, who are constantly aware and who sense the divine presence. In the Bible we refer to these people as prophets, and it is their prophecies which give us evidence that the Bible is not an ordinary book, but a volume that was inspired in a manner beyond the comprehension of men.

"In the Bible we find a statement that as a man thinketh, so he is. This is a deep, profound statement, and it means much more than having nice thoughts. As we look on the carvings of the ancients, we find the Square of Creation. On the left hand we find a vertical line, representing imagination. Across the top we find a horizontal line, representing desire. On the right-hand side we find a vertical line going down that represents fulfillment. Across the bottom and closing the square we find the next line, which represents thanksgiving.

"Here, again, we find that the secret to the mystery of man is spirit. Man was given the tools to create; first, his imagination, then desire, then fulfillment and thanksgiving. Thousands of people have had divine revelations that have changed their lives and brought comfort, peace, joy, and happiness to millions. Many of these began with an act of imagination of the better earth plane and with that came the desire that this be brought about and then the fulfillment of that desire.

"As I study the Kabala with its Tree of Life, with its story of Creation, I find that a certain basic, ancient wisdom has always been with us. As I study the Bible with the eye of the mystic, and I understand the symbols that are in Isaiah, Jeremiah, and Genesis, I realize again that the wisdom was with us even before Moses. When I study the Kahunas, I find again the same basic wisdom. In advanced Yoga philosophy, again I find the wisdom that goes back thousands and thousands of years. But it is the same today as it was then.

"I must conclude that God has never deserted man, that man was created in God's image and endowed with the gifts of Spirit, as Paul calls them, and that those through the ages who desired to use these gifts found that they were true.

"When man in the future rediscovers the great spiritual truths that the early prophets knew, our earth plane will be different. When man begins to see through the illusions of material things, then his senses begin to rise to his true spiritual value, then his awareness of the presence and the power of God will be much greater than it has been for the last two thousand years. He will find that revelation, the Divine Fire, has never left the human race. It has been that the human race has not understood it."

The great Jewish philosopher Maimonides conceived of

revelation as a continuous emanation from the Divine Being, which is transmitted to all those men and women who are endowed with a certain imaginative faculty and who have achieved a certain moral and mental standard. The revelatory transmission is filtered through the medium of the Active Intellect, first to the revelator's rational faculty, then to his imaginative faculty. In this way the distribution of prophetic illumination occurs in conformity with a natural law of emanation. Whether it is the sudden input of a transmission from the Divine Being that often so alters the personality of the revelator or whether there may be a certain tradition of possessing revelatory entities that brings about dramatic and rapid changes in the newly made prophet, the revelator's "putting on of the new person" remains an area for an increased amount of serious study.

At their Foundation for Mind Research in New York City, Dr. Robert E. L. Masters and Dr. Jean Houston have recognized the fact that throughout history people have sought altered states of consciousness as a "gateway to subjective realities." Although the husband-and-wife team are noted for their book *The Varieties of Psychedelic Experience,* they are currently engaged in nondrug procedures (sensory deprivation or reduction of sensory inputs, varieties of audio-visual environments, stroboscopic lights, electrical stimulation of the brain, an Altered States of Consciousness Induction Device) of inducing religious-type experiences in the laboratory.

"We call ourselves mind researchers and inner space explorers and differentiate our activities from those of psychiatrists and psychologists," Dr. Masters told me. "Our work is frontier and prescientific, although we do make use of scientific instruments and methods and endeavor to be dispassionate and objective (which may be as 'scientific' as possible in this area)."

An article in the October 5, 1970, issue of *Time* magazine stated that the Masters and Houston Foundation for Mind Research ". . . has concluded on the basis of hundreds of experiments with normal, healthy persons that 'the brain-mind system has a built-in contact point with what is experienced as God, fundamental reality, or the profoundly sacred.'"

Edward B. Fiske, writing in *The New York Times* (August 26, 1970), said that the Mind Research Foundation maintained that "encounters with God or 'ultimate reality' and other experiences described by great mystics such as Teresa of Avila can at least be approximated by ordinary persons. Fiske quoted Dr. Houston as saying: "People think that mystics are cut off from the world, but actually the opposite is true. The capacity for religious experience–including a deep feeling of unity with the universe–is built into human nature. It's simply a question of opening oneself up."

*Dr. Bruce Wrightsman*: I think the Holy Spirit is always present on the borders of human consciousness and human lives, but we set up resistances. One of the resistances has been the hardening of our own secularized consciousness, or modes of cognition, so we don't even see miracles anymore. I think that miracles happen to us all the time, but we don't apprehend the miraculous character of the hand that lies behind them.

Revelation is always available, but it is not always perceived as revelation. It often has to be accompanied by inspiration in order for it to be apprehended as a reality. And this is what I think is happening now. The revelation has been there; God has been transmitting, but we have not been receiving. We've been tuned into a different wavelength or something, and now all of a sudden, because of dissatisfaction, frustration with a lot of things that have been going on in the last ten years, people are looking around for other levels of meaning.

A. Dale Fiers, General Minister and President of the Disciples of Christ, Indianapolis, Indiana, told me that for him the presence of God had been a daily and meaningful experience from childhood. He further stated that he believed in a personal God who is "in communication with all His creatures."

Although he had not had the dramatic experiences reported by some, President Fiers commented that, "this, nevertheless, is not a contradiction of God's daily reaching out to touch my life and the others who truly seek Him."

A letter from Lee R. Gandee, author of *Strange Experience: The Autobiography of a Hexenmeister,* brought another interesting response:

"To say what I wish about the 'revelatory experience,' I must begin by stating that I am a pantheist, in that I conceive all that is to be in the phenomenon of energy which philosophers of science call the space-time continuum. I think of matter as a phenomenon, or aspect, of energy, given its appearance of solidity by a consciousness provided with very imperfect physical senses, and obliged by the limitations of a three-dimensional perception to experience and interpret what the senses report to human consciousness in terms of three-dimensional, tangible, 'solid' matter, whereas even in advanced science, matter is known to be no more than infinitesimal particles of energy in constant motion, the true nature of which can be understood only by persons with thorough knowledge of atomic physics and the mentality required to grasp the Einsteinian unified field theory, since the energy involved is electromagnetic, and true understanding of matter requires that the mind understand it in terms of electromagnetic behavior in space-time.

"I accept two kinds of reality. One is the everyday, earth-plane reality based on concepts formed by sensory impressions and associations, and valid only as long as I am sojourning on this plane. The other reality is greater and universally valid, but it is not 'human,' not 'physical.'

"I accept myself in both contexts. I believe that the Continuum (call it God if you like) created me of itself, and that this universal and nonphysical self (call it my spirit if you like) is still part of that from which it came, as is the universal and nonphysical self of every created thing. Thus, in that context, I am like every other creating thing, for we are all parts of the same thing. And since I believe that all created things are conscious, all are conscious of one another and are in relationship with one another in that all are parts of the same great consciousness.

"Call this superconsciousness 'Cosmic Consciousness.' I do not think that there can be any real meaning to life unless one relates it to this pervading universal consciousness; but I cannot think that contact with it involves anything supernatural, or that it constitutes a 'higher reality.'

"On the contrary, I think that contact with it is the only true natural relationship, and the only means of escape from sensory, three-dimensional limitation. The end of earth-plane, physical existence is death, but the spirit can never die. To share awareness of 'cosmic consciousness' is to lose all fears of death and to establish a kind of serenity which pays no great attention to those concerns which are temporal and mundane, knowing that they are transitory and illusory and of no real importance. When one accepts spirit as the real, and matter as the illusion, life as indestructible, and contact with Cosmic Consciousness as 'natural,' he acquires a kind of freedom which includes release from the limitations of the physical senses and dependence upon only the conscious mind. If I have anything more than anyone else has—rather, *everyone* else has—it is a greater sense of freedom. I do not impose limitations upon myself, feeling that I am slave to matter, and limited by my senses. I am not.

"I do not think of 'revelatory experience' only of perception. Like everyone else, I am habituated to 'see' in terms of the eyes, but the eyes cannot see reality, only three-dimensional impressions or reflections. When I wish to see the real, I close my eyes. Then I can perceive with spirit. Likewise, I blank out sensory impressions and still my conscious mind, and my subconscious receives impressions telepathically from other subconscious minds, and from the consciousness of nonhuman life forms, and from that of inanimate things. All this comes as symbols, and often my conscious mind intervenes in my interpretation of them, and I err, but when my subconscious interprets what it receives, and presents its interpretation in dreams, there is no error. When I dream a 'true dream,' I recognize it and remember it.

"Maybe that is what people call 'revelatory experience,' but to me it is only the natural way in which spirit maintains contact with the other embodiments of God, and with the consciousness of the individualizations and of the Creator. What is perceived thus by the spirit is true without possibility of deception, for it is (to use conventional terms) the God in man which does the perceiving and the created cannot deceive the Creator. Neither does one part of God attempt to deceive any other part."

On September 9, 1963, Jane Roberts, a young writer, had finished dinner and was settling down to her poetry. Her husband Rob was painting in the back studio, three rooms away. She had her ninth or tenth cup of coffee for the day at hand, her pack of cigarettes conveniently near, her cat dozing beside her on the rug. What happened next, she describes in *The Seth Material*, was like taking a "trip" without drugs:

> Between one normal minute and the next, a fantastic avalanche of radical, new ideas burst into my head with tremendous force, as if my skull were some sort of receiving station, turned up to unbearable volume. Not only ideas came through this channel, but sensations, intensified and pulsating. I was tuned in, turned on . . . *connected* to some incredible source of energy. . . .
>
> It was as if the physical world were really tissue-paper thin, hiding infinite dimensions of reality, and I was suddenly flung through the tissue paper with a huge ripping sound. My body sat at the table, my hands furiously scribbling down the words and ideas that flashed through my head. Yet I seemed to be somewhere else, at the same time, traveling through things. I went plummeting through a leaf, to find a whole universe open up; and then out again, drawn into new perspectives. I felt as if knowledge was being implanted in the very cells of my body so that I couldn't forget it—a gut knowing, a biological spirituality. It was feeling and knowing, rather than intellectual knowledge. At the same time I remembered having a dream the night before, which I had forgotten, in which this same sort of experience had occurred. And I knew the two were connected.
>
> When I came to, I found myself scrawling what was obviously meant as the title of that odd batch of notes: *The Physical Universe as Idea Construction*. . . .

Jane said the "revelation" came to her mind, but she tried to dismiss it in fear of the mystical implications of the word. The Divine Fire cannot be stopped by reluctant prophets, however.

In 1970 *The Seth Material* appeared—a marvelous, straightforward accounting of her life as a channel for an entity who calls himself "Seth," by a woman with both feet on the ground. Although the book is fascinating on several levels, we shall concern ourselves with some of the high-quality revelations which "Seth" channeled through Jane Roberts:

*The God Concept*

> [God] is not human in your terms, though he passed through human stages; and here the Buddhist myth comes closest to approximating reality. He is not one individual, but an energy gestalt.
>
> If you remember what I said about the way in which the universe expands, that it has nothing to do with space, then you may perhaps dimly perceive the existence of a psychic pyramid of interrelated, ever-expanding consciousness that creates, simultaneously and instantaneously, universes and individuals that are given—through the gifts of personal perspective—duration, psychic comprehension, intelligence, and eternal validity.
>
> This absolute, ever-expanding, instantaneous psychic gestalt, which you may call God if you prefer, is so secure in its existence that it can constantly break itself down and rebuild itself. Its energy is so unbelievable that it does indeed form all universes; and because its energy is within and behind all universes, systems, and fields, it is indeed aware of each sparrow that falls, for it *is* each sparrow that falls.

*Man as Co-Creator with God*

> What you call God is the sum of all consciousness, and yet the whole is more than the sum of Its parts. God is more than the sum of all personalities, and yet all personalities are what He is.
>
> There is constant creation. There is within you a force that knew how to grow you from a fetus to a grown adult. This force is part of the innate knowledge within all consciousness, and it is a part of the God within you.
>
> The responsibility for your life and your world is indeed yours. It has not been forced upon you by some outside agency. You form your own dreams, and you form your own physical reality. The world is what you are. It is the physical materialization of the inner selves which have formed it.

> There is no personal God-individual in Christian terms, and yet you do have access to a portion of *All That Is,* a portion highly attuned to you. . . . There is a portion of *All That Is* directed and focused within each individual, residing within each consciousness. Each consciousness is, therefore, cherished and individually protected. This portion of all consciousness is individualized within you.
>
> What you prefer to think of as God is, again, an energy gestalt or pyramid consciousness. It is aware of itself as being . . . you. . . . It is aware of itself as the smallest seed. . . . This portion of *All That Is* that is aware of itself as you, that is focused within your existence, can be called upon for help when necessary.
>
> This portion is also aware of itself as something more than you. *This portion that knows itself as you, and as more than you, is the personal God, you see.* Again: this gestalt, this portion of *All That Is,* looks out for your interests and may be called upon in a personal manner.

I must emphasize that I have, with permission, excerpted only bits and pieces from the wide range of topics in the two weighty Seth volumes and arranged them were according to thematic points of interest. Jane the channel, Rob the transcriber, and Seth the dictating entity have produced more than sixty-five hundred typewritten pages of "Seth Material." The two books, *The Seth Material* and *Seth Speaks: The Eternal Validity of the Soul,* deal with such topics as the nature of physical matter, time, and reality, the god concept, the substance of soul, probable universes, and reincarnation.

In her introduction to Seth's own book, *Seth Speaks,* Jane Roberts affirms that she was in no way involved in the creative endeavors of the entity's work:

> I went into trance as I do for our regular sessions. Seth dictated the book through me, speaking through my lips. The creative work was so distinct from me, that in this respect I could not call the product my own.
>
> Anyone can say, of course, that in Seth's book the hidden processes are so separate from my normal consciousness that it only *seems* to come from another personality. I can only state my own feelings and emphasize that Seth's book, and the whole 6,000-page manuscript of Seth Material, don't take care of my own

> creative expression or responsibility. If both came from the same unconscious, it seems that there would be no slack to take up.
>
> Despite this, I'm aware of the fact that I was necessary to the production of Seth's book. He needs my ability with words; even, I think, my turn of mind. My writing training aids in the translation of his material and helps give it form, no matter how unconsciously this is done. Certain personality characteristics are important, too, I imagine; the agility with which I can switch the focus of my consciousness, for example.
>
> Seth intimates as much . . . when he says: "Now the information in this book is being directed to some extent through the inner senses of the woman who is in trance as I write it. Such endeavor is the result of highly organized inner precision, and of training. [She] could not receive the information from me–it could not be translated nor interpreted–while she was focused intensely in the physical environment."

This seems as honest a statement regarding the interaction of an alleged independent entity with a medium's unconscious as one might find anywhere in the annals of psychical literature. Jane is convinced that she could not get the equivalent of the Seth Material on her own. The best she could do, she believes, is to hit certain high points, perhaps through the media of isolated poems or essays, but they would lack ". . . The over-all unity, continuity, and organization that is here provided automatically."

What was the entity's purpose in writing his own book? Why was he not content to permit his medium to channel his thoughts? Jane Roberts writes the following in answer:

> This book is Seth's way of demonstrating that human personality is multidimensional, that we exist in many realities at once; that the soul or inner self is not something apart from us, but the very medium in which we exist. He emphasizes that "truth" is not found by going from teacher to teacher, church to church, or discipline to discipline, but by looking within the self. The intimate knowledge of consciousness, the "secrets of the universe" are not esoteric truths to be hidden from the people, then. Such knowledge is as natural to man as air, and as available to those who honestly seek it by looking to the source within.

One of Seth's concepts that intrigued me very much lay in his description of "the Speakers"—"personalities who continually speak to man through the ages, reminding us of inner knowledge so that it is never really forgotten." Since Jane was always in the trance state when Seth was in control, and since she had decided not to make regular checks on Seth's progress but to leave the transcribing solely to her husband, she was able to come upon the comments regarding "the Speakers" with the same freshness and excitement of Seth's readers. Because the idea of "the Speakers" may contribute another facet to our understanding of the mechanism involved in the Divine Fire, I am quoting the "intuitive statement" regarding "the Speakers" and Seth that Jane wrote for her ESP class in Elmira, New York:

> We come together in ways that we do not understand. We're composed of elements, chemicals, and atoms, and yet we speak and call ourselves by name. We organize about our inner stuff the outer stuff that coagulates into flesh and bone. Our identities or personalities spring from sources we do not know.
>
> Perhaps what we are has always waited, hidden in the possibilities of creation, dispersed and unknowing. . . . We may have been sparked on and off into consciousness and unconsciousness a million times, touched by desire, by yearnings toward creativity and perfection we barely understood.
>
> And so there may be others now like Seth, also without images; but knowing—others who have been what we are and more—others who remember what we have forgotten. They may have discovered through some acceleration of consciousness other forms of being, or dimensions of reality of which we are also a part.
>
> So we give them names who are nameless, as basically we are nameless. And we listen, but usually we try to squeeze their messages into concepts that we can understand, cloaking them in worn, stereotyped images. Yet they are all about us, in the wind and trees, formed and unformed, more alive in many ways perhaps than we are—the Speakers.
>
> Through these voices, these intuitions, these flashes of insights and messages, the universe speaks to us, to each of us personally. You are being addressed, and so am I. Learn to hear your own messages, not to distort what you hear or translate it into old alphabets.

...I think we are responding to such messages, sometimes acting them out with an almost childlike wisdom, forming them into dramas that are original and individualistic—dramas that arouse within us meanings that cannot be put into words.

This may be the kind of play in which the "gods" indulge, from which creations grow, sprawling out in all directions. We may be responding to the gods in ourselves—those inner sparks of knowing that defy our own three-dimensional knowledge.

Seth may be leading us out of our usual imitations, into another realm that is ours by right—elemental whether we are in flesh or out of it. He may be the voice of our combined selves, saying: "While you are conscious bodies, remember what it was like and will be like, to be bodiless; to be freewheeling energy without a name but with a voice that does not need tongue; with a creativity that does not need flesh. We are yourselves, turned inside out."

# ELEVEN

## Judgment Day Isn't What It Used to Be

On May 11, 1957, Wayne S. Aho, a former Major with U.S. Army Combat Intelligence, saw a UFO land on the Mojave Desert, and in a sincere and quiet voice, he, too, will testify that his life did indeed change "radically." Today, Aho is the Director of the New Age Foundation, Inc., P.O. Box 867, Eatonville, Washington, a loyal co-worker with the Space Brothers, industriously doing his part to assist in ushering in the New Age.

It was on February 14, 1960, that Wayne Aho received what he considers his most dramatic revelatory experience. He awakened shortly before daylight into a state of ecstasy. "It was as though every atom in my body was reacting to a stimuli which I was to begin to understand as a spiritual experience," he said.

He saw a group of people. He heard beautiful, vibrant music. A personage who appeared to be Jesus Christ approached the group from the left. The personage spoke words "to be shared with others and [which] could be the basis of teaching and understanding that would help mankind in the days ahead." Aho reached for the pad and pencil which he always keeps beside his bed and wrote down the words as they were spoken.

According to Wayne S. Aho, the entity spoke of approaching time cycles of seven, nine, twelve, and fourteen years. These periods of work and preparation will bring us first to 1980, which, Aho writes in his booklet *What the Lord Said*, will bring us to

> ... the turning into the true New Age of Christ Consciousness or what many call the Aquarian Age. Man will have direction and spiritual leadership. Of course, during these times, great earth changes and changes in man's consciousness will be evident. There may be great upheavals and chaotic times as these changes manifest and man must give up the old ways for the new.
>
> The fourteen year cycle—1988 to 2002—was indicated as a time in which many upon Earth will come to know other realms of life, sister planets, etc. Earth will rejoin her sister planets, overcoming shortcomings which have delayed her unfoldment, and realization will dawn in the consciousness of all mankind of the magnitude of the true Creation.

Aho feels that his work has been indicated to him. "I feel that I have been guided to find persons, and I have been instructed to bring forth programs to prepare the way for the New Age."

In an earlier book, *The Aquarian Revelations*, I presented an extensive case history of the Light Affiliates of Burnaby, British Columbia, who began receiving urgent messages concerning forthcoming Earth changes from a Space Brother named Ox-Ho. Ox-Ho utilized twenty-two-year-old Robin McPherson as his channel, immediately changing her name to Estelle, his "little Star." Aileen Steil, Robin's mother, was rechristened Magdalene; Robin's friend Sally, who was to serve as her "energizer," was renamed Celeste; and a young man who had been present during the early transmissions from outer space was given the extremely common contactee name of Truman Merit (this name seems to be almost a title, "a man of true merit").

The Light Affiliates were told that they ". . . were the only people in this area whom we have found capable of receiving messages for our purpose. We have been preparing you for this task for quite some time. Yours is a very important task. Be grateful that you can help your fellowman."

The entire group was seized with a zealous missionary fervor. Judgment Day, they were told, had begun on November 22, 1969; but Judgment Day was "not to be one terrible day of salvation or damnation, but rather the beginning of the Final Hours, in which man is given a last opportunity to repair his decadent house before the terminal series of disasters." Ox-Ho told them that a series of cataclysmic Earth changes would precede the planet's tilting on its axis. Such a tilt would destroy the Earth as it now exists in its physical sense, but the Space Brothers would take away the Chosen and return them to Earth after the planet had once again crystallized. At that time, "The Earth will be totally new in every respect."

For the present, the Space Brothers were trying desperately to hold the magnetic force fields and frequencies of the planet together with their positive beams of light; but unless the people of Earth began rapidly to raise their personal "vibrations," Italy, Newfoundland, New York City, and most of California would soon be beneath the oceans. The compassionate Light Affiliates insisted that there must be something that they might do to help the Space Brothers in their work, and they were instructed to venture forth from Burnaby and to spread the message of the Space Brothers by whatever means presented themselves. In New York City, their sincerity and their intensity convinced an editor at Dell Books that I should be called to New York to hear the Light Affiliates out.

Through Robin-Estelle's channeling, Ox-Ho informed me that a Judgment Day, or period of cleansing, was necessary in order for the Earth to pass into the Aquarian Age. The following is a brief selection from Ox-Ho's revelations:

"A light shield is an encasement of light which is to be envisioned around the physical body as a form of protection against negative light rays. To create such a shield, you must be in harmony with light and love. You must be brotherly in your thinking. . . . Light is the element of God. Use it wisely and you will never have anything to fear.

"The ultimate "Last Day" must happen to each individual in his own way . . . Stand up and be proud to be alive, for Man is creating a great new step, a step which [the Space Brothers] are proud of, because it takes a long, monotonous time to evolve at the speed at which you have been evolving.

"There is a whole new world waiting for you people of Earth. The fourth dimension is one of subtleness, of lighter shades of beauty. With your increased vibrations, you will be able to see this subtleness with an intensity beyond your imagining. . . . There are seven dimensions of being. Each planet understands one dimension at a time, but as we aid your evolution, your Earth will be stepped up in frequency and vibration to the next level. Be one with this vibration, and you will become a different person from the old you. . . .

"Life is interdimensional, and so is man . . . Learn to flow with these dimensional frequencies and learn to become flexible. Do not allow yourself to become crystallized, for each man has a shattering point if he continues to resist the flow of dimensional evolution. . . . People of Earth, you are becoming fourth dimensional whether you are ready or not. Leave the old to those who cling to the old. Don't let the New Age leave you behind.

"The Great Change . . . is inevitable. Your world is contaminated to the very core. Earth must be cleansed. There can be no transition into a new dimension without this cleansing. But remember: the change is for the good. It is God's way."

"The world right now is feeling the effect of the Karmic pattern of the Atlantean culture. Your young people are Atlanteans reborn to once again work out their Karma . . . Their arts and their scientific technology is greater than ever before . . . Now their souls have evolved to a plateau wherein they seek only peace. Help the young to create harmony and peace, for they want it so desperately."

"The most important thing, of course, is to make yourselves adjustable and flexible to the subtlety and the refinement of the Universe. It is the Light wave, rather than drugs, to which all Earthlings should seek to 'tune' in, remembering that they must attune with it in love. Always keep in mind that love is a focal point when doing anything.

"The Light Beings try to create unity among God's creation. They can be of much service to you, my brothers, if you allow yourselves to listen to them. Those whom you have often called 'saints' have been but humans whom the Light Beings entered. The Light Beings herald God's words through the Universe and they are always at hand to ring in the new."

"There can be no transition into a new dimension without cleansing. But remember: the change is for the good. It is God's way," the entity Ox-Ho told the Light Affiliates in Burnaby, British Columbia.

Sut-Ko and other beneficent beings who contact Miss Marianne Francis are also concerned about man's vibratory rate and the difficulties inherent in making the transition from one age to another.

In one transmission through Miss Francis, Sut-Ko speaks of the raising of a higher vibratory frequency which is occurring on Earth:

"Many of your peoples are now aligning their consciousness with the realities of an inner world . . . from which Man has emerged onto the outer or exterior scene of the physical third-dimensional Earth. Man's home, however, is that of inner world and only as he is in tune with that god-self or god-consciousness can he journey in safety and in harmony beyond the levels of his own satellite . . .

"[Earth], in its frequency change, is rapidly orienting itself toward a more finely etherealized state of physical existence. . . . Our endeavor at this time . . . is to assist you in the raising of frequency, in order that you may be at one with the change as it comes upon you. We have so many times spoken of the shattering effect of this change upon those who are not so attuned . . . However, we do once more present to you our knowledge of the shortness of Earth time, of the ending of this cycle (and we speak of cyclic time now) and the imminence of gigantic change: Change with which Earthman *must* align or perish.

"Consciousness ... is the key to all change, of the cellular, the molecular structure which is taking place upon your planet ... Earthman, in his scientific might, has chosen to bypass the self which is the god-consciousness and has chosen in pride of intellect and achievement to attain to heights which cannot be scaled without the employment of a whole Man, or a whole being ... A time is coming of tremendous reassessment, reappraisal of values ... when Earthman must meet himself face to face, his self not only of the now, but his self of the incarnations of his being on the planet called Earth. A time is coming for the ending of a cycle and the beginning of a new; and at this time, Earthman meets spaceman in the one light and under the one sun of this universe."

"Voltra of Venus" has spoken through Miss Francis to deliver a lecture on "Density Level Transition":

"[The transition from one frequency or density level to another] will take place abruptly ... due to many events of a cataclysmic nature taking place, not only on your planet, but outside of your planet in the meaning of the Solar System.

"Your peoples have to undergo changes of consciousness, and at this time, only those whose consciousness is attuned with the things of a new dispensation will take into themselves, their beings, the increased energies and utilize these for their future transitional move.

"These energies taken into the ... aura of an individual, will emit such high-frequency radiation as to raise the molecular structure of the cells to a point whereby the body will then vibrate in the fourth etheric level. So will come the *change* spoken of by many, imperfectly understood by many, but grasped by some. The transition of matter into a finer, more etherealized matter will take place. You will still be yourselves, you will still function as human beings with all the sense perceptions of human beings. But you will be of a more rarified construction. Transition from physical to fourth etheric substance will take place.

"Many of us with whom you speak are of this composition in our bodies and therein has lain much of the misunderstanding among your peoples as to our nature. We can, and do, lower the frequency rate of our bodies to become visible to the physical retina of your eyes. We are physical-etheric, whereas you are physical-dense ... The composition of all matter upon your planet is rapidly reaching a point wherein it will either become a finer etherealized structure or will disintegrate. You will witness both of these phenomena taking place during your period on the planet.

"Our purpose at this time is to educate those of you who will work with us at, and after, the time of the frequency change ... We once more stress that you will not become discarnate beings: you merely step up one level and gain much by so doing. Your sense perceptions, rather than being eliminated, will only become heightened and an awareness of all that which is of beauty, of love, of eternal nature, will become as one with you."

If at least a part of Melanie's psyche might be obtaining knowledge from "a dimension above space," here is a portion of the information which she has relayed regarding coming Earth changes:

"I come to a chamber that is full of light like the sun. It is very bright and there is a ladder reaching as high as the eye can see. It is Jacob's Ladder, and I shall climb it now.

"I pass through a cloud that is cold and hostile. It is filled with entities and beings, and I must look neither to the right nor to the left until I reach the area above them which is warm and glowing. Now I see the Great Book as I stand in a chamber overlooking a dimension which is filled with life that is very different from Earth, yet very much like Earth. This is the place of Learning.

"I see a panorama of the United States. I see settlers landing. I see the country being declared a nation. I see people of the Negro race coming up from the South and people of the Indian race coming from the West and I see Oriental people coming from the North, and they all merge together at Illinois. They grow together with the white people, and they become one person. They have all come together, and yet they retain some individuality. This is what the United States must do, and this is what the races must do. They must become one person.

"I see a very black area over China, but this is not a governmental thing. This is a terrible famine.

"I see that there will be one major world religion. There will be two major world governments.

"Africa will develop mightily within the next few decades and will be separated into three basic subdivisions under the two major governments. Each of these governments will rule half of the globe. There will be a certain amount of tension, but not war, between these two nations. This is about 2025, after great changes have taken place in the surface of the Earth.

"There will be great geographical changes in California, reaching to Salt Lake. There will also be great changes in the region of the Great Lakes and in the Mississippi Basin.

"Russia will suffer great changes in the upper part of Siberia, down to Moscow, where there is the greatest congestion of population. They should disperse their population, beginning at once.

"Finland will suffer great damage. Holland will be largely destroyed. Germany and Switzerland will be generally unchanged. The coastlands of Sweden and Denmark will be radically changed. Copenhagen will be completely gone.

"The British Isles will remain basically unchanged, but their people will suffer many water deaths, because the English Channel will widen by many miles.

"Africa will be the least changed, but Australia will break up into several smaller islands. The western coast of South America will break away and disappear, as will a good-sized land mass on the eastern coast. This continent will resemble an elongated egg with the Argentinian point broken up into several islands. The breaking away of so much land mass in South America will cause the inundation of virtually all of the land between North and South America. Florida will separate from the rest of the United States and become an island, rather than a peninsula. Alaska will be virtually snapped off and will be moved down until it is nearly opposite the coast of Oregon.

"These Earth changes are underway at present and will continue until the year 3000. Many of these changes will take place in the year 2000, or shortly before."

*Miss Helen Hoag*: In probably fifteen years there won't be much left of the people on this planet, and the contour of Earth will be changed. Atlantis is rising. New York City will be no more. The whole edge of California is going to fall into the Pacific.

Since the beginning of time, the Creator has picked up his elect, his chosen people; those who are of angel status or higher will be picked up in spacecraft.

"What about the other people, those who do not have angel status?"

*Miss Hoag*: Last winter I got a message that I must interpret a revelation that our associate director had received. Sananda told me to put down my interpretation, even though it might not be one hundred percent correct.

I got that about one-third, maybe one-fourth of the people on this planet would be killed in earthquakes and other disasters. Another one-third or so will remain through the times of plagues, and they will cry for death. The people who are of angel status, or higher, will not have to go through that.

I don't know if you keep a force field around yourself or not, but we have been told to keep force fields around ourselves, around our cars, around our homes, around our loved ones. This force field glows so that the emissaries of the Lords can see the light and will pass over us. The Jews still celebrate Passover, you know, from that time of plagues.

"Are these rescuing spacecraft physical or etheric?"

*Miss Hoag*: I think they are etheric at the moment, but when they come down to pick us up, they will change and project a physical exterior.

"Then where do those of angel status go?"

*Miss Hoag*: To another planet. Some people will stay on the spacecraft and be taught on the craft, but most of us will go to another planet where we will be taught whatever is necessary for us to know to come back and help set up this planet the way the Creator wants it.

*Harold Schroeppel*: I have seen that there will be some rough days ahead, but I have seen no evidence whatsoever that the entire population of the world will be eliminated in the near-term future. This does not mean atomic bombs will not be dropped, but there won't be the major holocaust of destruction that some people seem to be hoping for. I have a rather nasty feeling that some of these people who predict global destruction are really kind of sore at the world, and they are hoping that it will all go away.

Deon Frey, Chicago mystic, believes that the Age of Aquarius must be prefaced by a process of destruction, but she had some positive impressions:

"Spirit says that 1973 will be a terrific year, so we will wait and see. I say that 1972 will have more than a few things in it to make us sit up and take notice and make us more aware of the fact that we should be more spiritual and get closer to the Source."

Joseph Jeffers, who says that the Creator's true name of Yahweh should be used more often, says: "The Peace movements of today mark the end of Babylon and the beginning of Yahweh's world peace in which there will be no fighting, no killing, no murder, no crime, no illness, no insanity, no hospitals. The spirit is peace, and when Yahweh's spirit is within you and controls your mind, you shall have perfect peace."

A sample from Louise Zimmerman's June 27, 1971, column indicates the strong female liberation undercurrent that is such a meaningful and vital aspect of this transitional period between ages:

> In the Aquarian Age, for which the vibrations have already gone forth . . . men will become much more secure because they will reap the benefits that the truly liberated women will bring into this ailing society. . . . As all those who are involved in the study of this new age know, the next 2,000 years will be the age wherein women excel in leadership. Recognition of the female aspect of the

Adam symbol, the Daughter of God, the Daughter of Earth, will bring new understanding and a new birth to the Earth. With confidence I predict that women will be "where it's at." We shall, in this new age, love our men more and the men will love us more, also, and that after all, will be the greatest liberating benefits that any age can reap.

White Bear, a chief of the Hopi Indians in Oraibi, Arizona, told those of us assembled at the Aquarian Age Conference in Honolulu that the prophecies of his people concerning the transition between ages were "right on schedule."

According to Chief White Bear:

"Those who are humble shall inherit the Earth. There are two forces in this Universe: those who destroy, and those whose spiritual power is trying to reach mankind.

"I come from the ancient people of Hopi. We are people of nonaggression, who have never declared war on anybody. We have tried our best to be neutral all these years and not do wrong to the people who have done wrong to us. When the old world [Lemuria] sank beneath the ocean, my fathers of the Bear Clan were the first to step foot on land, on what we today call South America. My fathers took with them a tablet which we still have with us. This tablet tells the story of what is going to take place in the Universe and in all the countries that we occupy at this time.

"I speak to you as a person who has had this knowledge given to me by my fathers. I meditated last night, and a great vision showed me that it won't be very long before we see great changes in the lands which we inhabit today.

"Many people have said that our picture-craft is nothing but doodling, but centuries and centuries ago the Hopi drew a jet airplane on a rock which depicted our people arriving from the birthplace of our fathers. Yes, centuries ago, we had a picture-craft of a flying saucer. . . . We are right on schedule. If the Great Plan says there will be a catastrophe tomorrow, we cannot make it happen on the next day.

"It is time now that all those people who have awareness, the true light, must come and see the truth and be aggrieved. No one wants to be aggrieved, but, alas, those of us who know what is coming must see the truth.

"Two and a half years before the Japanese bombed Pearl Harbor, I knew every step of the going. And now our nation is involved in a terrible thing in Vietnam. Are we strong enough to stand against the evil courses of nature and against those who wish us to participate in destructive ideas?

"I have suffered long, and I will suffer again, because we Hopis must reveal the truth. It is no accident that Hawaii is part of the United States today. It is a remnant of the great nation of my fathers that sank beneath the ocean. We knew years ago that our old land would one day be a part of our new land, the United States.

"We have so polluted all of our atmosphere with waste, and we have also poisoned all of our thoughts. That is why our brothers in the flying saucers are having a hard time coming in contact with us. This we know.

"The Hopis have known the truth for centuries. Before the old land sank under the Pacific Ocean, our people were communicating with the great civilization of Egypt by mental telepathy. We accept what has been written. Those educated folk [archaeologists] who seek our treasures in the ground try to learn from them what we are in our hearts. It can never be done. You cannot take the trash off the streets and the hills and try to interpret it to know the man who dropped it.

"Our President's trip to China was part of the schedule. The time is growing near. Two nations, Israel and Egypt, continue to fight each other with their lips, for there is a wedge of ungodly people between the two. The fight with the lips is only a temporary stall before the great conflagration. As I look over the whole plan of what is going to take place, every day I cry. I cry for the people, because I come from a people of peace.

"The Hopis had knowledge of the destruction of the first, second, third, and fourth worlds, centuries and centuries ago. In my tribe our people have a two-horn society, who are the custodians of the history of our knowledge. The horn on the right sees all knowledge that lies ahead. The horn on the left sees all knowledge which has passed. We know where we came from, and we know where we are going. We know how the world was formed, and that it will be destroyed by fire again. That is why we live in Arizona. This is the only place where in thousands of years, atomic radiation has never fallen.

"Find the man within. Gain a feeling of Oneness. Keep the third eye open. We will meet again in the presence of our Divine Source."

Jesus, writing through Mr. Padgett, has this to say:

> I am here, *Jesus.*
>
> ... When this gift [the possibility of becoming immortal] was bestowed upon man, it was also bestowed upon all those who were then living in the spirit world, but they could obtain it only in the way that was provided for man to obtain it. Understand me, everything that was lost by Adam's fall was restored by my coming with the restored gift; and it embraced every spirit who had ever lived as mortal and every mortal who thereafter lived up to the present time.
>
> My coming, of itself, or the death or sacrifice of me ... did not restore mankind to the condition that existed in Adam before his fall. I was only a messenger of God sent with that gift ... to teach the truth of its restoration to mankind and to spirits; and when, after my death, I descended into hell, as the Bible says (but which saying does not express the destination of my going, for the true meaning is that I went into the world of spirits), I proclaimed to the spirits the truth of the bestowal of this restored life which had been lost by Adam's disobedience.
>
> ... In the future, all men, either as spirits or mortals, will possess that soul quality or potentiality until the great day of judgment ... When that day comes, those who are without this divine essence in their souls will be forever deprived of the privilege of receiving this Great Gift ... And after that time, those spirits who have never acquired this divine nature will be permitted to live merely as spirits enjoying their natural love. This is the second death. Adam's was the first, and the great day of judgment will declare the second. And after that never again will man have the opportunity of partaking of this divine Essence of the Father and "becoming as one of the gods."

> . . . The opportunity is now given and will in the future be given to all men and spirits who become the children of the Father in the angelic and divine sense, and if they refuse to do so, they can have no grounds upon which to base the accusation of injustice against the Father or His Love.
>
> He will still be their Father, even though they may not accept His Great Gift, and they will from the natural love bestowed upon them be comparatively happy; but they will not partake of His heavenly kingdom. . . .
>
> . . . Ultimately . . . sin and error will be destroyed entirely, and men and spirits will live comparatively happy; but they will in death and not in life, so far as the life of the soul with its possibilities of becoming divine, or of enjoying the great happiness which the Divine Love of the Father bestows is concerned.
>
> So you see, immortality does not pertain to the physical body or to the spiritual body, or to the soul unqualifiedly, but to those qualities of the soul which make it possible for the soul to become in its nature divine. And immortality does not mean mere continuous existence, because every soul and every spirit may live through all eternity in their individualized form. And when it was said in the Bible that I brought immortality and life to light, it did not mean that I showed men merely that they would, as spirits, continue to live forever, but it meant that they would live forever in the Father's Kingdom with natures Divine. . . .

"Seth" has some fairly specific predictions about Christ and the New Religion of the Future:

> When the race is in deepest stress and faced with great problems, it will call forth someone like Christ. It will seek out and indeed from itself produce the very personalities necessary to give it strength. . . .
>
> There were three men whose lives became confused in history and merged, and whose composite history became known as the life of Christ. . . . Each was highly gifted psychically, knew of his role, and accepted it willingly. The three men were a part of one entity, gaining physical existence in one time. They were not born on the

same date, however. There are reasons why the entity did not return as one person. For one thing, the full consciousness of an entity would be too strong for one physical vehicle. For another, the entity wanted a more diversified environment than could otherwise be provided.

The entity was born once as John the Baptist, and then he was born in two other forms. One of these contained the personality that most stories of Christ refer to. . . . There was a constant communication between these three portions of one entity, though they were born and buried at different dates. The race called up these personalities from its own psychic bank, from the pool of individualized consciousness that was available to it.

These [individuals] were all males because at that time of your development, you would not have accepted a female counterpart.

These individuals were a part of one entity. You could not but imagine God as a father. It would never have occurred to you to imagine a God in any other than humanoid terms. These three figures worked out a drama, highly symbolic, propelled by concentrated energy of great force.

The three Christ personalities were born upon your planet, and indeed became flesh among you. None of these was crucified. The twelve Apostles were materializations from the energies of these three personalities—the combined energies. They were fully endowed with individuality, however, but their main task was to clearly manifest within themselves certain abilities inherent within all men.

The same kinds of dramas in different ways have been given, and while the drama is always different, it is always the same. This does not mean that a Christ has appeared within each system of reality. It means that the idea of God has manifested within each system in a way that is comprehensible to the inhabitants.

This drama continues to exist. It does not belong, for example, to your past. Only you have placed it there. This does not mean that it always *reoccurs*. The drama, then, was far from meaningless, and the spirit of Christ, in your terms, is legitimate. It is the probable God-drama that you choose to perceive. There were others that were perceived, but not by you, and there are other such dramas existing now.

> Whether or not the crucifixion occurred physically, it was a psychic event, and exists as do all the other events connected with the drama. Many were physical but some were not. The psychic event affected your world quite as much as the physical one, as is obvious. The whole drama occurred as a result of mankind's need. It was created as a result of that need, grew out of it, but it did not originate within your system of reality.

Additional information on the Three Christs was given by Seth in his *own* book, *Seth Speaks: The Eternal Validity of the Soul*, 1972:

> The third personality, mentioned many times by me, has not in your terms yet appeared, although his existence has been prophesied as the "Second Coming" [Matthew 24]. Now these prophecies were given in terms of the current culture at that time, and therefore, while the stage has been set, the distortions are deplorable–for this Christ will not come at the end of your world as the prophecies have been maintaining.
>
> He will not come to reward the righteous and send evildoers to their doom. He will, however, begin a new religious drama. A certain historical continuity will be maintained. As happened once before, however, he will not be generally known for who he is. There will be no glorious proclamation to which the whole world will bow. He will return to straighten out Christianity, which will be in a shambles at the time of his arrival, and to set up a new system of thought when the world is sorely in need of one.*
>
> By that time, all religions will be in severe crisis. He will undermine religious organizations–not unite them. His message will be that of the individual in relation to *All That Is*. He will clearly state methods by which each individual can attain a state of intimate contact with his own entity; the entity to some extent being man's mediator with *All That Is*. By 2075 all of this will be already accomplished.
>
> The third personality of Christ will indeed be known as a great psychic, for it is he who will teach humanity to use those inner senses that alone make true spirituality possible.

*Seth says elsewhere that Nostradamus saw the end of the Catholic Church as the end of the world and that his prophecies should be examined in that light.

The "new religion" following the second coming will not be Christian in your terms, although the third personality of Christ will initiate it. This personality will refer to the historical Christ, will recognize his relationship with that personality; but within him the three personality groupings will form a new psychic entity, a different psychological gestalt. As this metamorphosis takes place, it will initiate a metamorphosis on a human level, also, as man's inner abilities are accepted and developed.

The results will be a different kind of existence. Many of your problems now result from spiritual ignorance. No man will look down upon an individual from another race when he himself recognizes that his own existence includes such membership also.

No sex will be considered better than the other, or any role in society, when each individual is aware of his own or her own experience at many levels of society and in many roles. An open-ended consciousness will feel its connections with all other living beings. The continuity of consciousness will become apparent. As a result of this the social and governmental structures will change, for they are based upon your current beliefs.

Human personality will reap benefits that now would seem unbelievable. . . . From birth, children will be taught that basic identity is not dependent upon the body, and that time as you know it is an illusion. The child will be aware of many of its past experiences, and will be able to identify with the old man or woman that in your terms it will become.

Many of the lessons "that come with age" will then be available to the young, but the old will not lose the spiritual elasticity of their youth. This itself is important. . . .

As these changes come about, new areas will be activated in the brain to physically take care of them. Physically, then, brain mappings will be possible in which past-life memories are evoked. All of these alterations are spiritual changes in which the meaning of religion will escape organizational bounds, become a living part of individual existence, and where psychic frameworks rather than physical ones will form the foundations of civilizations.

Man's experience will be so extended that to you the race will seem to have changed into another. This does not mean there will not be problems. It does mean that man will have far greater resources at

> his command. It also presupposes a richer and far more diverse social framework. . . .

In the *Seth Material* Seth had said that the three personalities who made up the Christ entity had already lived and died; now, as we have seen, in his own book Seth speaks of the third personality *returning* in the next century. Jane, her husband Rob, and the others gathered at these sessions, wished a further explanation:

> The third personality, already born in your terms, and a portion of the entire Christ personality, took upon himself the role of a zealot. This person had superior energy and power and great organizing abilities, but it was the errors that he made unwittingly that perpetuated some dangerous distortions. The records of that historical period are scattered and contradictory.
>
> The man, historically now, was Paul or Saul. It was given to him to set up a framework. But it was to be a framework of ideas, not of regulations; of men, not of groups. Here he fell down, and will return as the third personality in your future. In that respect, however, there are not four personalities.
>
> Saul went to great lengths to set himself as a separate identity. His characteristics, for example, were seemingly quite different from those of the historical Christ. He was "converted" in an intense personal experience—a fact that was meant to impress upon him the personal and not organizational aspects. Yet some exploits of his earlier life have been attributed to Christ. . . .
>
> All personalities have free will and work out their own challenges. The same applied to Saul. The organizational "distortions," however, were also necessary within the framework of history as events are understood. Saul's tendencies were known, therefore, at another level. They served a purpose. It is for this reason, however, that he will emerge once again, this time to destroy those distortions.
>
> . . . When the third personality re-emerges historically . . . he will not be called the old Paul, but will carry within him the characteristics of all the three personalities.
>
> . . . Allegorically, [Paul] represented a warring faction of the self

that fights against his own knowledge and is oriented in a highly physical manner. It seemed he went from one extreme to another, being against Christ and then for him. But the inner vehemence was always present, the inner fire, and the recognition that he tried for so long to hide.

His was the portion that was to deal with physical reality and manipulation, and so these qualities were strong in him. To some extent they overruled him. When the historical Christ "died," Paul was to implement the spiritual ideas in physical terms, to carry on. In so doing, however, he grew the seeds of an organization that would smother the ideas. He lingered after Christ, as John the Baptist came before. . . .

John and the historical Christ each performed their roles and were satisfied that they had done so. Paul alone was left at the end unsatisfied, and so it is about his personality that the future Christ will form.

# TWELVE

## *Ego-Traps, Possession, and Parasites of the Soul*

For the most part the revelators whom the reader has met so far seem to be fortunate people: overnight their problems and doubts have been washed away and have been replaced by a new sense of faith, purpose, and well-being. But there is another, darker aspect to the Divine Fire: in short, not everyone is equipped to handle the burden of being a spokesman for the Light.

Superficially, it does seem that when the Fire descends, it does so immediately and completely. But I have wondered whether some kind of testing procedure might not be involved, a kind of trial period for revelators, during which their behavior and reaction designates success or failure.

It seems that when the "channel" is kept properly open and

ego traps are avoided, the material flowing through the revelator is of high quality. A very special kind of name may be given to the revelator, which, he is told, will enable him to more readily establish contact with the Source. Very often the revelator will be given glimpses of the future which later prove accurate.

In instances where the revelator allows his soul to become puffed up with ego and permits his material to be exploited by the personal demands of his group, the Source, I have noticed, will often announce that the revelator is a reincarnation of St. Peter or the Virgin Mary (depending upon the sex)—which truly inflates the revelator's ego beyond recognition. I feel great concern whenever a channeler excitedly announces to me that his Source has revealed to him that he is really an incarnation of some great and sainted figure from the past. To me, it signifies that he has flunked the test as a channeler of communications from some unseen realm and is about to be deflated in a most traumatic manner.

Coincident with this particular variety of spiritually aristocratic name-giving comes a great number of dramatic predictions concerning earthly crises, which the revelator is urged to make public at once. In Harold Schroeppel's words:

"There are certain basic aberrations that show up every so often on the spiritual planes, and they happen to a lot of people. These aberrations do not bring true revelations, and they get a lot of people in trouble.

"I am certain that you are thoroughly familiar with the pattern of the sect who claims a direct revelation from God, puts on its robes, goes and sells all its property, crawls up on a mountaintop, then sits there and waits for God to come and collect the entire group. Anywhere from forty-eight hours to three months later the sect comes crawling back down and tries to begin life anew. It has ever been so, and I think it shall continue to be ever so. This kind of thing happens about every twenty years.

"Right now there is a rather heavy prediction going around that there will be three days of darkness around the whole world. I think this is included in the prophecies from Garabandal and

Fatima and a couple of others; we ran into word of it in Hawaii recently. It is a garden variety spiritual aberration, and dire predictions about floods and global destruction by fire fall in the same category."

When the revelator's predictions prove to be false, ostensibly the ravings of a madman, the revelator is humiliated, the group is disbanded, and the "connection" is thoroughly broken. The revelator did not comply with Higher Intelligence's demands for pure channeling and broadcasting requirements, and his prophetic license is revoked.

Time after time I have observed such patterns. Perhaps I am but witnessing cause and effect in action, and what seems to me to be a rather cruel means of demoting an overzealous student is, in reality, a means of emotional purging to restore the revelator's psychic equilibrium to a point somewhere near where it was before the spark of the Divine Fire became an out-of-control, ego-driven holocaust. Most of these rejected revelators do bounce back. They may have to travel to another locale—and, in some extreme cases, even establish new identities—but most of them do reattain the rung of the social and spiritual ladder they occupied before they were touched by an intelligence outside of their own. Some revelators have even raised themselves a spiritual rung or two as a result of the experience, and they will be more cautious if there is a next time—and no doubt there can be.

There are casualties, however; and I am sorrowful for those who are left mentally, emotionally, spiritually crippled. Charles G. Finney was not the first man to compare the "Baptisms of the Holy Spirit" to waves of electricity pulsating through his body and soul. It may seem a bit disheartening to consider that man may have wasted his spiritual creativity in personifying an impersonal Energy that exists to be tapped by everyone without benefit of clergy or tithes and offerings. What we call prayer may be simply a condition, an attitudinal set that somehow attunes the psyche to receive waves of this Energy. The reception of an essential message can be blocked by "static" or can become misused and magnified in such a way that the message impulses can burn out the psychological "tubes."

I cannot help recalling the conversation which Diane

Kennedy Pike and I had on the subject of revelations. "It seems to me," Mrs. Pike said, "when this tremendous power enters one, it's something comparable to taking a psychedelic drug and flipping out on it. It throws you into a whole realm of consciousness for which you may not be prepared. What this does is to disorient you.

"Obviously all of us maintain our sense of balance in the world by a kind of reasoning process that makes order and sense out of everything; but if something happens to us that seems discontinuous with the ordinary stream of events in our lives, it can really flip us out. It can throw us right out of orbit, our expectation and understanding about what life is all about and how we relate to the whole of life, and so forth.

"I can give you an example of what I think happens to some people. I had a phone call the other night from a woman who had had a revelation that she was the Daughter of God. Well, the point was, as we talked on, that she felt she was the *only* daughter of God. I'm sure, though she was unable to say this, that no one's ever told her that such a fantastically powerful experience could happen, and, therefore, when it happened to her, she thought she was unique. But, in fact, this is a potential in each of us, and if we had some preparation, we could get in touch with persons who have had similar experiences and move with an understanding into this new realm of consciousness.

"A lot of this woman's revelation experience had to do with the coming of the Christ spirit and the end of the age that we're living in, and so forth. She had such a limited understanding that she felt that this thing that had happened to her was unique. She was not able to recognize that anyone else might even know what she was talking about.

"At the lower level of consciousness or awareness, which in our culture is called the psychic, the same kinds of things happen. People are having experiences without having any understanding of unseen spiritual forces; and, in a sense, they are becoming victimized by these forces instead of entering consciously into a relationship with them and maintaining some kind of control over them. We have people playing with Ouija boards who, in their rational orientation, don't believe that it is possible for there to be unseen spiritual forces, but who find themselves suddenly possessed by demons. It seems to me that this occurs out of a lack of preparation or out of ignorance of the spiritual forces."

It seems ominous, too, that many of the time-honored ways of inducing mystical experience involve practices that—to put it mildly—may be hazardous to your health.

Throughout the religious history of all cultures, we find that fasting, depriving the body of sleep, scourging the body, whirling it about dervish-style, and an enormous number of sensory deprivation and disorientation techniques have been employed. Psychical researchers have long noted that the mental functions categorically grouped under the ubiquitous initials ESP seem to be often associated with instances in which the subject suffered a weakness of body due to illness or exhaustion.

Dr. William Sargant, F.R.C.P., physician in charge of the Department of Psychological Medicine of St. Thomas' Hospital in London, sent me a reprint of his 1968 Maudsley Lecture, "The Physiology of Faith," in which he states that "prolonged excitement of the nervous system, the inducing of insoluble mental conflicts, the bringing about of mental tiredness, excessive strain, or extreme fatigue in a variety of ways, all tend to usher in . . . abnormal inhibitory brain activity."

The Russian psychologist Pavlov described "inhibitory brain activity" as a state similar to the hypnotic state. While in this particular state, the brain ceases to compute critically all the impressions being received by it.

"New impressions, new commands, new ideas become suddenly imperative in their need of acceptance, and ring absolutely true; and, moreover, are often completely immune to all the normal processes whereby the brain examines critically most of the new impressions received, compares them with all its stored impressions and experiences, and decides, on the basis of past knowledge and present balanced judgments, whether the new ideas are likely to be true or false. New ideas can then be accepted and believed in which are totally at variance to all the individual's other past and present experience and belief," Dr. Sargant writes.

A study of the literature of religious conversion, mysticism, and the acquisition of new faiths has convinced Dr. Sargant that there are two principal means by which totally new beliefs may be suddenly acquired, even though they may often be diametrically opposed to the individual's previous faith and beliefs:

> One . . . seems to be to excite the nervous system—and to overexcite it—by means of drumming, dancing and music of various kinds, by the rhythmic repetition of stimuli and by the imposing of emotionally charged mental conflicts needing urgent resolution. The brain then finally becomes overwhelmed by the imposed stimuli and conflicts imposed, and changes over from increased excitement into the progressive and varied states of inhibition described. . . .
>
> The other method seems to be one in which the same final end-point occurs, but is attained in an almost opposite way. States of abnormal brain inhibition are produced not by increasing the stimulus till inhibition finally supervenes but by starting off trying to inhibit most of the ordinary voluntary and even involuntary thoughts and activities of the higher nervous system. One tries to put oneself artificially in what is now increasingly called a state of "sensory deprivation." In states of contemplation and mysticism, which can create so much unsubstantiated faith, the individual has deliberately to learn, often by months or years of effort, how to empty his mind of all extraneous matters, and generally to center his thoughts, if he is finally thinking actively at all, on some subject on which he desires to obtain new enlightenment or faith. What then seems to happen is that, as the brain becomes more and more severely inhibited as regards its normal functions, one gets a greater and greater concentration on the one thing that matters . . . Then, as Pavlov also showed, such a focally excited small point of brain activity can also start to exhibit abnormal "paradoxical" and "ultraparadoxical" disturbance or function. Suddenly the particular god or devil being concentrated on is felt actually to enter into the person and become a very part of himself.

Later in his lecture Dr. Sargant states that in his classic work *Battle for the Mind* he gave numerous examples of how the brain of man can be reached and absolute faith created by "staging deliberate excitatory assaults on the nervous system with drumming, dancing, frightening threats." Numerous examples of the sudden creation of absolute certainty of faith has been recorded in every sort of "abreactive religion" throughout man's long religious history, Dr. Sargant says, and his studies have convinced him that, around the world, ". . . these varied means of excitatory conversion and the acquisition of new faiths, and the excitatory techniques used are practically always the same basically, whereever they are encountered, and whether the desire is to create new faiths in a religious or in a political or social setting."*

Robert Shell of Roanoke, Virginia, has spent the last two years researching occultism and mysticism and endeavoring to warn persons who are attempting to venture too far, too fast. Shell is convinced that ". . . the dangers that lurk outside man's known universe are great, and perhaps H. P. Lovecraft was right when he said, 'It was not meant that we should venture far.' "

In April 1971 Shell reminded me of the communication with alleged Higher Sources which Aleister Crowley began in Cairo in 1904:

"A being which called itself Aiwass suddenly took possession of Crowley's wife after she had uttered something to the effect that 'they' wished to communicate with him. At the time they were standing before the Stele of Revealing in the Cairo Museum. There followed three days of dictation by Aiwass to Crowley. The text of this dictation forms *The Book of the Law*, which was supposed to herald the coming of the Age of Horus, the Child. As can be easily seen from a reading of Crowley's autobiography, this was the turning point which led him from a relatively high attainment as an occultist and magician to the total collapse of his powers and the obscurity of his later years. The literature of occultism is flagrantly full of similar contacts. Madame Blavatsky and her absurd Koot Hoomi. . . .

"It seems that at any given point in history these entities, whatever they are, couch themselves in the form most likely to be accepted by the mind they contact. Thus the occultist has his invocations of spirits, good and evil, and the Saucerian has his space people. However, on one point only can we look to the

*For less drastic ways of kindling the Divine Fire, see Chapter Fourteen.

literature and be certain: that such contacts are always detrimental to the physical and the mental well-being of the contactee. Usually we see a relatively 'together' and down-to-earth person become a starry-eyed prophet, either of doom or of the coming of the Kingdom of Heaven.

"However, I should point out that my knowledge on this point comes not only from literature, but also from personal friendship with an unfortunate contactee. This young man, who was eighteen at the time of contact, was suddenly in communication with a powerful entity."

In the summer of 1969, Bob, his wife, and two friends named Reggie and Mark were living in an apartment in Richmond, Virginia, near the Richmond Museum of Arts. Bob and Reggie were actively pursuing their studies in magic, while Mark's primary interest lay in electronics, although he was experimenting with psychedelic drugs. Because Mark had always remained somewhat aloof from any discussions of magic, they were all surprised when he informed them that he had been contacted by what he referred to as an "entity." He told them that this being had offered him certain concessions in return for allowing it to use his body.

At first they dismissed Mark's claim as an attempt on his part to interject himself into their own studies and to attract attention to himself as an ego boost. But then the apartment began to be visited by poltergeistic manifestations. They would awaken in the morning to find bookcases turned over, furniture strewn about, the entire living room in a mess.

Once Bob had just opened a can of sardines and was unable to get a hold on the top with his fingers. He set the can down, went to get a knife. As he turned back to the can with knife in hand, he saw the lid lift itself slowly in the air, turn over two or three times, then plop gently and properly into the trash can! Four bottles exploded in Mark's room, showering glass all over the place. A knife that had last been seen in the kitchen, protruded from a windowsill. The door of the room also bore a much larger, heavier knife that was unfamiliar to them.

"It took two of us to pull this knife out of the door," Bob said. "It didn't look as though it had been driven into the door.

It looked as if it had been materialized inside the door, if that makes any sense."

It was soon after this incident that Mark began to confide in Bob:

"This being did not give itself a name, saying only that its name would be impossible for human vocal organs to pronounce. It claimed to be a multidimensional being whose substance was totally energy. It said that its being permeated the entire universe, but that by effort of will it could concentrate its force and being at any one point in the universe for the purpose of making contact with beings still bound to the physical plane. Its reasons for wishing to make such contact were always given in very vague terms, but it did claim on several occasions that it needed 'points of reference' on this 'plane of existence.' The exact function to it of these points I was never able to extract, but it was clear that this being had a deep interest in this level of reality for some reason that it did not wish to divulge.

"The entity had originally represented itself to him as being neutral in the affairs of man. As time had gone on, however, Mark had become rapidly aware that the being had misrepresented itself to him, and was, in reality, a very evil force. But by this time, Mark was committed to the entity and could find no way to drive it out of his head. It was holding him to the contract that he had originally made.

"Mark identified the being as Asmitor, and his description of it was something very similar to those H. P. Lovecraft uses in his stories of the Elder Gods and the Old Ones. The entity was infinite in its expanse, a tenuous network of energy that stretched throughout the universe, but which had consciousness and the ability to concentrate itself at any one point on this level of reality–but only when expressly invited, or unknowingly invited in this case. Mark had opened the door to the entity by his use of psychedelics without proper protective preparation.

"At one point I became reasonably lulled by Mark's assurances of the entity's good nature and accepted the proposal that I become a contactee, too. That night I was promised a visit, but because of my study of magic, I had developed a circle of protection about me through the construction of protective pentagram areas.

"As I lay half asleep, I felt suddenly as if a very great weight was being pressed down on my body. I had difficulty in breathing, and I could not move my body at all. I attempted to call out, but found that I could not. I felt what I can only describe as the feeling that something was fumbling around inside my mind. The physical sensations had by this time become extremely painful, and I was becoming frightened by my inability to move or to make any sound. I felt as if I were dying. Then, just as suddenly as it had come, the weight was lifted and I relaxed and fell almost immediately into a deep sleep. The next day Mark told me that I had been found unfit as a 'reference point.' I had been rejected as a contactee.

"According to Mark's cosmology, there were two beings: the one that had contacted him and another, both of which were, from the human point of view, evil, and both of which were basically equal in power and scope and perpetually at war over the ownership of the physical universe. In all of the previous battles the entity which had contacted Mark had been the loser. But Mark was convinced by the communications he received that the next battle was coming soon, and his entity was going to win.

"This was his original belief, at any rate. Later, I think, he became a little disenchanted when he found out that most of the promises that had been made to him by this entity were not fulfilled. None of the curses he levied upon his enemies took effect, and his claims of having the ability to levitate objects were never demonstrated.

"Along with the powers that this being supposedly granted to Mark came the commands to draw certain symbols on the floor, ceiling, and the four walls of his bedroom. The purpose of this, the entity said, was to form a landmark, a specific, easily accessible point for it to hold onto. The basic figure was the traditional pentagram with lettering and symbols drawn around it. The symbols were not of any alphabet with which I am personally familiar, and they caused very definite feelings of tension, a feeling that the room was "charged." I noticed that after Mark had drawn these sigils that on any occasion when I entered the room I could feel a definite tension, like static electricity.

"Asmitor told Mark that the conflict between it and the opposing entity, whose name it never gave, had been assigned by a Higher Ruling Force. The reason that it needed points of reference on this plane of reality was because the more points of reference it had, the better it would be able to fight against the other entity, which was also working toward gaining its own points of reference on this level of reality. Apparently these entities were not able to perceive our level of existence directly, but only indirectly through the minds of their servitors.

"The entity told Mark that 'Asmitor' was not actually its name but was only an approximation of its name that could be voiced by a human. It also said that its complete name was itself. The expression of its complete name would bring about the complete annihilation of this universe.

"Mark claimed to have been given the power to utter this name should it ever become necessary. I was skeptical of Mark's alleged powers, and I think the major blow that shook his confidence in Asmitor's promises came when he was arrested for possession of LSD and marijuana and thrown into jail. Mark had been promised total and complete protection from all physical harassment, and this experience showed him that his possessing entity either did not have the power to do what it claimed, or it was not working in his interests as it had promised.

"After Mark had served three months in jail, he was given a suspended sentence and released. At this point I was only in indirect contact with him through letters, because I was in a different city. He told me several times in his letters and in telephone conversations that the only way out for him was to destroy himself, because Asmitor was gradually taking more and more control of his body away from him. I'd been in his presence during some of these periods earlier, and it seemed from the change in his face and in the depth of his eyes that some other creature was looking at you through Mark's eyes.

"It came as a shock, but not really a surprise, to hear from a mutual friend of ours in Richmond that on April 1, 1970, Mark had committed suicide. I am personally convinced that, in his case, this act was justified and was probably the only solution to his problem. I do not think that most of the traditional methods and exorcisms would have had any effect after the being had become so firmly entrenched in him.

"The name 'Asmitor' meant nothing to me at the time when Mark first conveyed it to me. After his death I chanced across it in some of my study in medieval texts of magic—I believe it was in the works of Agrippa. I am convinced that Mark had never read this book; and I am also convinced that Mark did not simply make up this name. This was a piece of corroborating evidence to my mind to indicate that rather than a case of insanity, Mark's case was that of true demonic possession. I doubt that any higher-level entities would cause an appearance of insanity, but lower-level entities, demons, would certainly do so.

"I think that the poltergeist-type phenomena in our apartment were of a nature that would produce either a state of fear or a state of shock on the part of the observer. When a person is shocked or frightened, he sends out sudden bursts of psychic energy, and I believe that the entity fed on this released psychic energy. I am convinced that the energy derived to produce the phenomena came most likely from Mark and that the resulting discharges of energy produced by us as a result of the phenomena was used by Asmitor for his own purposes, whatever those might have been.

"The whole situation has a lot of similarity to the one in the news recently about the young man who was tied and drowned by his friends at his own wish because he'd been told by Satan that he would come back as the leader of several legions of demons. I am certain that the entity involved in his case was, if not the same, then a very similar entity to the one with which Mark was dealing. I am also convinced that promises of this sort are only made for the purpose of causing the individual to kill himself, because if sudden fright and shock can create a large surge of psychic energy, then the release of the entire life force at death would provide a much greater energy source for these entities."

Of course we must recognize the fact that a good many

psychologists and other researchers of inner space would maintain that Mark's summoning forth of "Asmitor" was a manifestation of paranoid schizophrenia, or some other illness. And, indeed, an uncomfortable segment of our psychiatric investigators would echo the words found in Hosea 9:7: "The prophet is a fool, The man of the Spirit is mad. . . ."

The vast majority of Biblical scholars will reject the suggestion of possession in regard to the prophets. They will be quite willing to acknowledge the universal belief among primitive people that certain men may be possessed by certain spirits which have entered their bodies for the purpose of revelation. They may even concede that these phenomena bear a rather pronounced superficial similarity to Biblical prophecy, but they will firmly denounce any kind of parallel.

Equally offensive, no doubt, would be the comparison of the Greek poets' invocations to the Muses with the Biblical prophets' prayers to Jehovah to put words into their mouths. Plato remarked that all good poets, epic as well as lyric, do not compose their poems by art but by possession. "There is no invention in him [the poet] until he has been inspired and out of his senses, and the mind is no longer in him . . . For not by art does the poet sing, but by power divine." It might surely be suggested that the Muses were entities summoned by the receptivity of those poets who had properly "tuned in" by fasting, meditation, dancing, or some other psychic mechanism. Although it is not obvious that the poets assumed the name of their inspiring Muse, they may indeed have been named by the possessing entity. No work of Greek poetry omits the invocation to the Muse with its holy breath and its divine madness of the soul.

In emphasis of the uniqueness of Biblical prophecy, Abraham J. Heschel writes in his *The Prophets*:

> . . . Man everywhere and at all times seeks guidance and help from the divine world, aspires to visionary experience and to the acquisition of supernatural powers, and longs to behold in dreams and visions the mysteries which are veiled from the common eye. Yet the prophets of Israel did not seek such experiences; they resisted their call. . .

The Biblical prophet, Heschel states, stands "in sharp contrast to the preoccupation with the phenomena of madness and possession in Greek literature." The Old Testament prophets did not claim that God spoke in them, but to them, by voice, vision, or dream—by command rather than possession.

It is never wise to attempt to reason backward in time, but let us examine some verses from only one of the Old Testament prophets. Jeremiah could not always have been a willing servant, or he would not have uttered the following lamentation:

> O Lord, thou hast deceived me, and I was deceived; thou art stronger than I, and hast prevailed: I am in derision daily, everyone mocketh me. For since I spake, I cried out, I cried violence and spoil.... Then I said, I will not make mention of him, nor speak any more in his name. But his word was in mine heart as a burning fire shut up in my bones, and I was weary with forebearing, and I could not contain them [20:7-9].

Formidable scholar that he is, Heschel tells us that in verse 20:7, the verb "deceived" should be translated as "seduced," and that "Thou art stronger than I" should be, in reality, "*Thou hast raped me.*" According to Heschel:

> The words used by Jeremiah to describe the impact of God upon his life are identical with the terms of seduction and rape in the legal terminology of the Bible. These terms used in immediate juxtaposition forcefully convey the complexity of the divine-human relationship: sweetness of enticement as well as violence of rape.... This interpretation betrays an ambivalence in the prophet's understanding of his own experience.
>
> The call to be a prophet is more than an invitation. It is first of all a feeling of being enticed, of acquiescence or willing surrender. But this winsome feeling is only one aspect of the experience. The other aspect is a sense of being ravished or carried away by violence, of yielding to over-powering force against one's own will. The prophet ... is conscious of both voluntary identification and forced capitulation.

Heschel does not interpret this surrender as at all similar to a state of possession. But might we at least consider the possibility that Jeremiah might have become dismayed at being used as a vehicle to condemn his countrymen with the wrath of a vengeful, jealous God. Might we wonder if Jeremiah really received a spark from the Divine Fire at all, but rather became possessed by a violent tribal god, wrathful at his subject's inconstancy?

British author J. Fred Justice refers to Gehokah, an early priest-king of Salem, a contemporary of Abram, who is mentioned often in various Egyptian inscriptions and in the *Book of the Dead*, as a "Constant Thorn in the Side of Egypt–both living and dead." Gehokah, (pronounced with a soft *G*) and his people were driven out of the Nile delta and forced to migrate to the hills of Sinai. In Justice's opinion, the fierce Gehokah became elevated to the status of tribal god after his death. Justice also believes that Gehokah and Jehovah are the same entity. Writing in the January 1972 issue of *Psychic Observer*, Justice states:

> They both had the same "stamping ground"–Sinai or Mount Horeb–and it was on Horeb that Moses had his pyrotechnic adventure with the bush–presumably above the settlement site of old Gehokah, who thereafter attached himself to Moses as his god or guide, Jehovah. Jehovah displayed many characteristics of a less than desirable nature: a god of war, vengeful, jealous, and blood-lustful, demanding much sacrifice (human sacrifice on occasion); all of which were mirrored in the cruel life of the barbarian priest-king Gehokah; and there is little doubt in my mind that the god Jehovah stems from the spirit of Gehokah, who carried over his natural instincts into the After Life.
>
> Jehovah was originally the god or guide of Moses, and afterwards the tribal-god, before he became the national god of the Hebrews.

In *The Divine Flame*, discussing Adolf Hitler, Sir Alister Hardy remarked: "It almost looked as if, in his ascendant phase, there was some superhuman power behind him, and he certainly seemed to feel it. Could it be possible that, as a part of nature, there might be, as a result of a sufficient degree of shared emotion, a kind of tribal (or racial) 'spirit,' either for good or evil, that can be generated by some extrasensory means and have such a force as almost to succeed in conquest?" One can see how a "Chosen People" might project a "sufficient degree of shared emotion" to create an independent, super-anthropomorphic racial spirit such as Jehovah.

Dr. R. R. Marett observes (*Faith, Hope and Charity in Primitive Religion*) that the "middle religions" of half-civilized people reek of blood because of the sacrificial rite. He writes:

> If religion is liable to unloose the beast in us even while seeking to free the man, we must learn how this deviation occurs, so that religion may be kept to the true direction. . . . Let us honestly proclaim that religious emotion is ambivalent, exciting the mind at once for better and for worse. At times, when man is apt to think that he has reached the heights, he has merely touched the lowest depths of his spiritual nature.

Dr. V. Truman Jordahl is Chairman of the Department of Philosophy of Millikin University in Decatur, Illinois. Truman did archeological research in Jordan and Israel on a State Department grant in the summer of 1963. Utilizing his study of the Dead Sea Scrolls, Truman has prepared an exhaustive study based on first-hand documentary sources in which he argues that pre-Christian Jewish immortality beliefs had a greater influence on the philosophy of the Hellenistic period than did Hellenistic philosophy on Judeo-Christian teachings on immortality. In his *The Dead Sea Scrolls and the Religious Movements of Their Time*, he examines the Scrolls in their original language as representative documents of Essene and proto-Essene reform movements which gave rise to the historical figure of John the Baptist:

"This subject of possession has always been of interest to me, particularly in light of my own research. Possession is not something that is entirely unexpected or completely unknown to those who study theology and ancient manuscripts and traditions. As a matter of fact, there is a very old tradition of this phenomenon.

"In the books of Enoch there is a reference to God dwelling *in* and abiding *in* people, or the household of people. 'And I will come and dwell among you and *within* you' is one of many such statements that occur in Enoch. We have a reference to Moses that is quoted again and again in the New Testament. 'And I will raise up a prophet in your midst like unto Moses.' This is a kind of reccurence phenomenon and begins to suggest, or hint, at the possibility of the kind of possession situation.

"We see this clearly in I Kings. The figure of Elijah, who literally comes back from the dead, is a tradition which is known among the early Christians. It was expected that John the Baptist was Elijah returned from the dead. Now it depends on how you look at the words 'return from the dead.' We may be speaking the language of ancient tradition more accurately if we use the term *possession*, rather than *return from the dead.*

" 'Sons of the Prophet' was a name given to the followers of the prophet Elijah, a very intriguing group mentioned in the Dead Sea Scrolls. According to the *Manual of Discipline*, a Scroll document, the Sons of the Prophet did not impose celibacy on their group and included women and children within the ordinances of their assembly.

"The Essenes were derided by the Hellenizers because they did not marry, but adopted other men's sons. Of course the term 'adopted' can perhaps be taken in a spiritual sense as well. As the Essenes were called 'Sons of Light,' it is most likely that members became sons of the community, in the sense that the Sons of the Prophet were considered the sons of Elijah; that is, they left their father and mother and took new names and acquired a new spiritual father in Elijah.

"Jesus called John the Baptist not only the prophet but directly by the name of Elijah. In Matthew 11 Jesus says that John was more than a prophet, he was Elijah, who was to return. Granting Jesus' prophetic presupposition concerning John, it appears that he places him above all prophets; I quote: 'Truly I say to you, among those born of woman, there is risen no one greater than John the Baptist' (Matthew 11:11).

"In Mark 9:11, after Jesus, Peter, James, and John are returning from the Mount of Jesus' Transfiguration, the disciples asked Jesus if it were true that Elijah must return again. Jesus answers: 'Elijah does come to restore all things; and how is it written of the Son of Man, that he should suffer many things and be treated with contempt. I tell you that *Elijah has come*, and they did to him whatever they pleased, as it is written."

It is clear through an examination of many documents and references that the resurrected prophet theme was an essential part of Old Testament theology. Elijah appears to be a helper in time of need in several traditions, so he was considered to be a sort of guide, or helper, one who was at hand.

In the light of Dr. V. Truman Jordahl's comments, I cannot help suggesting that perhaps Jesus became the *new Elijah*, the new prophet, the new guide, after John the Baptist was beheaded. If Jesus were an Essene, a follower of John the Baptist, then he shared the sorrow and confusion that must have spread throughout the group. As John's chief disciple, Jesus may have assumed the role of leadership in order to protect the cohesive unity of the Sons of the Prophet and the Sons of Light. Could Jesus have sought to be possessed by the Divine Fire, who, in the tradition of the Sons of the Prophet, was called Elijah? Did he set out to the wilderness to fast as had Elijah, as had John the Baptist, in order to encourage the revelatory experience that would draw Elijah to him?

Jesus' forty-day fast in the desert and the place of his temptation by Satan is thought to have been in the barren heights of the mountain region overlooking Jericho, above the brook Cherith, where the ravens had fed Elijah. Elijah had fasted for forty days on the way to the same mountain. Moses had fasted for forty days before he received the Ten Commandments. From the mountaintop where Jesus was fasting he could look eastward across the Jordan to the mountain ranges of Nebo where, centuries before, Moses and Elijah had ascended to God. Had Jesus been following some very carefully prescribed ritualistic steps that would assure his acceptance as a prophet by the clergy and the general populace?

When Jesus asked his disciples who people said he was, they answered that some people said he was John the Baptist returned from the grave after his beheading on the orders of King Herod, others that he was Elijah, the Old Testament prophet. Might he actually have been asking for a kind of progress report, a sampling of public opinion of whether or not he was receiving acceptance as the new Elijah?

Did the scene on the Mount of Transfiguration demonstrate

to the witnessing disciples that Jesus had received the Divine Fire, the *Elijah*, and that he was to be proclaimed the new prophet, the successor to the work begun by the Essene, John the Baptist? Did the revelators of the Hebrew tradition seek to become channels for the spirits of the great prophets Moses and Elijah? Might it even have been considered necessary to speak with the spirit of a revered, but departed, prophet in order to have one's revelations deemed valid? And did the spirits of these prophets possess new bodies in order to continue their godly missions? As Jesus hung dying on the cross, those who stood nearby thought they heard him calling to Elijah (Mark 15:35).

I have also wondered if possession might not explain the acquiring of a new name and a new personality.

Maybe the old Sunday school prayer that asks Jesus to "cast out our sin and *enter in*, be *born in us* today," might hearken back to a tradition so ancient that it has become lost to all but the collective unconscious: "Where two or three are gathered together, there will I be in the midst of them." Does this promise imply a direct melding or blending of the supplicants, the prayerful, with the deity?

"It distresses me to realize how much truth there is in the observation that if Jesus Christ had lived in our time, he would be committed to a mental institution," says Dr. Al Siebert, one psychologist who is not afraid to take another look at certain cases of "classic" mental illness: "My professional inquiries have led me to realize that the diagnosis of paranoid schizophrenia in young people is oftentimes more accurately understood as a developmental crisis, as a healthy thing to be happening," he remarked. "In my interviews I have learned to expect persons going through this to report psi experiences in which they have direct, or indirect, contact with a guiding and enlightening 'intelligence' from another realm of existence.

"When I hear about a young person who is supposed to be a paranoid schizophrenic, I am almost certain that they have been telling the professional shrink that they've been hearing voices talking to them, they've been talking to God, or there's some kind of religious and exceptional experience that is important to them. What I've been looking at is something else, and this is that the young person goes through a number of stages in growing up, but he or she never really takes control of his or her mind until adolescence. From my point of view in looking at this, I see that many of these young people in the past, who have had a so-called mental breakdown when they reached young adulthood, have really been experiencing an attempt to go through a developmental sequence or stage or crisis in order to reach for an even higher level of personality integration. It is with this crisis that they go through, at this developmental moment, that some of these revelatory experiences come through.

"What I have been trying to get through to some psychologists and psychiatrists is that when a young person starts talking about revelatory experiences, we should listen to them and not try to make them stop, because they need our help at that time, rather than our coming in and saying, 'Okay, you're a mentally ill person; we're going to cure you.' This puts more stress on them, and unfortunately most young people can't handle this and they end up being mentally ill patients all of their lives."

"In a sense," I put in, "they have been made mental patients because of interference at the wrong time, because of the intense desire to make them conform to a pattern approved by society."

"Well, yes, that and the fact that they provide the fodder that keeps this mental-health business going. An analogy I draw is that we all have the ability to drive down the street and see a house . . . that vandals are breaking down . . . but we can also recognize the difference when the owner is purposefully tearing it down because he wants to build something better on the property. At this time I see very few professional psychologists and psychiatrists who are able to see when a person is purposefully taking his own personality apart in order to build something better . . . "

Dr. Siebert states that professional psychologists and psychiatrists have been conditioned to interpret a number of experiences that people have as symptoms of mental illness. "There are a couple of factors that led to my breakthrough in this kind of thing," he told me. "One was when I began seriously to question . . . whether there really *is* such a thing as mental illness. I also found that I was curious about self-esteem, and I had this sort of hunch that if a person has been having a lot of things going bad for him, that some kind of self-regulating mechanism will go to work inside him. It will be unconscious, but it will be something to help his self-esteem and bring his esteem level back up. This may or may not be related to religious experience, but oftentimes it is."

In August 1965 Dr. Siebert was working as a staff psychologist at the Neuropsychiatric Institute, University of Michigan Hospital in Ann Arbor. A nineteen-year-old unmarried woman was brought in with the admissions diagnosis of "acute paranoid schizophrenia" and placed in a closed ward. She was very withdrawn, and she refused to talk to anyone. When her parents brought her in, they said that she claimed that God had been talking to her.

After a few weeks, the staff members agreed that she was so ill that she would probably have to spend the rest of her life in a mental institution. At this point Dr. Siebert asked the resident if he could interview the girl. Dr. Siebert received permission to do so, and before he spoke to the girl, asked himself these questions:

What would happen if he talked to her, believing that she could turn out to be his best friend? What would happen if he accepted everything she reported about herself as being the truth? What would happen if he just listened to her and did not allow his mind to put any psychiatric labels on her? What would happen if he questioned her to find out if there was a link between her self-esteem, the workings of her mind, and the way that others had been treating her?

A nurse brought the young woman to the ward dining room and introduced them. The patient glanced quickly at Dr. Siebert but did not speak. Dr. Siebert got her busy drawing and making some designs with blocks.

"Finally, after a while, she glanced at me, and it was the kind of look when you know you've made some kind of personal contact," Dr. Siebert said. Here are the highlights of their conversation:

"Why are you here in a psychiatric hospital?"

*God spoke to me and said I was going to give birth to the second savior.*

"That may be, but why are you here in the hospital?"

*Well, I'm talking crazy.*

"According to whom? Did you decide that when God spoke to you that you were crazy?"

*Oh, no, they told me I was crazy.*

"Do you believe you're crazy?"

*No, but I am, aren't I?*

"If you put that in the form of a question, I'll answer you."

*Do you think I'm crazy?*

"No."

*But that couldn't have happened, could it?*

"As far as I'm concerned, you're the only person who knows what happens in your mind. Did it seem real at the time?"

*Oh,yes!*

"Tell me what you did after God spoke to you. Did you start knitting booties and sweaters and things?"

(Laughing) *No, but I did pack my clothes and wait by the door several times.*

"One thing I'm curious about. Why is it that of all the women in the world, God chose you to be the mother of the second savior?"

*You know, I've been trying to figure that out myself!*

Dr. Siebert asked her what things had happened in her life before God spoke to her. She described how her parents never praised her for her accomplishments in school or the many helpful things she did around the house. She tried very hard to succeed in a nursing school course but received extreme criticism. Out of desperation she went to visit her high school boyfriend, but he announced that he only wanted to be friends. She said that she had felt sad and lonely after that. There did not seem to be anyone in the whole world who cared for her.

"And then God spoke to you."

*Yes! I felt like the most special person in the whole world.* (warmly smiling) *That's a nice feeling.*

In many cases such as the one recounted above, "They hear voices as real as mine sounds to you over the telephone," Dr. Siebert said. "It's God; it's Jesus; it's a personal kind of teacher or guardian that a person has had since childhood, and every once in a while this invisible guardian will come right out and talk to them a little bit. It makes them feel very special that they are the subject of special attention."

I asked Dr. Siebert if he could accept the possibility that these guardians might actually exist in an externalized form.

"Yes," he admitted. "Later on when I met the girl who had received the voice of God, she stopped me in the hallway and told me that she'd been thinking about everything and was wondering if perhaps she'd imagined God's voice in order to make herself feel better. I just said, 'Maybe.' I'm a very practical person. I took the position that if God really *had* chosen her to be the mother of the second savior, then He was watching; and I wasn't going to give her a rough time by declaring her to be a paranoid schizophrenic. I was going to be on her side!

"I'm open to the possibility that there may be an existence on the Other Side, and some entity just might attach itself to someone and appear once in a while."

# THIRTEEN

## *Testing the Validity of the Divine Fire*

Writing in *Christianity Today* (October 8, 1971), Clark R. Pinnock, Professor of Theology at Trinity Evangelical Divinity School in Deerfield, Illinois, and Grant R. Osborne, Instructor in Greek at Trinity, present "A Truce Proposal for the Tongues Controversy."

They begin by clarifying what they consider to be two important points. First, it matters not whether speaking in tongues in the apostolic age and today are real languages or ecstatic utterances. "The important point is that the nature of the gift cannot be the criterion for veracity. This must be determined from other considerations, especially the manifestation of the fruit of the Spirit (Gal. 5:22, 23) in the life of the tongue speaker."

Their other preliminary point is that Scripture upholds no distinction between tongues "as an initial sign of Spirit-baptism and as the gift of the Spirit." The twofold purpose of their paper, Pinnock and Osborne state, is to "show that tongues as a gift for this age is valid biblically" and to demonstrate that "glossolalia as the normative, initial evidence of Spirit-baptism cannot be upheld scripturally."

For the "nonglossolalist" they write:

1. *Tongues are a legitimate gift of the Spirit to the Church today.*

   The New Testament nowhere teaches that "the gifts were given solely to authenticate the apostles or that they were to cease after the apostolic age." The Apostle Paul did not teach the cessation of tongues at the close of the apostolic age, but he did indicate that "love is the context in which all the gifts must be exercised. The only cessation to which he refers is that which occurs at the [second] coming of Christ."

2. *The glossolalist should be welcomed into Christian fellowship and accepted into all cooperative endeavors.*

   Pinnock and Osborne state that the caricature of the glossolalist as a "neurotic, insecure person who can express himself only in unseemly emotional ways" must be smashed. They point out that some psychological tests have indicated that the opposite may be true and "in many cases the gift as a religious experience seems to contribute to mental health." Nor, as the gift appears on prestigious campuses throughout the United States, can the old stereotype of the glossolalist belonging only to the lower strata of society, "economically and intellectually," be considered as a serious charge. "Paul left room within the worship service for such manifestations . . . so long as certain guidelines were followed—edification . . . interpretation . . . self-control . . . order . . . and the absence of proselytizing. This last is the foundation stone of combined worship and continued unity."

For the "glossolalist," Pinnock and Osborne also present two suggestions:

1. *Tongues is not the normative sign of Spirit-baptism.*

   Although Pentecostals maintain that the Book of Acts demonstrates the normative value of tongues and in every case is "present as the conspicuous evidence of the power of the Spirit coming upon the individual," Pinnock and Osborne state that such an argument is weak "methodologically and exegetically." In their reading of Acts, "Each member of the body of Christ, according to Paul, enjoys a manifestation of the Spirit for the common good. There is not one gift that all Christians share. Glossolalia is simply *not* normative. The infallible sign of spiritual fullness is moral and religious." Pinnock and Osborne contend that the historical narrative of Acts does not establish the normative role of tongues. "Indeed, Acts seems to stress bold witness as a sign of a spiritual depth."

2. *The glossolalist should not take a superior attitude toward those who have not experienced tongues, nor should he coerce others to do so.*

The authors concede that the Pentecostals themselves are among the harshest critics of such a "spiritual aristocracy" attitude among those gifted with tongues, who tend to look upon those who have not experienced glossolalia as "spiritually stunted." Pinnock and Osborne maintain that glossolalia is not to be sought or propagated. "There is no room for active seeking, only for passive waiting for the particular gift the sovereign Spirit bestows on each one."

In their conclusion Pinnock and Osborne state that nonglossolalists run the risk of "quenching the Spirit," while glossolalists "often place too great an emphasis on the gift and engage in unscriptural proselytizing." They can see no reason why glossolalia should hinder the work of God or alarm nonglossolalists, "so long as the biblical safeguards are observed."

"I would really warn you, Brad," Dr. Donald Williams told me, "against confusing the counterfeits with the real thing. We believe that Satan is very much alive and doing well in this world. There are a lot of people who are being misled by astrology, by demonology, by witchcraft, by Black Magic, by all kinds of mystical experiences. Man is incurably idolatrous and incurably religious, and having given up the true knowledge of God, he continually tries to fill his life with substitutes.

"These substitutes have a lot of common characteristics.

They tend to be personal in terms of chanting or mystical experience or some identification with ultimate reality, but they don't talk about love and forgiveness and the reality of a living, personal relationship with God. They also tend to have an optimistic view of working one's way to God. Thus they are counterfeit to the true reality, which is not that we are trying to find God and achieve some spiritual state or some spiritual consciousness or some spiritual experience, but that God has come looking for us in Jesus Christ and he is seeking us and calling us into a relationship with himself. The quality of that relationship is dependent upon the kind of spiritual experience that we have on the truth of God's love for us and his faithfulness to us as we walk by faith.

"There are all kinds of spiritual experiences, all kinds of mystical experiences. People talk about love; they talk about peace; but we find a true test of that to be a life of discipleship in relationship with Jesus Christ, a discipleship that is willing to go through suffering and to endure whatever this world has to bring."

*Dr. Richard Rubenstein*: I do not deny the existence of other intelligences in other planes of being, but having no evidence that they are operative in my life, I have no way of commenting about them. I would, however, suggest that one must be very careful when one asserts that one is being controlled or harassed or informed by other intelligences that in reality what is happening is not simply a projection of one's own inner life into the cosmic sphere. A good deal of work has been done in the field of psychology on what it means to hear voices or to be harassed by other beings or to be guided by other beings, and while I could never in any instance tell a person who claimed to hear such voices or receive such revelations that he was wrong, I would tend to be initially skeptical of any claim that the voices came from anywhere but the person's inner being. Those of us who have done therapy and counseling with people have frequently heard people assert that they are being guided by other voices and other beings. When the course of the therapy was over, we found the people recognized the voices they thought they heard were in some sense coming from their own internal psyche.

If my hypothesis is correct that frequently the voices we hear, or the beings some of us seem to feel are guiding us, are projections of our own internal psyche, then we would project only what we want to project. We would project only a portion of what is real to us, and it would be no accident that some of the things that we heard are things that seem almost obvious and seem to relate very definitely to our own situation.

Father Ed Cleary, a Roman Catholic priest, said: "Subjectively, the revelator can never be fully certain of the revelation, nor of its origin. If it turns out to be correct and genuine, only then can it be traced to its certainness and its source. Before the fact of fulfillment, the revelator and his revelation cannot be validated."

How, then, might one distinguish the genuine revelatory experience from a parasite of the soul, paranoid schizophrenia, or a developmental crisis? Dr. Glen Lehman, President of the Independent Fundamental Churches of America, stated his conviction that the Bible clearly set forth the doctrine that "the Holy Spirit is a person with all the attributes of personality.

"If the Holy Spirit is a person, then it follows that any manifestation of his activity arises out of his personality attributes. Such characteristics as motive, emotion, will, volition, determine the purpose of his activity. For instance, the Scriptures plainly declare that the Holy Spirit will convict the world of sin in righteous judgment.

"Men and women under the convicting power of the Holy Spirit may exhibit physical signs of great stress, such as cold sweat, a shaking of some portion of, or of the entire, body, a sudden cry or a sudden stillness, uncontrolled weeping or great sorrow. I regard these not as visitations of the Holy Spirit, but only as reactions to what the Holy Spirit has already done.

"I believe the Holy Spirit especially manifests presence and power when Christians are assembled in Jesus' name. Jesus said, 'For where two or three are gathered together in my name, there am I in the midst of them' (Matthew 18:20). When such a gathering takes place in the true sense, then there may come a powerful ministry of the Holy Spirit. I have seen a congregation melted together in unity, in prayer, in a holy rush during which men feared to speak. I have witnessed a great joy bursting forth in spontaneous singing, a holy awe at the reading of the word of God, and a fresh new manifestation of love among the people.

"I believe that all manifestations of the presence and power of the Holy Spirit are in full harmony and accord with the Scriptures. I do not believe that the Holy Spirit is the author of confusion; neither is he limited, since as a person of the Godhead, his sovereignty is absolute.

"I believe that the supernatural events of the period of the Book of Acts took place during a transition period—the decline of Israel and the rise of the Church—hence not to be expected in our time except as the Holy Spirit in his sovereignty may act. I further believe that the modern tongues and healing movements are contrary to Scripture, and thus false manifestations of the real, as recorded in the Book of Acts. I do believe that bona fide healings and supernatural events do take place in this age in answer to prayer, which in itself may be initiated by the Holy Spirit."

Professor Milford Q. Sibley, Department of Political Science, University of Minnesota, answered my call for comments on the reality of the revelation experience by stating: "I believe strongly that there is a 'reality' called revelation, in which many have found guidance for their lives and creative (artistic, scientific, educational, etc.) activities. However, revelation may take broadly two forms—it may be a rather steady, slow, undramatic phenomenon or, by contrast, it may be sudden, dramatic, and earth-shaking. I personally have never experienced the latter form, but believe that in many of my life's activities, I have had some inspiration from the former type. The trouble, as Emerson used to say, is that it is sometimes difficult to distinguish what comes from God from what proceeds from the devil! Usually, I believe, we can make this distinction (is it a form of what Plato used to call knowledge as remembering?), but not always. Ultimate value judgments may be a form of 'revelation,' as may be the premises and assumptions upon which scientific work is based. And artistic inspiration, it seems to me, can be placed in the category of revelation."

In his *Watcher on the Hills,* Dr. Raynor C. Johnson sets forth the following three criteria to test the validity of mystical experience:

> (1) The pragmatic test. Has it led to well-balanced, happy, serene living of an enhanced quality?
> (2) Is it *consistent* with the well-established findings of reason? (This need not imply that it is *supported* by reason.)
> (3) Is it unifying and integrative, or isolating and destructive so far as the individual's relationship to an all-embracing whole is concerned?

Dr. Johnson writes that it is obvious that "... all psychotic products resulting in obsessional feeling-states cannot pass the first criterion. It is clear that all allegedly religious people who, as a friend of mine once said, 'have only intolerance in common, and are sure that if only people believed as they do, all would be well,' are ruled out by the third criterion."

Robert Shell, as we have seen, is extremely concerned with testing the truth of a revelatory experience. "It was always the claim of most of the legitimate magical and mystical societies of the past and particularly the Order of the Golden Dawn and the Ordo Templi Orientis, that the criteria employed to test revelatory experiences were basically contextual in that what would substantiate a revelation would be the fact that there was material contained within the text of the revelation that the person to whom it was revealed would have no legitimate access to. If I were ever to have a personal revelation, this would probably be the primary thing I would look for within it–evidence that something had been revealed to me that I would have had no way of knowing previously, and which later would prove to be correct or valid."

As I sift through the voluminous revelatory material which arrives at my office each month, I find certain shiny bits of truth in what may at first appear to be a murky swirl of metaphysical silt. But I also tend to note a good many outright fibs and lies on the part of whoever the revealing entities may be. The incongruities may result from the sometimes less than perfect vessels into which the Higher Intelligences chose to pour their material, or perhaps the ultimate revelation cannot be manifested until we are collectively ready for it. When we have reached a certain level of awareness, the bits and pieces of what appears to be a supercosmic jigsaw puzzle may at last make sense.

"Have you noticed that so much revealed material seems to contain certain half-truths or strategically inserted fibs?"

*Harold Schroeppel*: I would say that part of this is the individual's willingness to tolerate the material. It may be that the message could not be conveyed or forced through a particular mind. If you were to go back to the early Biblical revelators and theorize that, quite possibly, some of them had visions of modern cars or saw the atomic bomb, given their basic framework of information, how on earth could they write it up accurately?

If you were to see machines and equipment from the way-out future, not the near future, how would you put it down so that contemporary people could understand it and so that people two thousand years from now could read your revelations and see that you accurately foretold their present? I think you would have a real problem. Apparently, what is going to be here two thousand years from now is quite seeable. The only problem is whether or not you can tolerate the information.

*Lasca Schroeppel*: I think that the truths are as good as the person who receives them, and I feel that even a receiver in the course of development will have his "ups" and "downs." It simply depends on how much the revelator monitors, filters, and censors with his mind.

*Diane Kennedy Pike*: I think it is important to make a distinction between material coming through from the spirit world and the other dimension, because I think the two are quite different. I think that if Higher Beings choose to relate something, they do it in a very selective fashion. Say, for example, if Jesus chose to communicate with someone–and I think most Christians would agree that Jesus is alive in some sense–I feel certain that he would be highly selective in his choice of a revelator, so that the message would not be distorted unduly. I am sure that there is always some distortion that goes on when things are brought in from other states of consciousness into expression on this plane. I think the only confusion is that many times people seem to get into mental things that are really out of their own idea realm. They think they are communicating with Higher Intelligences, but really they are not. Of course, the trick becomes, how do you know the difference?

My personal feeling is that the test Jesus gave is really the safest one, and that is that you really can know the difference by the person's life. I think a person who has received a revelation from the Higher Realm will manifest high characteristics or qualities in his life and understanding. There will emerge in him a deeper sense of peace as a result of his communication and a deeper sense of wholeness. Physical health will begin to manifest. He will show great patience, speak of universal laws, and give evidence of the things that Paul calls the fruits of the spirit.

I think a person who is on his own mental trip will manifest what we call ego qualities, which is a kind of deceptiveness, self-assertiveness, pride, and so forth, which are not really characteristics of higher developed spiritual people.

And I think that anything that is fear-oriented—a so-called revelation that indicates that you should fear something coming to you from somewhere else or that incites fear in other people when you tell them about it—is obviously not of the higher spiritual realm.

Deon Frey, well-known Chicago medium, told me: "The one who has received spiritual insight must live it, that is my whole principle. Get knowledge, but also get understanding. You cannot receive understanding until you have had an illumination, a revelatory experience; and once you have had this experience, you will devote your life to helping others on the Earth plane. It isn't necessary for a revelator to proclaim that he has had the experience of revelation. If it was a true experience, it will show in his life, in his work, in his love."

Dr. Conrad W. Baars commented that the divine origin of revealed material is possible and likely "if it contains a message which enhances the love of God, encourages prayer and penance, encourages humility and obedience, and even more so, if the revelation is fully oriented toward the greater glory of God and does not seek any personal gain. . . . A true mystic is ever conscious of God present within him, and, as much as possible, unconscious of himself. The mentally sick and emotionally immature person is much too preoccupied with himself to be occupied with God and with neighbor in the way that a true mystic can be."

*Harold Schroeppel:* If the revelator had a true mystical experience, he should not fear death any more. He should know that he is immortal. If he had a full mystical experience, he should lose any hate he might have had for anyone or anything. If he had a genuine contact, he should look different. After a few months it will wear off; but, at first, he will have a rosy, newborn look about him.

Once a person has had a genuine visitation, he will be absolutely certain that there is a God, and nothing you might say or do will shake that idea out of him. He will be absolutely and completely certain of the existence of a Supreme God.

*Dr. Walter Houston Clark:* I believe there are criteria to be brought to bear on any awakening. Essentially these are pragmatic criteria of one kind or another. We still have the cathedrals of the twelfth century as concrete records of the vitality, multiform art, and spiritual thrust of those times, and we are told that a remarkable camaraderie led to the close cooperation of peasant and noble in the building of these expressions of what to that day was Ultimate Reality. Perhaps the communes of our day are groping toward some similar expression, which still may become concrete in this or other forms. Jesus said, "By their fruits ye shall know them," when a similar question was asked in his time. If the present awakening eventuates in cooperation, tolerance, social responsibility, vigor, creativity, and compassion, then those responsible may be looked on as truly revelatory of the Holy Spirit and the essential origins of Man.

"What if someone walked into your office at this very moment and told you that he had just had a direct communication from the Godhead. What would you say to this individual?"

*Dr. W. G. Roll:* To be certain that he and I speak in the same language, I would like him to tell me what his experience was . . . From my point of view, revelations are distinct from mental illness and other expressions of our ordinary kinds of self—the self we are in our ordinary, everyday lives. I would take the revelations to be expressions of some degree of self-transcendence, some degree of moving outside, or expanding, our experience of our ordinary, everyday self. If this hypothetical chap says that he is going to sort out the Christians or Muslims, or whatever, if that was his reaction to the revelation, then I'd say: You are just as you were before, maybe even worse. You haven't been anywhere. This is just an expression of your own egocentricity that's coming out.

"Let's say that he is going to preach peace, love, brotherhood, and man's greater relationship to the Cosmos. Then what would you answer him?"

*Dr. Roll:* First of all, I am not capable of hearing his consciousness, of hearing his experience. The only thing I could do is to see whether his description squares with descriptions of people whom I would consider as having achieved some kind of self-transcendence. Such statements about peace, brotherly love, suggest that he's experienced something wider than his own encapsulated biological organism, his own encapsulated personality.

Dr. Martin E. Marty is the Associate Dean of the Divinity School of the University of Chicago, author of many books, co-editor of the *New Theology* series, and a much respected contemporary theologian. Although the affable Dr. Marty protested that he had not really made a special study of the revelation experience, he assured me that he never let "ignorance inhibit some sort of discussion."

I told him that my book would seek to explore the mechanism that was involved in the revelatory experience.

*Dr. Martin Marty:* Okay, when you use the word "mechanism" in relation to revelation, this precommits a respondent to making an anthropological comment; that is, this is not the place that somebody jumps the gap and talks about faith or about the numinous and so forth. In other words, it is inviting phenomenonological comment, and it is in that context that I will make my remarks.

It seems to me that throughout history whenever someone makes the claim that revelation is occuring to him as a person, individually and exceptionally, the revelationary response is almost always borne by some sort of ecstatic or quasi-mystical experience. By the ecstatic, I mean the whole range, from the hallucinatory, the trance, the vision, the dream, to some other sort of way of transcending day-to-day reality. The person who apprehends himself as the bearer of a revelation doesn't think of it as happening in the humdrum, routine rhythms of the day. Isaiah has a vision of the temple, and his tongue is touched with a coal by an angel. The ecstatic types would be reached, as it were, by God and told to get on their horses and go into a town and prophesy.

The other root of revelation seems to me a quieter mysticism. Instead of an emotive, affective, experiential transcendence, it will be an inner, reflective attempt to find the void, the dark night of the soul, to have a mind free of distractions so the Spirit can speak. The mystical side of revelation, insofar as I can comprehend it, is more a transcending of categories of personality than it is a new infusion of these categories, so that the mystics pass through the dark night of the soul to the light and pass through the void to the center, or whatever. But mysticism is characteristically diffident about filling this experience with a lot of substantive detail.

There is another kind of revelational response that is more elusive, but I think I can demonstrate its presence throughout history, and that would be revelation apprehended socially, communally. The body social has no memory, has no collective voice, yet it still needs a name giver, a folk singer, a prophet, a chronicler. In this case, the personality of the person that serves this role is less important.

From the Hebrew Deuteronomists to John Dewey, the social process itself is expressive of transcendent values. In John Dewey's case this is rather a secular statement, but he does really believe that the democratic process in education or in the political order can generate what he calls a common faith which will tell people in the society more about themselves than they would have known alone.

Marcuse speaks very clearly of transcendence, as does Ernst Bloch in the Marxist world. Now they don't believe that there's a God-object out there revealing himself, but they believe that the participation in the social process, or experiencing as a group the revolutionary consciousness, leads one to have something revealed to him. In this kind of revelation experience, as we have noted, the philosopher Dewey, Marcuse, Bloch, the folksinger, the anonymous people who wrote the Old Testament Deuteronomic material, their personalities become secondary. In the case of the other kind of revelation, it matters that Meister Eckhart or Teresa of Avila is having a mystical experience. But in this kind of revelation, the individual has to stand aside and say that somehow God is speaking through the nation or the people or the race or the movement. That, to me, is a more elusive, but a more interesting form, or concept, of revelation. It's one that I think has a lot of roots in the West because of the Old Testament, the Hebrew scriptures in particular. The New Testament is a more focal revelation. Now the prophetic revelation is in Jesus Christ or through the scripture as written by Paul. I think that Jesus and Paul picked up the Old Testament experience, but now it's focused and less generalized.

"What criteria would you use to assess the revelatory experience of someone who came to you to recount his revealed material?"

*Dr. Marty:* Just as, in my ideology, there are no dumb questions—that is, every question imparts something to me of the person who's asking it and has to be taken seriously—so, in one sense, when the little old lady in tennis shoes runs up to me and says, "I've had a revelation" or "I've seen the Light" or "I've spoken in tongues," I can't simply dismiss it, though her revelation may have no possibility of enhancing my life or the world's life. I must begin by taking the revelation seriously on that person's terms. More or less, I guess, in the R. D. Laing sense that we really don't know who belongs in a nuthouse and who belongs outside it.

These people may be effectively constructing a world of reality that helps them function, without which they might be lost. It is enhancing for them. I might be amused by their revelation; I might tolerate it; I might be scientifically curious; and I might very often, I hope, be sympathetic.

But if I were to move beyond that, the question of authenticity would have to do with determining if there were a potential in this person's experience for benefiting other people's experiences. I would check out authenticity here, I suppose, by way of life, by tests I could make as to whether this person has some other kind of depth.

In other words, if Martin Buber, Paul Tillich, Martin Luther King, Albert Schweitzer, Pope John were to come along and say, "I'm having experiences that disrupt my normal order of things," then I would take them very seriously, because, in Kierkegaardian terms, they also belong wholly to the finite. They can return and let themselves be checked out. I can tell whether they write English sentences, whether they can think deep thoughts, whether they can sacrifice their lives.

The kind of person who can't be checked out in any other dimension—the chatterer at the local bar or the doddering boor at the VFW—who rushes off with his revelation to a vanity press, has placed me in a position wherein I can't say the experience is inauthentic for him; I can't even say it is all bad; I can just say that there is no reason for me to regard this revelation as having any particular psychological depth for me or for anyone else.

Dr. Bucke states that in order for one to achieve Cosmic Consciousness, he must first belong to the "top layer of the world of Self-Consciousness." One must have a good intellect, a good physique, good health, but above all ". . . he must have an exalted moral nature, strong sympathies, a warm heart, courage, strong and earnest religious feeling." Dr. Bucke's study of those whom he considered possessed of Cosmic Consciousness led him to consider the approximate age of thirty-six as the most propitious time in one's life to achieve this elevated state of consciousness. He found the marks of the Cosmic Sense to be:

1. *Subjective light:* The person suddenly finds himself immersed in flame, or a rose-colored cloud, or "perhaps a sense that the mind is itself filled with such a cloud of haze."
2. *Moral elevation:* The recipient is bathed in an emotion of "joy, assurance, triumph, 'salvation.' The last word is not strictly correct if taken in its ordinary sense, for the feeling, when fully developed, is not that a particular act of salvation is effected, but that no special 'salvation' is needed, the scheme upon which the world is built being itself sufficient."
3. *Intellectual illumination:* "He does not come to believe merely; but he sees and knows that the cosmos, which to the self-conscious mind seems made up of dead matter, is in fact far otherwise—is in very truth a living presence."
4. *Sense of immortality.*
5. *Loss of the fear of death.*
6. *Loss of the sense of sin.*
7. *Instantaneousness of the illumination.*
8. *Previous character of high intellectual, moral, and physical degree.*
9. *Age about thirty-six.*
10. *Added charm of the illumined personality.*
11. *Transformation, or change of appearance:* Although this change may gradually pass away, Dr. Bucke writes, "In these great cases in which illumination is intense, the change in question is also intense and may amount to a veritable 'transfiguration.' "

Among those individuals whom he saw as having definitely attained Cosmic Consciousness, Dr. Bucke included Gautama the Buddha, Jesus the Christ, Paul, Plotinus, Mohammed, Dante, Francis Bacon, Jacob Behmen, William Blake, and Dr. Bucke's friend and idol, Walt Whitman (Dr. Bucke saw illumination occurring more often to men than to women). He added chapters on several others whom he considered lesser, imperfect, or doubtful recipients of Cosmic Consciousness—men such as Moses, Gideon, Isaiah, Socrates, Spinoza, Swedenborg, Ralph Waldo Emerson, Henry David Thoreau, and Ramakrishna Paramahansa.

In *Varieties of Religious Experience,* William James cites the features which he believes form a "composite photograph of universal saintliness, the same in all religions":

1. A feeling of being in a wider life than that of this world's selfish little interests; and a conviction, not merely intellectual, but as it were sensible, of the existence of an Ideal Power. . . .

2. A sense of the friendly continuity of the ideal power with our own life, and a willing self-surrender to its control.

3. An immense elation and freedom, as the outlines of the confining selfhood melt down.

4. A shifting of the emotional center toward loving and harmonious affections, towards "yes-yes," and away from "no," where the claims of the non-ego are concerned.

William James also proposed four criteria which may denote a mystical state of consciousness from other state of consciousness:

1. *Ineffability*—The handiest of the marks by which I classify a state of mind as mystical is negative. The subject of it immediately says that it defies expression, that no adequate report of its contents can be given in words. It follows from this that its quality must be directly experienced; it cannot be imparted or transferred to others. In this peculiarity mystical states are more like states of feeling than like states of intellect . . . Lacking the heart or ear, we cannot interpret the musician or the lover justly, and are even likely to consider him weak-minded or absurd. The mystic finds that most of us accord to his experiences an equally incompetent treatment.

2. *Noetic quality*—Although so similar to states of feeling, mystical states seem to those who experience them to be also states of knowledge. They are states of insight into depths of truth unplumbed by the discursive intellect. They are illuminations, revelations, full of significance and importance, all inarticulate though they remain; and as a rule they carry with them a curious sense of authority for after-time.

3. *Transiency*—Mystical states cannot be sustained for long . . . Often, when faded, their quality can but imperfectly be reproduced in memory; but when they recur it is recognized; and from one recurrence to another it is susceptible of continuous development in what is felt as inner richness and importance.

4. *Passivity*—Although the oncoming of mystical states may be facilitated by preliminary voluntary operations, as fixing the attention, or going through certain bodily performances . . . yet when the characteristic sort of consciousness once has set in, the mystic feels as if his own will were in abeyance, and indeed sometimes as if he were grasped and held by a superior power. This latter peculiarity connects mystical states with certain definite phenomena of secondary or alternative personality, such as prophetic speech, automatic writing, or the mediumistic trance. When these latter conditions are well-pronounced, however, there may be no recollection whatever of the phenomenon, and it may have no significance for the subject's usual inner life . . . Mystical states . . . are never merely interruptive. Some memory of their content always remains, and a profound sense of their importance. They modify the inner life of the subject between the times of their recurrence. . . .

In his chapter on "Basic Mystical Experience" in his superb *Watcher on the Hills,* Dr. Raynor C. Johnson, Master of Queen's College, University of Melbourne, lists eight characteristics of illumination:

1. *The Appearance of light:* "This observation is uniformly made, and may be regarded as a criterion of the contact of soul and Spirit."
2. *Ecstasy, love, bliss:* "Directly or by implication, almost all the accounts refer to the supreme emotional tones of the experience."
3. *The Approach to one-ness:* "In the union of soul with Spirit, the former acquires a sense of unity with all things."
4. *Insights given.*
5. *Effect on health and vitality.*
6. *Sense of time obscured.*
7. *Effects on living:* Dr. Johnson quotes a recipient of the illumination experience who said: "Its significance for me has been incalculable and has helped me through sorrows and stresses which, I feel, would have caused shipwreck in my life without the clearly remembered refreshment and undying certainty of this one experience."

Dr. Johnson places "the appearance of light" at the top of

his list of illumination characteristics, and although his list may not coincide precisely with Dr. Bucke's marks of the Cosmic Sense, it is quite clear that they are speaking about the same type of experience.

In her *Ecstasy: A Study of Some Secular and Religious Experiences,* Marghanita Laski lists five principal manifestations of the ecstatic mystical experience:

1. *The Feeling of loss:* i.e., loss of time, of place, of worldliness, of self, of sin, and so on.
2. *The Feeling of gain:* i.e., gain of a new life, of joy, of salvation, of glory, of new knowledge, and so on.
3. *Ineffability:* experiences which the person finds impossible to put into words at all.
4. *Quasi-physical feelings:* i.e., reference to sensations suggesting physical feelings, which may accompany ecstatic experiences, such as floating sensations, a feeling of swelling up, an impression of a shining light, and so on.
5. *Feelings of intensity or withdrawal:* i.e., a feeling of a "winding up," an accumulation of force to the point at which it is let go, whereas withdrawal is the opposite—an ecstatic condition reached "not by accumulation but by subtraction," a feeling of withdrawal of force and energy.

Among Miss Laski's conclusions on the nature of ecstasy are the following:

> I do not believe that any explanations of these experiences can be satisfactory if they suggest that ecstasies are *only* this or *only* that—only a phenomenon of repressed sexuality or only a concomitant of some or other morbid condition. Certainly convictions are an insufficient substitute for evidence, but both people's convictions of the value of these experiences and their substantial influence on outlook and language persuade me that these are of some evidential value in justifying the conclusion that ecstatic experiences must be treated as important outside religious contexts, as having important effects on people's mental and physical well-being, on their aesthetic preferences, their creativity, their beliefs and philosophies, and on their conduct. . . .
>
> . . .To ignore or to deny the importance of ecstatic experiences is to

leave to the irrational the interpretation of what many people believe to be of supreme value. It is, I think, significant that we have no neutral adjective to distinguish the range of emotions, values, moral compulsions, felt truths that arise from ecstatic experience. *Spiritual* implies acceptance of pre-suppositions rejected by rationalists, and those who reject such pre-suppositions have sought rather to deny importance to ecstatic experiences than to examine them on the basis of their own pre-suppositions and to supply a vocabulary in which such examinations could be made....

In *Varieties of Religious Experience* William James quotes Dr. W. R. Inge as stating:

It will be found that men of preeminent saintliness agree very closely in what they tell us. They tell us that they have arrived at an unshakable conviction, not based on inference but on immediate experience, that God is a spirit with whom the human spirit can hold intercourse; that in him meet all that they can imagine of goodness, truth, and beauty; that they can see his footprints everywhere in nature, and feel his presence within them as the very life of their life, so that in proportion as they come to themselves they come to him. They tell us what separates us from him and from happiness is, first, self-seeking in all its forms; and secondly, sensuality in all its forms; that these are the ways of darkness and death, which hide from us the face of God; while the path of the just is like a shining light, which shineth more and more unto the perfect day.

# FOURTEEN

## *Should We Seek the Revelatory Experience— And If So, How?*

If we recognize that there may be certain hazards involved in opening our psyches, should we encourage the revelatory experience in our own lives? And if we believe that a visitation of the Divine Fire should be encouraged, are there certain practices which we might employ that may stimulate such experiences?

In one way or another, I have asked those two questions of a good many men and women over the past several months. Here are some of their responses:

*Dr. Bruce Wrightsman* (Professor of Religion): Oh, yes, we should definitely encourage the revelation experience in our lives. Without that, there is no knowledge of God. I think one who doesn't seek it is turning religion into a kind of moral code, and that's all he's got left. If there is no numinous experience, no encounter with the divine, then all that's left is ten little rules for daily living—pretty sterile and pretty futile.

"Do you think that we should seek personal revelatory experience?"

*Dr. Martin Marty* (theologian): I'll put the question a different way, and I think I'll come out with a similar answer. I think we know very little yet of what human consciousness is, what its limits are, where it ought to go. I consider man to be, in Nietzschian terms, an indeterminate being. Restricted, constricted by an awful lot of inheritance and traditions and social forms which were themselves born of other kinds of remembered experiences, we ossify, petrify, and we forget the origin of everything from our gestures and manners and habits to our mating forms and our ecclesiastical lives, and so on.

I do believe that the race regularly needs a new infusion of experience, and I think that we should welcome the people in our midst who say: "Are you sure that the set of experiences that have gone into the development of our consciousness so far should define the outer limits of what we're doing?"

Personally, I prefer this expansion of consciousness when it is done without drugs, but I can't a priori rule out drugs as a solicitation of a larger range of experience. We know it has happened to saints in the past: they chewed something and saw something, so I don't rule it out a priori, but I do think it is a different level of controversy.

It is hard for me to see how a person can be in a religious tradition, as I am in the Christian tradition, and say that once upon a time we encouraged prophecy and listening and speaking and now we don't. It is itself a very heavy theological commitment to suggest that once there was a Holy Spirit and now the world is abandoned to itself.

I must confess that I am usually skeptical about what comes up—in Biblical terms, I *test* the Spirit—and I am not easily impressed. To put it another way, I often enjoy these experiences more at scientific distance than close up. I'm not particularly eager to have my wife go running off speaking in tongues or my kids to be freaks, and yet I'm glad that these things are around and that people are speaking in tongues.

In general, though, insofar as revelation is a theological translation of a code word for altered consciousness, or enlarged range of human experience, I would just have to say, why not? Bad things can happen in the name of revelation: people start wars; they kill people; they turn fanatic; they start crusades. But people do those things without revelation, too.

*Peggy Townsend*: Now is the time of God. Right now is our time to look to God and open the doors to the knowledge that He is out there for anybody to receive. We will have this opportunity for a little while longer before the doors start closing on us. Maybe it sounds a bit ominous, but I feel that we have a lot of work to get done very quickly.

*Dr. Walter Houston Clark* (Emeritus Professor of Psychology of Religion): There are many practices that will release the revelatory experience–from Yoga exercises and sensory deprivation to biofeedback and chemical alteration within the body. An ancient (and also modern) source of the latter is dieting and fasting, as well as the ingestion of psychedelic herbs. A modern practice is the ingestion of psychedelic synthetic chemicals, like mescaline, psilocybin, and other LSD-type drugs, which, it has been clearly demonstrated, release mystical states of consciousness.

What about drugs as a means of encouraging the revelatory experience? We have, of course, the extremists, such as John Allegro, whose *The Sacred Mushroom and the Cross* maintains that Jesus Christ was the personification of a fertility cult based on the use of the psychedelic mushroom *Amanita muscaria*, and in a new book, *The Chosen People,* claims that Judaism is rooted in a similar mushroom cult; but we must not permit an overstatement of a case to bias us against its possible truths.

Wilson Van Dusen has remarked that the discovery of the central human experience which alters all other experiences–*satori* in Japanese Zen, *moksha* in Hinduism, religious enlightenment or Cosmic Consciousness in the West–appears to be facilitated by the drug LSD.

Dr. Huston Smith has observed that "given the right set and setting, the drugs can induce religious experiences indistinguishable from ones that occur spontaneously."

When Dr. W. T. Stace, Professor Emeritus at Princeton and a leading authority on mysticism, was asked about the merits of psychedelic mystical experience as opposed to the natural kind, he replied: "It is not a matter of its being *similar* to mystical experience; it *is* mystical experience."

In his *Varieties of Religious Experience*, William James reported his thoughts concerning a personal experience of his own with the inhalation of nitrous oxide:

> One conclusion was forced upon my mind at that time, and my impression of its truth has ever since remained unshaken. It is that our normal waking consciousness, rational consciousness as we call it, is but one special type of consciousness, whilst all about it, parted from it by the filmiest of screens, there lie potential forms of consciousness entirely different. We may go through life without suspecting their existence; but apply the requisite stimulus, and at a touch they are there in all their completeness, definite types of mentality which probably somewhere have their field of application and adaptation. No account of the universe in its totality can be final which leaves these other forms of consciousness quite disregarded. How to regard them is the question—for they are so discontinuous with ordinary consciousness. Yet they may determine attitudes though they cannot furnish formulas, and open a region though they fail to give a map. At any rate, they forbid a premature closing of our accounts with reality.

Dr. William Sargant, in his Maudsley Lecture, "The Physiology of Faith," from which I have previously quoted, commented:

> Drugs have been used from time immemorial by all religions to induce sudden alterations in brain activity which are often accompanied by the certainty that a new revelation has been acquired. Often, as soon as the drug wears off the newly acquired faith goes with it, but this is certainly not always so. Aldous Huxley and many others have come to believe that mescaline has revealed to them the personal presence and the certainty of God. . . . [mescaline and LSD] create varying faiths in beliefs as diverse as those of the "hippies" in their need for universal love and brotherhood in all its many aspects and at the other extreme

> the alternative need for castration, supposedly to resist all life's many hippy-emphasized temptations! Probably the faith created by the Eleusinian Mysteries in Greek times and the faith of coven witches that they could and did fly through the air were helped by the use of drugs.

Joseph Havens, writing in his "A Memo to Quakers on the Consciousness-Changing Drugs," states: "It is just possible that God, in His inscrutable Grace may wish to shatter all our Pharisaic pretensions, and through these remarkable chemical substances gracefully provide glimpses of the realm of the Spirit precisely to those whose path would otherwise never have come near it. . . ."

In their *The Varieties of Psychedelic Experience*, Masters and Houston conjecture:

> Undoubtedly it would be the supreme irony of the history of religion should it be proved that the ordinary person could by the swallowing of a pill attain to those states of altered consciousness a lifetime of spiritual exercises rarely brings to the most ardent and adept seeker of mystical enlightenment. Considering the present rapid assimilation on a mass cultural level of new discoveries, therapies, and ideologies, it then might not be long before the vested religious interests would finally have to close up shop.

Perhaps the aspect of LSD-cube mysticism for everyone that most offends the traditional spiritual teacher is the indiscriminate manner in which psychedelics are often utilized and the "drugs for kicks and thrills" philosophy which relegates potentially religious experience to just another "high." I am in no position to speak authoritatively about drugs. In the words of comedian Woody Allen, I never turn on with anything more powerful than chocolate-covered baby aspirins, but I have no objection to the reverent approach to psychedelics suggested by such men as my friend Fay Clark.

In 1950 two doctors in Cedar Rapids, Iowa, asked Fay to be a guinea pig in some drug experiments. Fay consented, and took mescaline over one hundred times in dosages of 50, 150, 300, 375, 400 and 475 milligrams. He would prepare himself for these experiments by strict adherence to diet and by maintaining the same kind of spiritual approach he had attained during his pubertal initiation into the Winnebago Indian tribe.

While under the influence of the mescaline, Fay moved toward a Light and beyond it to a place of peace and quiet, a place where no time and space existed, just the God-force.

"The doctors were able to keep me talking in that condition, and they were apparently able to move me forward and backward in time," Fay said. "They were able to watch my body temperature lower to 93 degrees with apparent physical death—no heart beat, no pulse."

Each year, hundreds of college-age men and women, who have read Fay Clark's book, *Beyond the Light*, travel to his home in Perry, Iowa, to ask his advice on how to control or how to kick drugs. "I'm able to look at the individual and see if he is ready to drop drugs," Fay told me. "He has to do it himself. Life is a do-it-yourself kit. I convince him that he has a 'George,' another part of himself that will help him.

"I tell the young people that they should take the drug only once a year, once a year with two weeks of preparation. For two weeks they should drink no coffee, no tea, no alcohol; they should smoke no cigarettes; they should not go to sexually suggestive movies; and they should not engage in sexual intercourse. They must give themselves two weeks of this very rigid discipline; and three times a day, they must ask their concept of God to guide them in the drug experience they are going to take. If they take their drug after that preparation, they'll never have a bad trip. And they will certainly have learned something, so much that most of them will *never* take the drug again. I've recently talked to three young people who went the whole year as I directed, underwent their two weeks of preparation—then asked why they should take the drug at all."

I asked Fay if, in his opinion, a genuine revelatory experience could come from drugs.

"Yes, but only with preparation," he answered. "I would not say that a revelatory experience might *not* happen if you did not undertake the preparation. But the drug is only a vehicle, the same as a bus or an airplane. Where you are going to go on this vehicle is determined almost completely by the preparation that you have made. I would never take any form of drug without undertaking the preparation, without asking my concept of God three times a day to direct me and to protect me during the experience. Then just before taking the drug, I would again take a moment for prayer, to ask the God mind to guide me while my body was not under my full control."

Dr. Walter Houston Clark also sees drugs as a means, not an end:

"Drugs, I have come to believe, are useful chiefly in revealing to a person his essential nature, which is spiritual and mystical. Once he learns this, he must understand that a simple repetition of the drug experience is not enough. He must discipline his life and organize it in such a way that these insights are expressed in his living. Drugs are not the best road to mysticism, but there are millions of Americans who will attain the mystical state in this way or not at all. Once spiritual insight is attained, drugs then should be used either sparingly, or not at all."

After discussing the matter of drugs with numerous psychic sensitives, mystics, and theologians throughout the United States and Canada, it would appear to me that the majority of spiritual teachers favor the "natural way" and readily dismiss as delusions the experiences obtained through drugs. Again and again I hear the words of the Avatar Meher Baba being quoted: "The experiences which drugs induce are as far removed from Reality as is a mirage from water. No matter how much you pursue the mirage, you will never quench your thirst, and the search for Truth through drugs must end in disillusionment."

Dr. R. E. L. Masters was kind enough to send me a number of research papers on the nondrug induction of religious-type experiences which are being conducted on an experimental basis by the Mind Research Foundation. One device that has yielded several successful religious-type experiences in its subjects is the ASCID, the Altered States of Consciousness Induction Device:

> It is essentially a metal swing or pendulum in which the subject stands upright, supported by broad bands of canvas and wearing blindfold goggles. The device containing the subject moves

> from side to side, forward and backward, and rotating motions generated by the subject's body. Typically, in from two minutes to twenty, an altered state of consciousness or trance state results. Trance depth ranges from light to profound sonambulistic, but in almost all cases the subject experiences vivid eidetic imagery, imagery in other sense modalities, and other phenomena characteristic of trance and psychedelic drug states. The trance is different from a hypnotic trance, especially in that the usual hypnotist-subject relationship does not pertain and the experience of the subject occurs with a high degree of autonomy and spontaneity—he goes, if you will, on his own trip.

Another device employed by Masters and Houston in their experiments with the induction of nondrug "trips," is the AVE, the Audio-Visual Environment, a program which consists of dissolving 2 X 2-inch slides, projected by two projectors, accompanied by a coordinated taped sound sequence of principally electronic music. The husband-and-wife research team point out that "AVE" was the famous salutation of the Angel Gabriel to the Virgin Mary, which has the twin meanings of hail and farewell. "When one is dealing daily in visions and ecstasies," they observe, "it is best to keep a sense of humor in the armamentarium."

The sound tape of the AVE controls at programmed intervals both the changing of the slides and the one- to twenty-second duration of the slide dissolves. The 120 to 160 slides are mostly abstract paintings chosen either to suggest emotional and projective responses or to facilitate free projection.

"Slides are projected over the whole surface of an 8 X 8-foot semicircular rear projection screen, behind which the subject is sitting," the researchers explain. "This gives the effect of an 'environment,' of almost being *in* the painting pictured. Sound comes to the subject through a headphone or from speakers at each side of him. We work usually with a single subject, but have utilized the program effectively with small groups of simultaneous viewers."

Responses to AVE range from marked time distortion to euphoria to religious and erotic feelings. Masters and Houston emphasize that AVE is not just another "light show," but that it "... suggests film and multimedia possibilities which we may have to contend with in the near future. And it also may disclose in a magnified form alterations of consciousness with heightened suggestibility which already occur in milder forms with multimedia, television viewing, and films."

A well-known theologian who experimented with the ASCID device, nicknamed the "witch's cradle," spoke of having descended through darkness, then water, then fire, until he reached a vision of the Platonic forms:

> It is as if my mind were united to the mind of God. I am expanding, expanding . . . and I can read secrets of the universe and glimpse the form of things . . . Beautiful forms, mathematical forms, geometric forms. They are all alive, colorful and brilliant. This is the Source of the Forms, the World of the Divine Ideas, the Creative Source. It is the *Fons et origo*. It is the unity unified; it is the experience of the Unity, the *Nous*, the *Logos* of the soul, as if all unified in me!

*Time* magazine Religion Researcher Clare Mead underwent a half-hour-long "inner odyssey" with no stimulus other than the direction of Dr. Houston.

She flew ". . free, joyous, yet peaceful, ever deeper to the center of my being, until I was conscious of an indescribable unity within myself and with all things. Finally, I felt as if I had flown to the core of life itself."

Queried about whether there was anything that she wished to understand better "while in this sacred place," Miss Mead answered that the problem of injustice had, for her, been the most difficult reality of life to accept:

> Then I had vivid mental images of real-life horrors throughout history, like the Inquisition and the Holocaust of the Jews during World War II. I saw the petty injustices that people commit against each other every day . . . I saw the poor strangling in the disease and dirty ugliness of the slums. . . . I was aware of my unity with all the people who have ever suffered, from the victims of petty lies to those killed by untold wars, persecutions and centuries of mistrust and hate. But simultaneously and paradoxically I understood quite vividly that life triumphs over all this

misery even though it cannot erase it. Life is indeed "stronger than death"—not just in the religious sense, but quite literally stronger than death's ultimate absurdity. . . .

How do Masters and Houston regard the validity of the religious experience produced by their laboratory experiments?

The experimenter must ask himself if the Presence of God, so intensely experienced by the subject, is delusion, reality—and, if so, what kind of reality—or what? If God is truly present in some religious experiences, but not present in those that occur during our experiments, then we are assisting in the production of an inauthentic religious experience which, nonetheless, can powerfully and beneficially transform the deluded individual and awaken in him or intensify a dedicated spiritual life . . . It is our feeling that these experiments and explorations are permissible given the experimenter's open-mindedness, respect for the subject and the subject's experience, and dedication to the pursuit of knowledge. Given these attitudes and aims, there seems no reason why the experimenter should not venture upon terrain he shares with traditional gurus of the East and spiritual directors of the West. If man comes equipped with a spiritual core that can be made conscious to the end of health and enrichment, then it should be desirable to join in the effort to study that core and to make it more readily available to consciousness. If religious and mystical experiences are *only* regressive and nothing more than products of the activation of brain mechanisms and chemicals, then that harsh fact had best be made plain and adjustment made to it. . . .

With regard to the cases already described ["The Experimental Induction of Religious-Type Experiences" by Jean Houston and Robert E. L. Masters], it probably would be more accurate to say that we helped *enable* the experience to occur, rather than that we *induced* it. Each of the individuals in question brought to his session a degree of development and an orientation that made possible the depth and richness of the experience on the one hand, the formal characteristics of the experience on the other. And throughout our work it has been our observation that the profound and possible authentic experiences occur only with those persons who could be considered well prepared for such experience.

Hatha Yoga, the ancient Hindu system of disciplined postures, breathing rhythms, and meditation, brings a conscious control of all body processes to achieve the ultimate goal of the arousal of the vital, universal energy called "kundalini." When this energy has been aroused and controlled, the various psychic centers are said to be activated. The kundalini may then be directed to the head-center where it may bring about the blissful awareness of the great consciousness that is God and which is in man.

As Dr. Walter Houston Clark says:

"Whatever the method used is usually promoted for others by those who have found them personally useful. However, *all* of these methods are best looked on simply as tools, spiritually beneficial when properly used, and potentially harmful and even very dangerous when abused. Whether they are legitimate or not will depend on how they are used, and particularly on how the experiences they release are followed up."

"Are there certain practices that might encourage the revelatory experience?"

*Harold Schroeppel:* I would say that depends entirely on why you want revelation and the visitation of the Holy Spirit. I would definitely encourage the visitation of the Holy Spirit to anyone, because, among other things, opening up and allowing the Holy Spirit to flow through should help the individual in terms of healing. It should help him in his relationship with the people around him. It should help him to function better and to have more spiritual consciousness.

*Lasca Schroeppel:* Every individual has to decide who he really is. Is he the conditioning he got in his educational system? Is he the product of demanding or coercive parents? I feel that the revelation is inevitable once a person begins to know himself and become attuned with the various strata in the Universe. Once an individual gets over and above his own conditioning, then he is at the stage for the visitation of the Divine Fire.

Miss Marianne Francis does not believe in men and women attempting to become channels for the Space Brothers until they have put themselves through a program of self-discipline and self-knowledge. Over the last few years she has observed dangerous, juvenile antics and ego-inflation taking place in untrained and unprepared individuals. She feels quite strongly that if Space Intelligences want to contact someone, *they* will do the choosing.

In an issue of her interesting *Starcraft* journal, she presented the following questions and comments for self-examination to be employed by all those who might wish to make themselves a suitable candidate for contact by the Space Brothers:

> 1. Have you dedication of a spiritual nature?
>
> 2. Have you courage to stay with your convictions without bravado, quietly, reasonably, *peacefully*?
>
> 3. Do you really know yourself inside and out, through hell and high water? If not, start a self-knowledge program.
>
> 4. Have you an inferiority complex or a secret desire for power? If so, forget about Space People and go to work to balance your ego and attain inner poise. When you truly know self, you will find knowledge of others follows.
>
> The Space Brothers need highly *stable* individuals. Are you one?
>
> Astral interlopers, masquerading as Space Intelligences, clutter up the Space field. They flourish in the purely psychic realm. They feed on vanity and ego.
>
> Space men and women from the Solar and Galactic Confederations are concerned with the good of all peoples, of any nationality on Earth, whom they can reach. They preach no dogmas nor creeds, nor do they feed "ego food" to their channels. All *true* channels are part of a plan to assist the Earth and its peoples through the great change or initiation. Some play a greater part, some a lesser, but all are part of the Plan, Cosmic and spiritual in nature. The desire to serve, to love, and to understand, is the real mark of a *true* Light server.

*Robert Shell* (occultist, Ordo Templi Orientis): The question of whether one should encourage visitation with higher-level entities depends mostly on the goals of the individual and also on the individual's prior preparation for such things. Practices such as breath control, some of the Yoga breathing exercises, and more recently . . . psychedelic drugs are all openers of the way.

They open the normally unused pathways of the mind to experiences that normally are not had by humanity. Also, in the process of these experiences, they generate a large amount of psychic energy, which unless it is controlled or channeled, sort of dissipates into space around you. This dissipation of large quantities of psychic energy can attract all sorts of beings. Some feed on this energy and some use it as a means of tracking down human hosts, much in the same way that classical vampires and natural parasites would act. I am convinced that there are such things as psychic parasites, entities which exist off the psychic emanations given off by people who are not properly shielded.

Visitations from higher-level entities can be of extremely great value to a person if the source is very carefully controlled and checked beforehand. The only people in the recent past who are able to do this properly were the British Order of the Golden Dawn, and this through a series of rituals which they had partially developed and partially derived from older sources. These rituals build up a wall of protection about the individual and allow the individual to vibrate out through this wall only certain forms of radiation, only the type that he himself desires to radiate, so that the type of entity which is being attracted can be controlled.

Even this is not a certain thing, and this is one of the dangers for the beginning magician . . . One of the cautions that you are always given when you embark on any of these experiments with different rituals is that it is perfectly all right to meditate on these various entities; but for God's sake, don't try to contact or communicate with any of them until you are much farther along in your development. This is something that far too few people realize.

"In order to receive the prophecies which we have received," Dr. Joseph Jeffers says, "we Yahwist people eat fresh fruits, raw vegetables, and we eliminate most breads and other starches, so that our stomachs will not get sour and our breaths will not get bad.

"You will find throughout the years that the greatest

spiritual leaders and teachers of prophecy have followed a very strict diet and kept their minds clean and pure so that the clean and pure spirits can possess them."

*Irene F. Hughes* (psychic-sensitive): Yes, indeed, we should encourage the inflow of the Holy Spirit. First of all, *we must believe that we can have such an experience.* Most people are not prepared for the inflow of the Spirit, however, and I suggest that they prepare themselves by prayer, self-discipline, and meditation. I believe that the inflow of the Spirit will lead to a richer, more spiritual life.

When I was fifteen years old I was attending a service at a Church of the Nazarene where a Baptist minister was speaking. When he gave the call to come down to make a confession of faith, I recall very vividly that that was the moment I decided that this was the time and the right place. I'll never forget it, because it seemed to me like a fountain opened up inside of me, and I heard beautiful singing and a voice that said to me, "If you will always listen to my word, everything will be all right."

I have learned in the years after to really listen and to really experience the tremendous ecstasy and the calming peace within me, and I believe that this calm and peace is something that everyone might acquire if he prepares himself through prayer and study. He must learn that it is not enough to *ask* for something when he prays. He must *affirm* that it is so. Affirmation shows faith, and in faith comes an overwhelming experience of knowing. I feel that man, in small groups or by himself, is becoming more aware that God is within him and not in some far distant Heaven, and that he does not have to seek Him in strange places, but that he can find Him where He really is.

According to Dr. Harmon Hartzell Bro, author of five books on Edgar Cayce's life and readings, the seer of Virginia Beach offered four simultaneous fronts for building a closer communion with God:

1. *Act on your chosen ideals.* (Dr. Bro comments that almost all mental illness is caused by trying to live up to other people's ideals.)

2. *Learn to risk your love in relationships with other people.* ("This means risking love and trust and forgiveness even when dealing with minorities, outcasts, and strangers," Dr. Bro said.)
3. *Study your own experiences of growth.* ("What are you like when people love to see you arrive and hate to see you go?)
4. *Enter into daily meditation.* ("In Cayce's terms, meditation was a serious, daily cultivation of attunement to God, where the individual will and reason were subordinated to wake up something else.")

*Diane Kennedy Pike:* Based on my study of the early Christians, Jesus, and the Dead Sea Scrolls, it seems to me that there are two things we should seek. One is to purify and order our own lives in the physical dimension and in the emotional and mental dimensions so that we do all we can to make ourselves as perfect an instrument as we can for the Spirit.

Secondly, we should seek to alter ourselves to God for the experience of unity with Him, or we should seek to achieve the higher states of consciousness so that we can experience unity with the Cosmic forces or with the whole Universe, or however the experience comes.

My feeling is that revelation, or insight, will follow naturally. However, if we *seek* a message or a new understanding, our mind will almost inevitably get involved in the formulating of what we would like to come by way of revelation. We have somehow set up a precondition, and I think it's apparent in Biblical literature that man, if he is to be in a live relationship to God, cannot set up any preconditions. Even though we have lots of promises of what we can expect, we just have to be expectant and not set up the conditions upon which the revelation will come.

My feeling is that we should seek higher states of consciousness or union with God or the gift of the Holy Spirit, but we should not set up preconditions as to how that gift should manifest. This, by the way, is one of the things that I think is a limitation on some of the spiritual movements in our culture. They, in effect, have already decided *how* God will give the gift of the Spirit to everybody. It says in the New Testament that the Spirit moves where it will, and I don't think we have any say over that. I don't think we can say, for example, that if a person has not spoken in tongues, he hasn't received the gift of the Spirit. To the contrary, I think there are a great many people who have spoken in tongues who do not manifest as many of the qualities of the gift of the Spirit as some who have not spoken in tongues.

I feel that we should aspire to the highest level of spiritual consciousness that is possible in our lives, and then wait to be given whatever gifts God chooses to give us and not have any predetermined ideas about that. If we receive revelation or new understanding or new messages from some higher beings, then we should consider this a great gift and a great responsibility; because those who are given those gifts are expected to do something great with them.

*Dr. C. W. Baars* (psychiatrist): The only way to encourage the visitation of the Holy Spirit is by a proper mental and spiritual attitude and by a passiveness so that the Holy Spirit can make himself known at his convenience, so to speak. There is great danger that any active practices on a person's part to encourage revelatory experiences are going to result only in pseudo-experience, pseudo-revelations. I think there are too many real outpourings of the Holy Spirit that are appearing in everyday life that people are just not aware of, but overlook because they are concentrating on the abnormal, the unusual, the sensational.

In my personal opinion, I believe the greatest obstacle in making progress to be more receptive to the outpourings of the Holy Spirit is the fact that we have matured relatively little as whole human beings and that we still have a long way to go to get a very well balanced personality. History has shown us that people have been either much too intensely rational or were much too intensely emotional, and we are still far away from having a balanced relationship between the physical, the emotional, the intellectual, and the spiritual.

*Miss Helen Hoag:* First you must want to serve the Creator. This desire helps to raise your spiritual vibrations so that he may come through to you.

We have learned that the Creator expects us to contact the Higher forces at least twice every day. But most people do it once a week if they feel like it. Or maybe only once a month. In between times their vibrations fall back down, because they aren't keeping them up. Those of us who have seen twenty lives and gone up the planes keep our vibrations up and go to see the Creator at least once a day.

"How can someone who has not seen his past lives keep his vibrations up?"

*Miss Hoag:* He would do it by prayer and meditation.

*Harold Sherman* (psychic-sensitive): Apparently we have a highermost level of consciousness which we very seldom touch. It establishes our relationship with the God-process. We can't even comprehend in what form the God-conscious mind exists, but we can feel its presence; we can express it in terms of light. When one is suddenly surrounded by a radiance of light, he is often given an awareness of some particular tremendous spiritual truth, or maybe some inventive awareness. This doesn't seem to be something we can make too much of a conscious effort to achieve. Trying too hard might even short-circuit the experience.

I have learned in my psychic work that you have got to let go. If you try too hard, you activate your imagination and then you self-hallucinate. That is a very important point. It isn't the case of deservability, as we would try to determine our meriting of that kind of experience. It is a condition that exists, and when our own mental attitudes or emotional natures happen to be right, we hit a higher frequency for a moment, and all of a sudden something happens.

When some people receive this experience, they make the mistake of interpreting this very unusual occurrence as though they have become missionaries and must spread the wonder of it all. They are so eager to have someone share the experience that meant so much to them.

I don't believe it is possible to receive a genuine revelatory experience through drugs. I think drugs eventually result in a disorientation of personality, no matter how vivid the experience may be and how intriguing it may seem to the mind once it is caught up in that kind of very realistic seeming cosmic experience.

If young people could be encouraged to develop their ESP powers in a rational way and let this experience develop naturally through their own application of meditation and concentration, they would receive the most satisfying revelations of who they are and what they are and their relationship to the God-consciousness within. In my book *How to Make ESP Work for You,* I have presented a simple method of concentration that has brought results for thousands of people. People have proved to themselves that these powers do exist and do work. In the process of doing this, they are making themselves susceptible on unconscious levels without aspiring to it, and they are getting some of these marvelous experiences people are seeking in terms of Cosmic Consciousness. This is a by-product of cleansing the mind, getting the hates and the resentments and the fears out of consciousness and making consciousness a clear and true channel for contact with the Cosmic Conscious level of the mind.

*Dr. Bruce Wrightsman:* I think the revelatory experience can be sought, but I don't think it can be manipulated. Everything depends upon the quality of mind and heart that a man brings to life, and that's one of the imponderable things that makes it impossible for us to predict who's going to receive it and who isn't.

I think that one can make himself more receptive. I think we do have that responsibility to make ourselves more receptive through prayer, meditation, worship, which if it doesn't create the conditions for revelation, at least offers the opportunity for God to get through.

*Henry Cole* (author, expert on the Occult): Try this in "slow motion" for reaching a level of higher consciousness: Following a period of relaxation, a tingling throughout the body begins, and at some point of increase (yet to be determined, I dare say) the tingling begins to act as a vibration, which slowly (at least in my case) separates from the body—from toes and fingertips simultaneously, then increasing up legs and arms, up torso and down head until it feels like all the skin from these areas has decided to congregate at the heart area; full and heavy tingling at the heart, no feeling whatever elsewhere.

Vision throughout this time is blackness. The congregated vibration (for lack of anything else to call it) seems to seek an upward level and tugs up with a feeling somewhat of taffy being pulled by an unknown hand.

Coincidentally a pinpoint of light appears at first "tug" and increases in direct relation to the tugging, giving the feeling of rising to a skylight while prone on an elevator floor—except that what feeling the body still possesses is that of dropping (a rather odd dichotomy). Immersion into total light and lightness seems to time exactly with the leaving of the "taffy-pull" from the body.

*Dr. Richard Rubenstein* (Professor of Psychology of Religion): Yes, I believe there are practices which would encourage revelatory experiences. I think meditative practices are certainly helpful, and I would encourage people to have them. However, I would not see the workings of the Holy Spirit involved in such practices. I would see that through meditation one becomes more aware of one's own inner self, one's own unconscious self. Furthermore, I believe that it is possible for many people, as a result of the techniques of the psycho-therapeutic sciences, to become much more conscious of the depths of their own being. I think that is all to the good. What interests me is not the manifestation of the Holy Spirit, but the ability of people to come into contact with their own depths.

*Father Ed Cleary* (Roman Catholic priest): The best way to encourage the revelatory experience is to steadily cultivate contemplation, the condition of stillness or quiet of all the outer principles, powers, and acts of mind, emotion, sense, and body so that the inner principles and acts of soul, spirit, and God can manifest, or surface, in consciousness.

Contemplation offers the best climate for the revelatory fruit. Whatever happens in this condition has the most chance of being genuine, though the outer ego still has to express it, and this necessarily causes a loss of degree of its authenticity.

I would say that most of what popularly passes as revelation of one form or another is not authentic or genuine, but only a distorted glimpse or peek at one angle of a problem, event, or condition. The Spirit of God is just too much for any human soul or mind or faculty to handle. The overwhelming majority of predictions about people and events are not of spiritual origin (in soul, spirit, or God). Their source is in either the mind or emotions, belonging to what is commonly called mental and astral phenomena.

I go along with those who maintain the better course is to let these experiences develop spontaneously, rather than go into training for their growth. However, nothing is fundamentally incorrect in *either* course.

*Dr. Joseph Jeffers:* The name Yahweh has the highest vibration of any word ever released in the atmosphere. In order to achieve the results of which I am speaking, you must repeat this name aloud, if possible. If not, whisper it mentally when you open your communications or prayer or meditation.

No evil spirits or negative vibrations can remain for any length of time in your presence when the vibrations of Yahweh's name are about you. This name can, and will, mean life to you in the coming Armageddon and the crisis which is before us. And use the name Yahoshua (Yah-HOSH-u-a) for Jesus. I used "Jesus Christ" for the nearly forty years of my Baptist ministry, but that name did not bring the results of Yahoshua.

And we should pray, Our Father who art on *Orion,* not Heaven. Orion is Yahweh's headquarters—the constellation where all things began in the universe. Even the book of Job, written thirty-six hundred years ago, tells us, "Do you know the Pleiades and the belts of Orion?" Our *Father* who art on Orion, hallowed, sacred, be thy name.

### *How to Communicate with Yahweh*

First of all, use the name of Yahweh in all of your communications, meditations, and prayers in order to usher you into the presence of the Almighty Creator. The second step is concentration. Your mind must be relaxed. Worry, fear, noise, confusion—all hinder you from receiving the message.

One of our greatest spirit teachers told us: "I imagine a huge blackboard in front of me. I can see nothing but darkness. With my eyes closed, I keep concentrating on the black wall before me. I close my mind and my consciousness to all outside forces. I don't think; I keep my mind blank; I let the spirit receive the message.

Keep repeating Yahweh's name and ask him to hear your requests. Ask Yahweh to fill you with his power and spirit. You may have to repeat this procedure a number of days before you receive anything. Don't be discouraged; the message will come.

At first you may have just a feeble amount of electricity. Perhaps your body may need a cleansing before you can attract enough of Yahweh's power to yourself. If you purify your body and your mind, your spirit will then become open and Yahweh will speak to you.

A thought will flash before you. You may receive an impression. You may see or hear a word, a sentence. If this happens, repeat it out loud, then more words will come.

Each day you will develop a little more. The time will come when you can write down the words as they come, or you will be able to speak into a microphone and tape record them. You will be able to get prophetic messages. You will be able to receive information about yourself. You will be able to receive messages about your former lives. That is the way these prophecies come. We have thousands and thousands of fulfilled prophecies that Yahweh has given us, and we know other things that have not yet happened.

### *How to Receive Yahweh's Prophetic Messages*

Keep in the spirit by singing praises to Yahweh. When you pray, let the spirit within you pray, and not your mind. Your spirit must direct your mind. Let the spirit move you.

When the message in the spirit comes, the letters, syllables, and words are given to the mind by the spirit. Spirit projects on the screen of the mind; the mind, in turn, converts the picture to words. The mind calls the mental forces together, and they move and activate the vocal cords. That is the spirit, mind, and fulfillment.

Through the Holy Spirit, Yahweh will give your own spirit an impression to speak his message. Do not speak hastily, but remain silent for a moment to permit the message to grow clear.

As you wait, the impression grows stronger. Most often a strong impression will be relayed by a voice. At first you may hear nothing. You will see a picture. Keep listening. You will feel Yahweh moving. If words come, they will be followed by more words. I have received millions of these words, and they are now being published by the Ambassadors of Yahweh [P.O. Box 23060, San Antonio, Texas 78223].

When you surrender to the spirit and to Yahweh, you become part of Yahweh. One of the first things you must learn in order to become a good prophet is that you are an instrument of Yahweh. You must be pliable and yield completely to the spirit. The spirit must take full possession of your body, your mind, and your emotions. You must never force a preconceived notion of what Yahweh is going to tell you. Don't try to tell Yahweh what to say to you. Let the spirit take charge; let the spirit give you the right answers. If you attempt to force it, you will receive nothing. If you have fears, the mind will play tricks on you.

To be a good messenger, you must be absolutely neutral. The words that Yahweh gives you by the Holy Spirit are not of your own. It is Yahweh who puts the message in your mouth. Your own spirit must be humble, otherwise Yahweh cannot use you. If you have love and wisdom, you can use the gifts of prophecy and be a blessing to the people of Earth and to the Kingdom of Yahweh that he is building now on this planet.

When you speak Yahweh's name, the air about you becomes charged with fire, electricity, magnetic force. When you speak Yahweh's name out loud, your own aura becomes intensified.

Yahweh has billions of spirits, or messengers, in this universe. Several are with you constantly—a loved one who has left this life, a dear friend, or some guardian spirit. Among the Yahwists, we call them spirit guides. These spirits guard and protect you until death, unless you abuse them by rebelling against Yahweh and becoming so corrupt that the good spirits flee from your presence.

The greater you are in the spirit, the more good spirits you will attract. They will be drawn to you like a magnet, unlimited to you by space or time.

Sir Alister Hardy is convinced that with the experimental method applied to theology, "we could have a new flowering of faith that could reshape our civilization." He foresees this faith in a spiritual reality as matching that of the Middle Ages, ". . . but one based not upon a belief in a miraculous interference with the course of nature but upon a greatly widened scientific outlook."

It is Sir Alister's contention that one can test the power of prayer, experiment with it to see if it really works. "However unlikely it may seem to one from one's rationalistic upbringing, try the experiment of really imagining that there is some element that one can make contact with beyond the conscious self," he writes. "Have that amount of faith and see."

In his *Divine Flame* Sir Alister outlines a method that he is certain will bring positive results if used in the right way. He admits that it is really a very old method with a very recognizable origin.

The approach should be made as if one were a child speaking to a loved Father, realizing at the same time that "the form of this relationship is almost certainly a psychological one based upon one's own former filial affection." Although one knows the reality must be something very different, Sir Alister explains, the visualization of a person enables one to have the emotional sense of devotion that is a necessary part of the process. "The analogy, if you like, sets up the relationship with this element beyond the conscious self."

Once the proper relationship has been established, Sir Alister sets forth the following experiment to "test" the efficacy of prayer:

> Ask in all humility to receive help in trying to bring about a better state of the world ("Thy Kingdom come, Thy will be done") and think in what ways one might oneself do something to this end.
>
> Ask to be shown how one can keep oneself in better health to play a better and more active part in the world. Ask oneself if one is abusing one's own body by taking more than one's proper share of daily bread.
>
> Ask that we may realize our own faults and how to mend them, and how to forgive those who have trespassed against us.

> Ask that we may recognize with thought what are the real temptations and evils that are making our lives less worthy than they could be.

Sir Alister Hardy fully believes that if one carries out this experiment with deep feeling and devotion and will not simply rattle the prayer through in a matter of seconds as if it were a magical incantation, he will come to feel a new power in himself, and feel in touch with a *power* and a *glory* beyond himself "which can make the world a different place, a new kingdom." Sir Alister feels that prayer of the kind outlined above is as essential to one's mental health as a bath is to the body—"it clears and uplifts the mind and gives on a zest."

*"Seth" on Prayer:* Prayer contains its own answer, and if there is no white-haired kind old father-God to hear, then there is instead the initial and ever-expanding energy that forms everything that is and of which each human being is a part.

"This psychic gestalt may sound impersonal to you, but since its energy forms your person, how can this be?

"If you prefer to call this supreme psychic gestalt God, then you must not attempt to objectify him, for he is the nuclei of your cells and more intimate than your breath."

Dr. L. P. Jacks (*Religious Perplexities*) suggests that prayer may set in motion some action which draws the required solution for each supplicant from his own subconscious mind rather than prompt the intervention of a personal God. He hastens to add, though, that such a concept need not diminish the Divine:

> All the evidence of religious experience shows us that man makes contact with this Power, which appears partly transcendent and felt as the numinous beyond the self, and partly immanent within him. I also think it likely, however, that it may well be this uplifting Power which does in fact activate the subconscious solution-providing mechanism in a way which would not otherwise be possible. . . .
>
> In its essence the Gospel is a call to make the same experiment, the experiment of comradeship, the experiment of fellowship, the experiment of trusting the heart of things, throwing self-care to the winds, in the sure and certain faith that you will not be deserted,

forsaken or betrayed, and that your ultimate interests are perfectly secure in the hands of the Great Companion. . . .

Each of these various prescriptions for religious experience, in one way or another, speaks of proper preparation through prayer or meditation and the cultivation of a passive, receptive attitude that does not set up preconditions for the revelation by actively seeking or forcing the experience, thereby encouraging hallucination, self-deception, and, in some cases, parasites of the soul.

Peggy Townsend maintains: "Once you have opened the door, then there is no closing it. Things just keep coming through constantly."

*Deon Frey* (psychic-sensitive): If the revelatory experience comes, you become one with it. You must grow into it, become a part of it, let the light become a part of you.

But learning to grow into the light is a process that cannot be rushed with the idea that, "Now I'm great!" You must learn to experience the light, let it flow through you, giving it force so that others may feel a portion of it through you. Become a channel for the light, and you will leave a portion of it with whomever you meet. I think that everyone should seek illumination, the process of becoming one with the spiritual principle.

"How would you define this spiritual principle?"

*Deon:* I look at it as an energy, a source, something that works within and without and all around us. Something that we can tune ourselves in to.

"How can one tune in to this spiritual principle?"

*Deon:* By constant meditation, by wanting to help others, by desiring to become one with the universe. By becoming one with the spiritual principle, you, in one sense, give up your life, but you balance your life because you still must live on the Earth plane and do the things that other people do. But you must work more and more for others; you must always be ready to help; you must be ready to do whatever is needed of you. You must remember that you are only a channel for God, the spiritual principle; and you must help others become fully aware so that if they should receive this illumination, this spiritual unfoldment, they will know how to handle it correctly.

"Do you mean to suggest that it is possible to subvert this force?"

*Deon:* Any force that can be used for good can be used for evil. There is a positive and negative aspect to everything. We must keep our own light strong. We must be constantly aware, working in the light, becoming light, because that is why we have been set on the Earth path.

Although the revelatory experiences we have examined in this book may seem decidedly different, we must learn to look beyond the specifics of strange words and unfamiliar concepts and see universal and timeless precepts:

1. Each of the revelators speaks of a Higher Being from which every man might draw power and inspiration. Some see this Higher Being as immediately accessible to man, while others cite the necessity for the intercession or guidance of more advanced spiritual intermediaries.
2. The revelators state that man has within him all that is necessary to establish harmony with Higher Intelligences or a Higher Being, provided certain spiritual conditions are encouraged and maintained. These conditions generally have little to do with an organized priestcraft or a dogmatic theology. Most of the revelations point out that the individual ego requirements and cultural needs that are realized in an ecclesiastical hierarchy are almost certain to distort the universality of the communications from Higher Intelligence.
3. The revelators stress a sense of unity with all things. Man is one with all other men in spirit. Man's soul is both universal and individual.
4. Nearly all revelators tell us that we are entering a New Age, another progression in our evolution as spiritual beings. The Age of Secrets that encouraged priesthoods, Keepers of the Secrets, will soon be ended. We are moving toward a state of mystical consciousness wherein every man shall be priest.

We each of us have within us the potential to receive a spark from the Divine Fire and to be elevated to higher realms of consciousness and spiritual communion. But if such communication should be established in our lives, we must avoid traps of ego by remembering that we have not thus become unique in our relationship to God, we have rather become one with an Eternal and Universal Brotherhood and Sisterhood.

In the final analysis, it may matter little whether one conceives of his God Concept as a single, individual intelligence, or as the entity Seth puts it, "an absolute, ever-expanding, instantaneous psychic gestalt." The important thing, as that same informative multidimensional being or superconscious creation said, is that, "There is a portion of *All That Is* directed and focused within each individual, residing within each consciousness."

It is the focusing of this Higher Intelligence that creates the Divine Fire—a continually accessible line of communication with an ever-powerful energy source. The Divine Fire will eternally transmit universal truths so that man may draw power and inspiration from a source of strength outside himself as he evolves as a spiritual being and progresses out of his old, physical limitations into a higher realm that is his by right of his cosmic inheritance.

# *Bibliography*


Bach, Marcus, *The Inner Ecstasy.* New York-Cleveland: World Publishing, 1969.

Bach, Marcus, *Strangers at the Door.* Nashville and New York: Abingdon Press, 1971.

Berger, Peter L., *A Rumor of Angels.* Garden City, N.Y.: Doubleday Anchor Book, 1970.

Braden, William, *The Private Sea: LSD and the Search for God.* New York: Bantam, 1968.

Castaneda, Carlos, *The Teachings of Don Juan.* New York: Ballantine Books, 1969.

Clark, Fay M., *Beyond the Light.* Perry, Iowa: Hiawatha Publishing Co., 1962.

Clarke, Arthur C., *2001: A Space Odyssey.* New York: New American Library, 1968.

Dyer, Luther B., Editor, *Tongues.* Jefferson City, Missouri: Le Roi, 1971.

Eliade, Mircea, *Cosmos and History.* New York: Harper Torchbooks, Bollingen Library, 1959.

Eliade, Mircea, *The Sacred and the Profane.* New York: Harcourt, Brace and World, 1959.

Eliade, Mircea, *Myths, Dreams, and Mysteries.* New York, Evanston: Harper Torchbooks, 1967.

Ferm, Vergilius, *Classics of Protestantism.* New York: Philosophical Library, 1959.

Fisher, Vardis, *Peace Like a River.* New York: Pyramid Books, 1960.

Freemantle, Anne, *The Protestant Mystics.* New York: New American Library, 1965.

Gaver, Jessyca Russell, *Pentecostalism.* New York: Award Books, 1971.

Gelpi, Donald L., *Pentecostalism.* New York, Paramus, Toronto: Paulist Press, 1971.

Heschel, Abraham J., *The Prophets.* (volumes I and II). New York, Evanston, London: Harper Torchbooks, 1969.

Huxley, Aldous, *Heaven and Hell.* New York, San Francisco, Evanston, London: Perennial Library, 1971.

Huxley, Julian, *Religion without Revelation.* New York: Harper & Row, 1957.

James, William, *Varieties of Religious Experience.* Garden City, New York: Masterworks Program, 1963.

Johnson, Raynor C., *Watcher on the Hills.* London: Hodder & Stoughton Ltd., 1959.

Jung, Carl G., *Modern Man in Search of a Soul.* New York: Harcourt, Brace, World Inc., 1933.

Jung, Carl G., *Man and His Symbols.* New York: Dell Books, 1968.

Kavanaugh, James, *The Birth of God.* New York: Pocket Books, 1970.

Keel, John A., *Strange Creatures from Time and Space.* Greenwich, Conn.: Fawcett Gold Medal, 1970.

Keel, John A., *Our Haunted Planet.* Greenwich, Conn.: Fawcett Gold Medal, 1971.

Lawson, James Gilchrist, *Deeper Experiences of Famous Christians.* New York: Pyramid, 1970.

Lilje, Hanns (tr. by Olive Wyon), *The Last Book of the Bible.* Philadelphia: Fortress Press, 1967.

Leibman, Joshua Loth, *Peace of Mind.* New York: Bantam, 1955.

Lewis, C.S., *Miracles.* New York: MacMillan, 1970.

Lindsay, Gordon, *The Gordon Lindsay Story.* Dallas: Voice of Healing Publishing Co.

McPherson, Aimee Semple, *Fire from on High.* California: Heritage Committee, Foursquare Publications, 1969.

Nahal, Chaman, *Drugs and the Other Self.* New York: Perennial, 1971.

Otto, Rudolf, *The Idea of the Holy* (tr. by John Harvey). New York: Galaxy Book, 1958.

Otto, Rudolf, *Mysticism East and West.* New York: MacMillan, 1970.

Potter, Charles Francis, *The Great Religious Leaders.* New York: Simon and Schuster, 1958.

Schlink, Basilea, *Ruled by the Spirit.* Minneapolis: Bethany Fellowship, Dimensions Book, 1969.

Schonfield, Hugh J., *The Passover Plot.* New York: Bantam, 1967.

Schonfield, Hugh J., *Those Incredible Christians.* New York: Bantam, 1969.

Schwarz, Berthold E., *Ordeal by Serpents, Fire and Strychnine.* Utica, New York: State Hospitals Press, (pamphlet 1960 Psychiatric Quarterly).

Sherrill, John L., *They Speak with Other Tongues.* New York: Pyramid Books, 1965.

Spalding, Baird T., *Life and Teachings of the Masters of the Far East, Vol. 1.* Los Angeles: DeVorss & Co., 1937.

Stace, Walter T., *The Teachings of the Mystics.* New York: New American Library, 1960.

Suzuki, D. T., *Mysticism, Christian and Buddhist.* New York: Perennial, 1971.

Swedenborg, Emanuel, *Heaven and Its Wonders and Hell.* New York: Citadel, 1965.

Tart, Charles T., *Altered States of Consciousness.* New York, Sydney, London, and Toronto: John Wiley & Sons, Inc., 1969.

Underhill, Evelyn, *Mysticism.* New York: Dutton Paperback, 1961.

Watts, Alan W., *Myth and Ritual in Christianity*. Boston: Beacon Paperbacks, 1968.

William, Michael, ed., *They Walked With God.* Greenwich, Conn.: Fawcett, 1962.

Young, Barbara, *This Man From Lebanon.* New York: Borzoi Book, Knopf 1970.

# Index